Teaching in FE

What should you put in to get the best out?

A paperback or kindle with
access to further online resources

The companion volume to
Managing Teachers in FE (isbn 978-0-9926088-4-2)

It's not about you. It's about them

www.justifiedtext.co.uk   wwwbpfe.org.uk

Contents

1 – What is FE, and why?   **p8**

encompassing the sector – the dynamics that shaped FE – a potted history of industry's relation to education and FE's role – professionalism in FE

2 – The clients for FE, and how we relate to them   **p43**

a natural market? - pre-16 – mature students – de-schooling and commodification – andragogy - the previously excluded – the social mix

3 – Differences and how we respond to them   **p60**

differentiation and significant differences – previous experience – discovery learning – advanced organisers – readability measures – learning styles and metacognition – gender – support needs – cultural and socio-economic differences - confidence and self-esteem – choosing techniques - so what is personalised learning?

4 – Skills and metacognition   **p119**

what should be questioned? – transient, enduring, transferable, basic, key, functional – employability – an educated mind? – thinking and learning skills – writing frames - evidence of learning – formative assessment – ipsatic referencing – medium and message - what is a lesson anyway? - social networks as social judo (blogging back to happiness)

5 – Behaviour – theirs and yours   p158

levels of response - what is unacceptable? – defining the problem – diet and behaviour – Maslow – labels and syndromes - motivation and persona - managing the context and energy levels – disciplinary systems - teacher variables: style, stress, temperament and personality

6 – Tutorials and transition, paperwork and reality   p223

our ends in our beginnings – why bureaucracy should be taken seriously - added value and distance travelled – sharing data – why tutorials – tutoring skills – motivational interviewing - self assessment – questioning methods - the stages of change

7 - Equal opportunities   p259

conceptualising equality and fairness – what is reasonable? – balancing needs in diverse microcosms

Bibliography   p273

Introduction

This is a text for practitioners in Further Education (FE) or
Life Long Learning (LLL), the people who relate to students to
bring about learning. You may work in a college, a voluntary
agency, a community centre, a private provider or some new
hybrid yet to be imagined as we continue to be reorganised and
reformed. It draws on both research and experience to answer
three questions:

Why are things the way they are?

What does that mean?

What can you do about it
as you try to make learning happen?

It looks for a way to understand FE that will help you
become more effective, and offers basic principles, practical
advice, material and ideas you can try for yourself, adapt or
reject as you think best.

You may be experienced and looking for new ways to deal
with a changing sector, or new to teaching and looking for ways
to get to grips with the whole complex business. The text will
assume that you always want to know the reasons behind any
idea or suggestion, but also that no idea is worth pursuing
unless it has a pay-off in terms of increased learning. The
balance between reflection and application is fundamental.

The first edition was released in 2006, as an e-book entitled
Making the Difference as a Teacher in FE. Although 2006 may
sound quite recent, it is still one year before the first Kindle.
Now, of course, the new text is formatted for both Kindle and
I-phone. Change is increasingly rapid and that will be one of
your problems (which, of course, most people will encourage
you to call 'challenges'). Small changes can have widespread and
unexpected effects. It is hard to keep up, let alone judge wisely
which new ideas or sources are worthy of attention in a busy

schedule.

A great deal has changed in that time. Major agencies have been formed, abolished or redesigned; Learning and Skills Council, Dept. for Children, Schools and Families Education Funding Agency, Skills Funding Agency Young Peoples Learning Agency, Learning and Skills Improvement Service, Centre for Excellence in Leadership, Quality Improvement Agency, Adult Learning Inspectorate, Institute for Learning – the list goes on. If you haven't heard of some of those they may have been formed *and* abolished in the last few years. Cunning Plans have come and gone (baccalaureate - again), the Ofsted grading system has changed from five to four options and the Equality Act tightened up previous duties towards staff and students.

The basic principles of good teaching have not changed, although the research that underpins it continues to develop, sometimes controversially. Consequently, the way this book works has also adapted.

All the links and many of the sources, references have been removed from the main text, along with the sample materials. This makes it a lot shorter - hooray! Instead, if you go to www.bpfe.org.uk you will find two pages you can use on line. One of them is 'materials' and here you can gain access to The Learning Suite, a set of downloadable files for classroom use which I shall explain later. The other is 'links', and here you will see live links to a whole range of forums, agencies, research sources, jargon busters etc. They will always be up to date and you can use as many, or as few, as you need. In this way, the printed text works with on line sources to remain up to date.

Another site you have access to is a web-based information system on Executive Function and barriers to learning. This is at www.personalisedlearningforum.eu and will also be explained later. In both cases, where you need a username and password to use the resources, you can log in with TIFE1/ISBN2.

Education is a co-operative form of creativity. Ideas and material pass freely between colleagues, evolving in the process. It is sometimes very difficult to know where a particular example originated. Almost as soon as I entered FE, I was shown a page for testing students' ability to take tests. Nobody knew where it originated. I used it, found it helpful and passed it on. Thirty years later, leafing through material used by a private company, I saw a version of the original for which they were cheekily claiming copyright. My hope is that this text and the online backup contain only ideas and material that are (a) duly acknowledged and referenced or (b) communally owned or (c) original contributions by the author. For classroom use or staff training sessions, you are free to make photocopies or to project anything that contributes to the cause, and to adapt or pass it on, so long as you acknowledge the source and include any original attributions. [1]

If you happen to recognise something over which you think you have moral rights that were not recorded, please get in touch. Equally, if you wish to comment on opinion, correct errors or typos or contribute to the common weal, your contributions or improvements can be passed on through info@bpfe.org.uk.

---

[1] That legal permission applies to anyone who owns their own copy of the paperback or kindle, or borrows it from a provider's library.

Chapter 1

What is FE?

> Accurate scholarship can
> Unearth the whole offence
> From Luther until now
> That has driven a culture mad.

> W.H. Auden, *Sept. 1st 1939*
> in version printed July 1942

Encompassing the sector

It may be a long time before we stop using the phrase 'further education', but it no longer describes a clearly definable sector.

There used to be a system, largely college-based, that served educational needs 'further to' the age of compulsory schooling. It had its own Further Education Funding Council (FEFC). Then we had 14-19 planning and a Life Long Learning Sector (LLL) involving elements like the Learning and Skills Council (LSC) and Sector Skills Councils (SSCs). Then the LSC was replaced with the Skills Funding Agency (SFA) and Young People's Learning Agency (YPLA) until the YPLA disappeared as the Dept for Business, Innovation and Skills (BIS) exercised its new muscles. Changes of agency are sometimes presented as ways to increase efficiency but are also, usually, ways to impose a new ideology or set of priorities. We shall come to that later.

Historically, FE as we know it is a recent phenomenon, but in personal terms many people think of it as something that has always been around, a feature of their local environment with certain comforting structures that were constant in their lifetime, and that of their grandparents. Radical change will be difficult for them to understand. Popular images by which they might recognise or identify such the idea of FE might include:

Young apprentices and others learning a trade on day-release or full-time courses in carpentry, construction, hairdressing, motor mechanics, care, catering, engineering and other familiar vocational areas.

Full-time courses in the newer vocational areas, such as media and multimedia, web design, popular music and music technology.

Workers seeking promotion or a career change through further qualifications, on day release or in evening classes. This might include cleaners learning to be cleaning supervisors, graduates learning new software programmes or accountants taking their next qualification.

Evening classes in academic courses – GCSE Maths or A Level Psychology – either for general interest or for mature students to enter university, a process also served by Access courses during the day.

Evening classes with a potentially vocational outcome, such as sound recording, furniture restoring, web design or programming.

Adult education defined as leisure courses – drawing, flower arranging, wood turning and holiday Spanish. The concepts of 'leisure' and 'vocational' learning can be difficult to disentangle, as hobbies become vocations in unpredictable ways.

Degree courses – full or part time - sometimes the first year of a course continued at a local university, which may or may not be an ex-polytechnic.

Service to certain groups in the local community, including English as a Second Language, perhaps for refugee groups, asylum seekers, or new citizens. This may include

unexpected hybrids, such as English with Plumbing for
Asian Women.

Adult literacy and numeracy courses for Adults with
Learning Difficulties or younger students with Special
Educational Needs.

A place for the unemployed and the presently
'unemployable', to come to retrain so they can enter the
system and join other courses later. Courses labelled NEET
(Not in Education, Employment or Training) often involve a
combination of practical skills and a form of 'socialisation',
learning how to behave so they can be accepted into the FE
and employment systems.

Link courses for school students aged 14-16 to pursue
vocational options.

This is by no means a complete picture - what about sixth
form colleges; would some academies fit in? - nor are any of
those single elements necessarily part of the future of a given
provider. In many cases, HE will also be pursued in FE,
perhaps with apprenticeships leading to new vocational HE
modules, or one of a range of new vocational degrees.

Taken together, that is a lot of beneficiaries. Depending on
who you count, an annual figure of six million is not an
unreasonable estimate[2] and most of the sector takes its clients
disproportionately from lower social-economic groups. As
government pressure increases to make clients pay for their
own education, replacing grants with loans, that will create its
own difficulties and may (a) reduce the clientele and/or (b)
create a need for more flexible ways to learn; part-time,
modular, on-line, e-learning etc. Classroom teaching will almost
certainly not be the only form you engage with over the next
ten or twenty years. It is hard to imagine it ever disappearing,

---

[2] Key data sources are on bpfe.org.uk/links

but then it was hard to imagine paperbacks giving way to kindles when I wrote the first edition, and in my first year of teaching they hadn't invented PCs. Many of the basic principles of learning may be constant, but the media and social systems through which we apply them will change dramatically in your professional lifetime.

It is worth reflecting historically on some of the defining elements of what we now call FE, with a rich diversity of purposes, and discovering the inherent tensions that will shape its next stage of evolution. These will include the charge that FE is trying to achieve too much, but has consistently achieved too little, that it has been poorly organised for most of its purposes, is a major element of economic development and social justice and can be bought and sold on the open market.

Asking 'what is FE?' is also asking 'what are the purposes and inherent problems of FE?' and we will start with one of the most ironic, tracing a development that runs roughly as follows:

early apprenticeships (on-the-job training) before FE existed

early technical education, from which FE developed

a more complex and academic vision of further education

FE including an element of work-based learning (wbl), often as a poor relation in terms of departmental influence and managerial attention

an expansion of wbl to the point where it looks like a major element of the future of FE, with or without the local colleges, some of which may cease to exist. FE does not have to mean college in any sense that its old clients would recognise.

In tracing this development, we shall have to abandon some of

the comforting terms that are often used to categorise FE. Post
16? No longer. Post-compulsory? Not really. Legislation will
raise the compulsory age of involvement in training to 18,
although it remains to be seen what that 'training' will be in
most cases.

We shall also have to consider very carefully what it means to
be 'professional' in the context of FE. Is it different to being a
professional school teacher?

The dynamics that shaped FE.

What does FE do and what is it for? What kind of students,
or clients, or customers, undertake what kind of experience?
What sort of people work in it, why and how?

Any provider attempting to fulfil even some of the purposes
outlined above might be seen as a haven, a stepping stone for
the local community, whatever their starting point, to develop
their personal potential and to find an active role in society.
That is not an unattractive image and many teachers in FE were
initially motivated by it. Some local residents still think of it in
those terms, and often fondly. Local employers may have
become qualified through a local apprenticeship.

The people who use the service won't necessarily
understand about paymasters and sources of policy for client
colleges, nor about all the agencies and policies meant to create
qualifications and ensure the relevance of learning to economic
needs. They won't realise how much training is now done
privately, or by voluntary bodies and charities. Until recently,
FE could be thought of as a building, or at least as a multi-site
local institution. Now it has to be thought of as a multi-agency
process. There is a tension between performing a social service
and running a business, to which we shall return. Nor is it a
simple opposition of good and bad influence.

It used to be referred to as the post-compulsory sector
because, after the age of 16, education becomes voluntary.

Then we encouraged 14-16 year olds leaving school to attend FE colleges for vocational GCSEs, usually volunteering to go there but during the compulsory stage. Some of those attending vocational training post-16 do not do so because they want to, but because somebody in authority said they needed a qualification to get a job, or to keep the job they already have.

The need for paper qualifications is increasing in most sectors, and this compulsory element drives adult employees into FE, although not necessarily to a local college. They may obtain a National Vocational Qualification (NVQ) on the job through a private agency. But gaining a qualification does not automatically equate to having more ability. The confusion of paper qualifications with employable skills has led to a number of problems, including a kind of inflation as more and more pieces of paper are required to do the same job. This gives work to the FE employees who provide the paper, but does not in itself improve the economy. It means some people are left behind in the paper chase and become permanently unemployable - an underclass without academic 'permits to work', whom nobody wants.

> Ainley & Corbett (1994) took shelf-filling in supermarkets as an example: the requirements for this task have changed remarkably. In the mid-1970s, special school leavers with moderate learning difficulties were shelf-filling in some supermarkets. By 1986, the National Council for Vocational Qualifications renamed shelf-filling 'stock replenishment' and set it at NVQ Level 1. Competence in stock replenishment was then part of the NVQs demanded of trainees on retail YTS. It was later placed at NVQ Level 2 as 'stock control' and has become significantly more complicated through the inclusion of ICT. Graduates at NVQ levels 3-4 may now be employed as 'trainee managers' to perform this task among a range of others.   Ainley (2005) p10

Those who cannot find employment will be told that they

need retraining, preferably leading to qualifications, and even refused state benefits if they do not accept it, creating more post-16 clients for the FE sector. Interestingly,

> Some researchers have noted how empathy and concern for particular groups, such as 'disaffected young people', quickly become strongly moralistic and judgemental, signifying an underlying fear of deviance and portrayals of ' the other' - Ecclestone (2002) p26

This may be a government minister recommending ASBOs or an experienced lecturer, faced with the results of badly managed widening participation, complaining that students behave badly and don't want to learn, and such people have no place in their classroom. We shall return in other sections to the fear invasion and anarchy that affects some teachers faced with new cohorts, and some ministers faced with the stubborn facts of unemployment.

Notwithstanding the element of coercion in some areas, it remains true that adults of all ages do return willingly to education for a variety of reasons, from retraining for a new job to leisure courses, from mid-career to post-retirement. FE is often a second chance for those who did not benefit from the more traditional routes first time round, including mature students with no qualifications wanting to go to university by taking evening classes or Access courses. But it is not only a form of remedial activity for the unqualified or dispossessed, and you may find post-graduates taking short courses to continue their development. You may also find degree courses taking place in the same building as basic literacy classes, and provision for special educational needs sharing space with consultancy work for local employers.

To an outsider, and to some insiders, the picture can seem confusing, as if the term FE covers so many different kinds of provision that it is almost meaningless. Indeed, it is a criticism of some colleges that they try to fulfil so many different roles they cannot hope to fulfil them all adequately. That was the view of the old Adult Learning Inspectorate (ALI):

> ... further education institutions are buffeted by change. They are often very big, very diverse and subject to frequent demands for limitless responsiveness. Grade profiles show that, almost certainly, that degree of responsiveness cannot be reconciled with consistently good provision. Even in the best managed colleges, there will always be areas of learning which have been newly introduced, or are overburdened with student demand, or are in the process of transition to meet changing circumstances of one kind or another in the wider world ... very few colleges can sustain generally high standards for long. Only 45 of the 125 colleges (about 36%) that inspectors judged to be consistently good between 1993 and 1997 have stayed so since. Twenty five of those were sixth form colleges. It may well be time to review the form of governance of incorporated colleges and their relationship to government. ALI (2004) pp27-28

As a result, private enterprise and/or voluntary groups were invited to take over some of these functions, because they could offer a more narrow but more clear focus and a degree of efficiency that big, old-fashioned, muddled colleges cannot:

> Inspectors found too many providers still equating good performance with simple contract compliance (ibid p7). In the area of work-based programmes, the private providers do better...greater proximity to employers...closer in structure and ethos to the companies it. p13

One might suspect that a rational response to such criticism is to abandon much of the work done by a large college and focus more narrowly on just a few specialist markets, those you can do particularly well. These may or may not be those that

are most profitable, and certainly this does not imply that a
more narrow focus would abandon concepts of social purpose.
Ofsted published their opinion that most successful colleges
"have an exemplary response to educational and social
inclusion." (Ofsted WCS p6). On the other hand, the 2006
White Paper stated very clearly that

> As general FE colleges focus increasingly on the core
> economic mission, local authority and voluntary
> providers may focus on wider personal fulfilment and
> community programmes - DfES (2006) forward para 20

FE colleges are subject to deliberately fostered competition
from private providers, with business expertise being imported
to sharpen up the way they manage themselves. Potential
structural reforms include consortia and even the formation of
educational charities with colleges as one element of a
public/private mix.

This situation is most easily understood by considering the
origins of FE, looking at the forces that shaped it, and caused
stress within it, since the very beginning.

Potted history

1 – Whose problem is it to train employees?

One of the interesting tensions within FE is between
college-based training and work-based learning (wbl). College
employees, used to dealing with full-time and day-release
courses, have had to come to terms with an increasing pressure
for training on-the-job, in which their input is reduced and may
be entirely replaced by employers and private agencies. FE
colleges are told to be more responsive to employers, to their
need for a well-trained workforce with the skills to fuel
economic growth. That such a demand needs to be made
requires an explanation. How does a sector considered
primarily vocational manage to be disconnected from

employers? On 14th March 2013 Nick Clegg made a public announcement that:

> Employers will be empowered to design and develop their own Apprenticeship standards and qualifications, so they can address skills shortages that are threatening growth.
> www.dpm.cabinetoffice.gov.uk/news/employers-design-their-own-apprenticeships.

and this was treated as if the idea were somehow new. Let's put in in historical perspective.

Mediaeval trades throughout Europe were highly organised by employers as what we would now, disapprovingly, call restrictive practices. Nobody could operate as a shoemaker, mason, goldsmith, tanner or carpenter unless they had served an apprenticeship to a master from the guild, qualified as a journeyman and, capable of making their own 'master-piece', emerged as a potential member of the guild themselves.

Nobody would take on more apprentices than they needed, and you might pay handsomely for the privilege of becoming one. Quantity and quality were controlled by the trade. This might protect the public - Roman fishermen had rules about the size of nets, to protect fish stocks, and insisted that fishmongers used scales with holes so the public didn't pay for water. It might also protect the guilds from competition - a Florentine skilled in silver and gold brocade work was forbidden to take that skill to another town, on pain of assassination. What was not in any doubt was that someone was in charge and there was order in the system. Insiders could be secure, outsiders were controlled.

The student experience

John de Walton was a mercer (dealer in textiles) in Preston. On 22nd December 1393, he took John Adamson as an apprentice for the term of six years. In return for what he was about to learn, and for food and clothing, the apprentice agreed to pay

---

the master for materials used, to act as guardian of the house
and to refrain from carnal knowledge of the maidservants (on
pain of doubling the term). If he survived these rigours, John
would qualify and receive ten shillings.

(pre-decimal, a penny was 1d, twelve = one shilling (1s or 1/-) and 20
shillings = £1 (= 240d). In 1393 you could live simply on a penny a day.)

Increasingly, apprentices would have to pay the master for
the privilege of qualifying. By the early 16th century that fee
might be anything from 3s4d to 40s (about 17p to £2). An
archer on active service at Agincourt in 1415 would have
earned 6d a day, so it would cost him 80 days active service just
to pay for his son's 'graduation fee'.

Henry V111 later reduced the fees to a maximum of 2s6d to
enter the training, and 3s4d to qualify. Central government
interfered with local self-regulation if it threatened national
interest but, for the most part, let them control their own
affairs.

The student experience

In was in Henry's reign that John Harbard bound himself to a
seven year apprenticeship to William Tebe, Lord Mayor of
Leicester and master baker. He was to be paid 8d a year until
qualified, then 6d a week, plus food and clothing. In return for
not gambling and not becoming engaged without permission,
John would eventually also become a master baker.

By the time apprentices like John were running their own
businesses under Elizabeth I, a school teacher only earned £50
a year and Shakespeare would be handing over copyright for
whole plays at between £3 and £6 a time. Craft skills meant
security and status.

By the time Shakespeare was retired, there were plays like
The Shoemaker's Holiday (Dekker) or Four Prentices of

London (Heywood) reflecting the power and satirising the pretension of the new middle classes, encouraging apprentices to mock their masters and, by implication, flattering them as an important group which no theatre owner wanted to alienate. Ekirch (2006) refers to "upwards of 25,000 apprentices" in London alone by the early 17th century. "roughly 12 percent of the population". It was considered throughout Europe "a popular means of socialising adolescents", certainly "young males of modest origins", although, of course, "large numbers failed to complete their training" (p232). Being an apprentice might have meant membership of an increasingly radicalised group - Harrison (1984) refers to "several thousand citizens and apprentices" enlisted with the Earl of Essex in 1642 and mustering at Turnham Green to prevent the royalist cavalry taking London (p.194).

By the 19th century, industrialisation had led to large towns and satanic mills, in which mass work forces were often not formally qualified and had no hope of becoming their own master, but the apprenticeship system was still taken for granted as a means of controlling labour. Harrison describes how a labour shortage in the early 1800s was solved by taking pauper children from the London workhouses and binding them to northern mill owners. "In one notorious case ... a Lancashire mill owner agreed to take one idiot with every twenty normal children" (p218). He also cites an experience from 1815-16, when up to 150 pauper apprentices would be lodged in a single Prentice House:

The student experience

We went to the mill at 5 o'clock without breakfast, and worked 'till 8 or 9, when they brought us ... water porridge with oatcake in it, and onions to savour it, in a tin can .... This we ate as best we could, the wheel never stopping. We worked on till dinner time (Derbyshire oatcakes, one buttered, the other treacled). We then worked on till nine or ten at night. (p218)

Of course, it was still possible for those who had contacts or financial backing to enter the more traditional trades to gain a more independent future.

The student experience

In 1886, Josia James Goozee signed up for five years to learn the trade of cooper from James Frewin of Battersea. For a 60 hour week with no sick pay, he received 7s 6d a week in year one, rising to 18s a week in year five. This being a year of depression, the average wage was cut from 30s to 27s. Sewing machine hands earned 8s a week. That signed agreement meant security and a potentially profitable future.

Then, when technical colleges and later the FE system emerged, power moved away from the masters, the foreman and employer, to teachers and a growing educational bureaucracy beyond their reach. Training and education became the province of national and local government and for a brief period, from the mid 20th to early 21st centuries, employers were not the main influence on the training of employees.

The student experience

By 1976, an apprentice electrical engineer working for a local authority on the south coast spent 40 hours a week earning £23.88 p.w. with a £6 supplement for shift work. He had more legal rights and freedoms, but was not significantly better rewarded with short term income. It was probably slightly harder for him to start up his own business, but the greatest difference between the 20th century sample and all his antecedents is that he spent a day of each week at a technical college, learning what his employees chose not to teach him themselves. This included most of the electrical theory, and classes in General Studies and 'how to communicate'.

His qualification was formally called a City and Guilds
Certificate but was awarded or withheld by a paper-based
system operated by teachers and central examiners. A degree of
literacy was assumed to be in his interest and was thus insisted
upon. There is evidence (below) that many were less than
grateful for that 'opportunity'.

Four decades later, it is difficult to gain an apprenticeship in
many vocational areas. This is partly because many businesses,
from independent trades people to medium sized
manufacturers, now complain they have no time to train young
people and cannot afford to pay them until they can earn their
keep. They prefer to receive them either unqualified, to fulfil
menial tasks cheaply, or ready-made. Central government is
working hard to persuade employers to take on trainees, and
often prefers young people to be trained 'on the job', which
more cost-effective than full-time college courses.

As Kathryn Ecclestone points out (2002 p17) despite a
record of poor investment in training amongst British firms,
the 'needs of employers' are cited regularly as a driving force
for educational change even though some employers "do not
want, or need, highly skilled workers"

The teacher's experience

In 2003, wondering how to find work for young male students
and what industry needed from FE, an FE Director spoke with
an employers' representative who explained that they did not
want young male employees. They required a small number of
highly trained staff, but a much larger number of semi- or
unskilled people.

Young men expected a career ladder and they couldn't provide
one. They preferred to employ mature married women, as they
were more reliable and more malleable, asking less from the
firm and willing to carry out mundane tasks without

frustration. The 16-18 year olds were often merely a nuisance to local employers, he argued.

The Sector Skills Councils were designed to give employers more influence over vocational qualifications. The present 'reforms' are partly a movement towards a traditional situation which, in historical terms, was only recently changed, and apparently not for the better. However, there is an important change of emphasis. A guild member training an apprentice tanner or mercer was offering a trade for life. The Specialist Diplomas discussed in the early 21st Century, although based in vocational areas, must accept that their task is to make people work-ready not job-ready, and the nature of that work may change radically over a single lifetime. It is likely to be the large firms who have time to take part in designing any new vocational qualifications. Small or medium enterprises (SMEs) and the sole trader are unlikely to affect the outcome directly. But one thing is very clear – FE had its chance to dominate the process and blew it. What went wrong and what can we learn from it?

2 - Training, education and accountability.

Norman Lucas has written a study of FE teaching which analyses the upheavals of the recent decades but begins by placing it in historical perspective. He outlines the

> impoverished legacy and unplanned development of the FE sector and the neglect of FE colleges by policy makers. Lucas (2004 a) p3

and in doing so illuminates several elements of the dynamics that shaped the sector.

Reaching back as far as 1792, he points to the Sheffield Societies formed by mechanics for self-education and radical political organisation, and to schools of industry set up after 1795 for self-improvement. During the 19th century, as well as the voluntary apprenticeship schemes that provided training for young workers, there was continued growth of working class 'self-help' education, involving

> working class literacy, general culture and, above all, political awareness

and it was certainly voluntary for a variety of groups

> reading circles of working men and women ... Owenite halls of science, the 'schools' organised by the Chartists, Christian Socialists, night schools and others.

Unfortunately,

> The principal precursors of the late nineteenth century technical colleges were the mechanical Institutes

which

> did not win credibility as genuinely mass education providers because their major emphasis was access to scientific knowledge through the reading of tracts and pamphlets ... and assumed a high level of literacy (ibid p5)

He cites a complaint in 1857 that an evening school in Shoreditch enrolled volunteers for learning who soon found that the level of reading expected of them, and the sheer tedium of some of the teaching methods relying upon it, led to poor retention (p6). One and a half centuries later, we have identical problems. There is clearly something fundamentally wrong with the relationship between an FE system set up to 'educate' the workers and the clients who feel out of their depth within it, and are not able to learn.

The student experience

When the young apprentice in 1976 entered a college, he was entering a national system with notoriously high failure rates. He was also forced by the college to take tests in written communication. In many cases he, or in rare cases she, would be introduced to the culture of the middle classes by well-meaning General Studies teachers who wanted to elevate them to another form of thinking or responding, perhaps by encouraging them to read a short story. Cupboards full of Jane Austen, rubber stamped as property of the Technical Institute, can still be found in the depths of some college store rooms, left over from the era when it was thought that apprentices could benefit from such an acquaintance, whether they liked it or not. By the seventies Austen was more likely to be replaced by Roald Dahl, who in turn was dismissed in favour of practical tasks, such as learning how to apply for a driving licence or bank account by filling in blank forms. This eventually gave way to the unpopular idea of key skills, with equally poor attendance and high failure rates.

Meanwhile, the turgid hand-outs used by their teachers were sometimes so badly written that Austen would have had difficulty understanding them.

VanderEyken and Barry (1975) cite cases in the seventies where young workers could devote their time to studying whilst at work and, after 3 years, 40 per cent did not receive the qualification.

There is a complex relationship between failure rates and assumptions behind the way those young workers were treated, and a long, dishonourable tradition of expecting young workers to cope with complex written material because it is supposed to be good for them, leaving many not significantly more literate, and too many branded as failures. Too many people have been failed for too long, partly because of unreasonable demands placed upon them by teachers who think it is necessary and reasonable to organise the process of learning on a set of abilities that learners do not possess. That they ought to possess them is an argument to be made, and that is explored in chapter 4, but that is not the same as teaching them as if they already did. If you throw enough people in the deep end, many will drown.

Lucas also describes how the legacy of 19th century technical education was impoverished because it was

> part-time, intellectually narrow and it never acquired a status comparable with that achieved in other continental countries.

It lacked

> any legitimated notion of general culture and general education within which to frame technical skills (9)

Technical subjects never had the status of classical subjects; engineers were not considered 'educated' in the same sense as lawyers. And when technical schools were eventually founded, in the early 20th century, they were poor relations to the grammar schools, and relied on workers being released by employers or, more commonly, turning up after work. It was hard for employers to see what benefits were gained by such an imposition.

The student experience

In 1976 it was still not unknown for young bakers to work a full shift from early in the morning and then attend college for the theory lessons. Unskilled in reading and making notes, not screened to ask if any of them were dyslexic, a group was observed sitting tired but obediently in front of a teacher/baker, who wrote notes upon the board for them to copy, and thus 'taught' them, in preparation for an exam, that a baker's yeast, which they had been mixing all day, was called

---

saccharomyces cerevisiae. Their employers were not keen to subsidise such an experience, but a City and Guilds certificate required attendance at college. To stay in the class, and thus keep their job as bakers, they had to write and remember that technical term.

So, among the strands that can be seen in the historical legacy of FE are:

> Working people trying to better themselves by an educational process that included political awareness, sometimes though self-help groups.

> Institutes that wanted to help working people to enter the culture of the middle classes – reading their books and using their language - but often did so by demanding of them an ability to use that language already which they did not possess

> A centralising force that set up technical schools or colleges with a limiting, ungenerous notion of what technical education might become.

The former have now been largely replaced by evening classes, which one may attend as a client, paying increasingly high prices. Nothing in the latter two took adequate account of what young workers needed, or how they learned. Retention and achievement was low.

Throughout the 20th century, as LEAs were encouraged to take over responsibility for technical education, the strands that emerged from the 19th century have remained stubbornly present and undermined the system:

> A separation between employers and colleges so that the former do not trust or value what the latter insist on providing

An assumption that being competent in a trade enabled someone to teach it to large groups in a college classroom, as opposed to passing on skills at work, although what was passed on and how it had to be learned was quite different

Expectations that students would cope with long hours and high order reading/writing skills in order to learn

Poor records of retention and achievement, so that FE as a sector tended to create failure on a regular basis and was thus poorly viewed by those who funded it

Had the economy remained the same, the problems may also have remained the same. In fact, as the economy changed, the problems grew worse, and more ironic.

3 – FE and the economy

The Department of Education and Science was set up in 1853 to "stimulate and co-ordinate" technical education (Lucas 2004), which was still local and voluntary. Exam boards were set up - Royal Society of Arts (RSA) in 1856 and City and Guilds of London Institute (CGLI) in 1879. The late 19th century saw a growth of technical and polytechnic institutions, intended to bring about useful, vocational knowledge. This was required by the economy but not valued in the same way as the liberal, classical education. It was practical, not theoretically based, and necessary to wealth rather than valued as part of national culture.

The 1902 Education Act, or Balfour Act, laid the basis for post-primary expansion, including evening institutes and junior technical colleges (Lucas 2004 p10) but those were characterised by poor attainment and retention, partly because their 'beneficiaries' were expected to combine work and study.

Development was ad hoc and had low status. We can call 1944 the year that saw "the birth of FE as we know it" when the Education Act required LEAs to provide for 'further' education – further in the sense of coming after the official school leaving age, now raised to 15.[3] There were 680 establishments by 1947 and in 1959 the Crowther Report identified FE as a "crucial sector for generating economic growth" (Lucas 2004a p15). Unfortunately, the old apprenticeship schemes were part of the old economic model. Narrow and restrictive, they took too long to complete and did not provide sufficient skilled workers, nor provide for the semi-skilled or for female aspirants (ibid 16). The newly formed college system reflected the old trades and practices, with teaching staff who were often better qualified as tradesmen than teachers, using pedestrian methods.

It is ironic that at this stage complaints about FE saw teaching staff as too much a product of their industry rather than professional teachers, who might be able to move the system away from old industrial practices, whereas in the 21st Century colleges are criticised for being too remote from local industry to understand their needs. On the other hand, it is still sometimes argued that FE teachers gain their notion of professional pride more from skills in their trade than in their teaching. The Institute for Learning was set up in 2002 to manage the notion of professionalism in FE teaching. It briefly oversaw a compulsory system of registration for a licence to practice that involved CPD and reflective practice. At the time or writing, the licence had become a voluntary matter and quite will be required to operate legally within FE in future remains to be seen.

The growing economy needed something more flexible and dynamic to provide flexible new workers for new kinds of

---

[3] In 1893 it was 11 years, 1899 = 12, 1918 =m14, 1944 =15 and only in 1972 became 16.

industry. FE grew as it tried to supply those needs, but it did so with the cultural inheritance of the old system that was part of the problem. Moreover, as they saw old industries decline, and whole departments started to be underemployed, technical colleges struggled to re-define their markets. They expanded into new vocational areas and, crucially, into more academic and adult-ed courses, to become more like the community-based FE colleges of the late 20th century.

The problem with adding new purposes to old staff and structures is that they might not be able to manage the new ideas. BEC and TEC were introduced and then became merged as BTEC, demanding that staff manage cross-modular assignments and interdisciplinary teaching. A new, more 'educated' and flexible worker was envisaged for the new industries, requiring new, more educated and flexible teachers.

The teacher's experience

By 1989 the new BTEC methods were dominating colleges and centrally devised curricula were intended to change the way teachers behaved, bringing about a more active, flexible, inter-disciplinary kind of learning. A central element of the BTEC philosophy was the cross-modular assignment, which asked students to bring together different subjects to explore a particular issue or theme relevant to their vocational area. Guidelines on how to manage the process and what should arise from it were, depending on one's point of view, generously flexible so teachers could react with creative design, or so vague they didn't know what to do, or could carry on as before with a few superficial changes.

In some cases, it led to serious stress among those who could not understand exactly how their notion of learning – a clear syllabus and teachers in front in control – could survive when students managed their own time for projects. That is why I was told by a teacher in 1989:

> I'm there to implant information... You can look up
> knowledge, but you can't look up skills. Any student
> arriving here who can look up stuff for themselves in
> Maths and Finance didn't ought to be on the course.
> They're too good for it----You've got to pour it in - you
> can't expect them just to look it up.
>
> The notion of pouring in skills is odd, but the concern for
> student welfare was genuine and the stress considerable.

Lucas refers to the effects of the Technical and Vocational Initiative (TVEI) and the Certificate in Pre-Vocational Education (CPVE) in the 1980's, arguing that prevocational courses "showed an approach to pedagogy which emphasised learning as a process (p139). He cites Harkin's finding (1995) that while teaching and learning within GNVQs showed diversity, the more traditional A level teachers found it difficult to adopt a more interpersonal style (p140-41) . "The introduction of AS exams after one year has led to an even more didactic approach by some teachers" (p134). He questions the effects of employer dominance on new standards applied to teacher training for FE, so another interesting tension within the sector is who is supposed to be the source of authority when deciding how teachers should be trained and what sort of experience they should be encouraging. In FE, teachers are drawn from a wide variety of trades at a wide variety of levels. The source of staff is necessarily much more varied than in schools or sixth form colleges, which is both a benefit and a problem in this context.

As employment became harder to find, government started to organise schemes such as Youth Opportunity Scheme (YOPS) and Youth Training Scheme (YTS) to bring students into the colleges and then encourage employers to take them on. CPVE was introduced to offer a flexible model for students to choose their career. Instead of training people for specific jobs, FE started to train people for work in general, and for the problem of finding it (Lucas 2004 p23). In this context, it could be argued that training was what you received after your education enabled you to find someone to take you on. That is a far more complex notion than passing on simple job skills, and colleges were not notably successful at even those.

In a haphazard and often confused manner, colleges responded to market forces and government initiatives, trying to redefine their role, or at least retain their employment. Unfortunately, the pace of change often increased more quickly than the colleges' ability to deal with it, and any new systems tended to inherit many of the dysfunctional strands of the old models. This included the fact that colleges had tended to grow in size without becoming integrated as whole systems. Notions of what constituted the purpose of the college, good teaching, functional literacy or unacceptable behaviour could vary significantly between departments with different vocational cultures.

The more government worried about the problems of workforce and economy, the more it valued FE, and the more it worried that FE was not delivering what it thought it needed, no matter how much it imposed new schemes upon it. Classes were often small and received generous teaching in terms of hours allocated, but results were still poor and dropout rates high. In 1993 dropout rates in FE were 12% for A level and 18 % for vocational course, with exam failures at 20% for both, with funding that ranged between £1,000 to £7,000 for students on similar courses (Lucas 2004a p29). Clearly, reform was essential.

Between 2004 and 2013 a flurry of new Acts continued emphasise the new role and priorities, with FE being hailed as a sector of major importance to our social and financial development even if it was not entirely trusted to deliver without much more 'improvement'. More are added at regular intervals, so to keep this chapter shorter and up to date you can find a brief summary of all the major publications, with their intentions, at www. bpfe.org.uk/materials. You can skim them now and/or return to them as necessary.

> *The tyrant grinds down his slaves and they don't turn against him, they crush those below them. - Emily Bronte*

Allowing for the dangers of generalisation, the effects of Incorporation, in 1993, might be summed up as follows:

Colleges were no longer part of an LEA, defined largely by social purpose, but independent businesses who had to pay their way in an open market.

Managers had to compete for business and, if they failed to control budgets, the college could close.

They would receive large contracts from the local Learning and Skills Council (LSC) but only if the LSC, Ofsted and ALI all agreed they were maintaining standards, so that regular and thorough inspections had financial consequences. These contracts might reflect social purposes approved by central government, but they had conditions and penalties attached.

A new and complex way of funding courses – the unit of activity – meant managers had to measure what students did in terms of the financial consequences and, if they were quick to master the system, could make considerable profits by changes in curriculum design. This system was abused and later dropped.

Students became customers, teachers and managers became sales people, in a system that was asked to behave in a more business-like fashion (= accountable and efficient) but instead started to think of itself as a business, like any other (= profit-driven).

It is understandable that some senior managers, faced with

such pressures, focused their attention on pleasing the new masters and, in their nervousness, insisted that FE staff should comply in all particulars with the new regulations on pain of unemployment. Sometimes, nervously, local managers interpreted regulations more stringently than was actually necessary. This 'compliance culture' was a rule by fear, which does not encourage clear thinking. FE is still recovering from this period, when the parent state lost patience with its errant and expensive children. As Margaret Thatcher famously proclaimed at her Party Conference,

> We want education to be part of the answer to Britain's problems, not part of the cause.

Lucas reminds us that

> The tendency of technical and FE colleges to identify primarily with their vocational, industrial and, later, their subject expertise... contributed to the isolation of FE teachers within their specialisms, thus re-enforcing the diverse and fragmented teaching and learning traditions which still characterise FE today (2004a p62)

The general distrust of the educational establishment felt by central government is ably illustrated by Kathryn Ecclestone. Focusing on the particular example of General National Vocational Qualifications (GNVQ) she shows that surprising amounts of time and money were spent by central bureaucracies trying to find ways to control teachers, to manage what happened in the classroom by laying down ever more complex guidelines on content and process.

> *They constantly try to escape*
> *From the darkness without and within*
> *By dreaming of systems so perfect*
> *That no-one will need to be good.*
> T.S. Eliot, *The Rock*

The process, in fact, created

> Major contradictions in goals and practices for teachers
> and students having to implement them.
>
> Ecclestone (2002) p3

So it made worse a situation that was already seen by central
government as so bad it could no longer be run by its own
managers.

> Government agencies intend, probably implicitly, that
> burgeoning guidance and regulation will compensate
> for poor staff development and an absence of regular
> discussion of criteria and requirement among teachers,
> students and awarding bodies (p179)

Ecclestone shows how the policy of central government
becomes "encoded in complex ways through political and
organisational struggles, compromises and the ensuing public
interpretations of policy intentions" (p6). By looking back from
what happens in the classroom, comparing it to what is said by
government agents, we can decode the system.

Part of the decoded message is that teachers cannot be
trusted.

> An important aim in NVQs and GNVQs was, then, to
> reduce the influence of teachers with assumptions that
> learning is not a social but an individual process –
> Ecclestone (2002) p49

An NCVQ official admits:

> One can't have great faith in teachers. They aren't going
> to change overnight to become inspirational. Improve
> teachers, by all means, but there must be other means....
> Autonomy is therefore associated with independence
> from institutional timetables and teachers' idiosyncratic
> and often lacklustre approaches (ibid p60)

As Lucas points out, FEFC inspections tended to conclude that

> Poor teaching in FE colleges was … a consequence of insufficient knowledge by teachers of how learning takes place, particularly within the context of a growing diversity of students (85)

A system designed to bring about autonomous learning in students denies any autonomy to the teachers supposed to manage the process because it doesn't consider them professionally able. It is not surprising that the workforce started to lose confidence and that recent calls for a professional workforce include a requirement to re-build that confidence.

Towards the end of the 20th century, when government took increasing control of the curriculum and assessment regimes that dictate classroom interaction, they did so on the assumption the teachers were the weak element of education, and if central planning could not replace them it had to shape the learning process by controlling it from outside. At the same time, LSCs were asking colleges to become centres of vocational excellence. Teachers were asked to take the lead in raising standards but were controlled by external guidance to the point that they began to lose confidence and became fearful of transgressing the assessment and inspection regimes. As external tests were increased because they were more rigorous than coursework assessment, Moderators were replaced by External Evaluators (EVs) because, as one ex-moderator put it to me at the time, "they think we tend to go native".

This was a time of newly independent management, nervously insisting on a compliance culture. Creative, independent professionals were not a likely outcome. It was in this context that the idea of formative assessment was supposed to take root, encouraging teachers to use feedback loops to encourage learners to analyse their own processes, but the weight of paperwork and lack of confidence did not encourage such movements. Reforms came thick and fast, often contradicting and certainly undermining each other.

Students, faced with a need to qualify to get jobs, wanted to know how to please examiners and EVs. External bodies laid down guidelines to control the learning process. Thus "images and values within teachers' notions of professionalism are squeezed in subtle ways" (Ecclestone 2002 p173)

Research would help concerned teachers to understand their predicament, if they had time to read it and the confidence to respond. But Ecclestone is aware that

> Low morale and intensification of work in FE colleges can tempt researchers and teachers themselves to see policy and its facets as the main cause of problems and themselves as powerless to influence policy.

so that

> Researchers need to find new ways to engage practitioners more deeply with issues raised by research (178)

This is a major concern for Ashcroft and James (1999), who argue that

> Many reforms have occurred in a climate of consumerism, marketisation and increased accountability and have either reduced professional autonomy or *appeared* to do so (p1-2)

Thus FE teachers now need to have their confidence restored.

Ashcroft and James think one means to do that is to involve practitioners in research, although they admit this is a process that might involve a short-term reduction in confidence, or at least comfort, as teachers explore their practice and its context (4 & 45). Of course, they lack time to reflect – workloads were deliberately increased under the new contracts that followed incorporation. They are under pressure to perform in class all day every day (p43) and don't have the support systems often required by researchers (p44), but reflection will show them, for example, that there is no magic bullet solution to teaching, no recipe to be followed, but that teachers need to be able to respond with a range of solutions according to context (p52-55).

They need also to resist the 'proletarianisation' of their work as decisions are made centrally and they are stripped of certain skills and autonomy (p111). This process will not be helped by a tendency for colleges to ride out economic problems by using increasing numbers of part-time (=disposable) staff, what Lucas refers to as "unhealthy levels of casualisation and insufficient emphasis on improving professional skills" (2004b) p37.

Models of research incorporated into education tend to be subject based, and need 're-contextualisation' to be truly relevant and useful. The training of teachers was ruled by standards that used to be from the Further Education National Training Organisation (Fento) but then went to its replacement - Life Long Learning UK (LLLUK)[4]. They became "increasingly restricted to skills and behaviours that are easily assessed and observed" (117). Walker and Ryan (in Aschcroft and James ed 1999) argue that teachers need to be empowered to make decisions on a professional basis, and if students had more control over their work they would have better motivation (p144) so issues of control, autonomy and what makes for educated, professional practice are related.

Lucas reminds us that

> The new roles full-time teaching staff are expected to undertake in FE colleges include counselling students, marketing and promoting their own courses, managing

---

[4] Lifelong Learning UK closed in March 2011. Many of its s responsibilities transferred to the Learning and Skills Improvement Service (LSIS) but at the time of writing that is also being reshaped. Try bpfe.org.uk for updates.

> budgets and course teams and developing open and
> flexible learning systems as well as new learning
> techniques for distance and independent learning (2004
> a, p84)

The very people mistrusted and dismissed by some elements in central agencies are also supposed to become multi-talented professionals, as they take up increased teaching loads and a new set of responsibilities. How much of the life of a graduate in English or a master plumber prepares them for these roles? And how much of the managerial culture of colleges encourages such creativity and independence?

Fortunately, there are signs that the very agencies who helped to create such problems have learned from it and are now working hard to reverse the process. Experiments with Advanced Practitioners (APs) were followed by Subject Learning Champions (SLCs), who could take materials and ideas from the DfES and spread them through their college. But, of course, the materials for SLCs were centrally prepared, and the SLCs themselves approved by central agencies to remain 'on message', but the potential existed for creative teachers to feed their own ideas into the system. Similarly, good practice is recorded and shared through 'good practice' sites. [5]

The model as we enter the 21st century is of a moderated exchange of ideas by professionals informed by research and by each other's experience. And, slowly, reforms seem to be working. Although we still have a low rate for participation post-16 by international standards, success rates (and by implication FE's efficiency) are improving, although financial constraints will discourage post 16 study. In Feb 2013 the latest statistical release from the DFES (Feb claimed that:

> The proportion of 16-18 year olds in full-time
> education fell from 68.6% in 2010 to 67.7% in 2011.
> This is the first time it has fallen since 2001.

---

[5] Up to date list on bpfe.org.uk/links

Overall participation in education and work-based
learning rose by 0.5 percentage points (ppts), to 79.0%.

The proportion of 16-18 year olds NEET rose by 0.8
ppts, from 9.1% in 2010 to 9.9% in 2011.

Of course, one always has to interrogate figures carefully.
Steedman et al (2004) highlight an interesting contradiction:

> The 2003 OECD PISA study[6] showed that even our
> poor performers score better than their counterparts in
> some other countries. Yet half the English students
> scoring at Level 3 on PISA tests may have failed to gain
> a grade C pass in English. Are we setting the bar too
> high too early? Other countries with a more socially
> equitable distribution of educational achievement (e.g.
> the Scandinavians) do not set a formidable hurdle at 16
> and have very few high achievers, but also fewer very
> low achievers at age 15. (p3)

Because what we ask of them at 16 is so difficult to do,
many give up trying. Even bright students may fail the GCSE
English because it asks too much too early. So perhaps
complaining that too few students possess it at grade C is not a
complaint about their potential, or about poor teaching, but
about the nature of the crude and outmoded GCSE system?
What *exactly* are we worried about? That argument will wait
until chapter 4.

Conclusions?

So, after all that, what is FE?

---

[6] Programme for International Student Assessment , an internationally
standardised assessment, jointly developed by participating countries and
administered to15-year-olds in schools. OECD = Organisation for
Economic Co-operation and Development

It might have been relatively easy under the Further Education Funding Council to talk of an FE sector. Now, we have a 'learning and skills sector'. This includes further education and sixth form colleges, schools with sixth forms, local authority and adult education institutions and private and voluntary sector providers. There is much reform centred on the 14-19 age range which involves new partnerships between several of these players, in various combinations. FE and sixth form colleges work with schools, private training companies and independent charities to serve the needs of the community as defined by ... whom? It might be a priority for economic development identified by national government and passed down through national or local planning agencies. or a need identified by a local group of employers, taken up by the college and approved by such agencies. It might be a need identified by local groups for which funding is sought and a contract negotiated through them.

It might involve colleges providing consultancy services for local business to make income that pays for better buildings or higher salaries, or is used to subsidise courses for the less fortunate to whom it feels a responsibility. That is a choice for managers to make. So, if you enter FE to serve the needs of local communities, you may have to decide which element of the FE market place to join, and how to find a role within it that best fulfils your purpose. It may or may not be a local college, and colleges will continue to vary greatly in size and type. FE colleges might decide to buy themselves a local school or set up their own academies. Some will slim down to smaller, more focused units whilst others will grow. It may be that the new 'Tescos' of FE will drive out the old educational corner shops in your high street, which may or may not increase quality and choice.

As for career structures, as work is increasingly multi-agency it may be that future careers will span several agencies. In a 'Tesco' mega-college there will be room for many different roles internally. It is not clear at the moment what qualifications will be required or how those pieces of paper will relate to an ability to bring about learning. Ofsted is convinced that poor teaching equates with lack of formal training, so, there may be more formal training, more competition, more influence of business expertise and employer bodies upon education and yet more reform, which this time encourages a more fluid market, which may invent under market forces a form of provision that is yet to be imagined. But good teaching will still be good teaching, whoever pays you to do it. And bad teaching will have consequences far deeper than just a bad day for the teacher. We must focus now on the clients, or students, or customers, or beneficiaries, as you may choose to conceptualise them.

Chapter 2 looks at the range of clients that FE might choose to serve, and their different needs and purposes. Chapters 3 to 7 then look in detail at the basic elements that make up any rational plan when approaching those clients to try to help them.

Chapter 3 - how do you prepare material for a wide range of different people in one group, and include them all in the learning process? How do you know the information you are offering can be read and/or understood? How do you help students to think about learning, and feel responsible for their own? What is being learned when you try to teach them?

Chapter 4 - how can students learn how to learn? What exactly are they supposed to be good at, and why? Who says so, how do we know and what should we do about it? How can you use feedback to allow students to improve their performance, and do so efficiently as part of the daily routine? What do we mean by all these 'skills' they are supposed to develop?

Chapter 5 – behaviour is often a major concern. Some of the clients for FE may have rejected learning or been rejected by it. How are these factors manifested and how should we respond? How to manage energy and stress levels - theirs and yours.

Chapter 6 - what is the purpose of a tutorial and how can you use them to get real benefits? What sort of information is available to tutors and teachers and how should it be used? How can paperwork serve the teaching process and not simply take time away from it? Why does all that bureaucracy exist and what is the most productive way to respond?

Chapter 7 - Equal opportunities - what does this mean for teachers? What are the real issues and how do they affect planning and delivery?

As we start the next stage, it is worth considering that in Ofsted's report on the Learning and Skills sector for 2011/12 the percentage of really outstanding teaching they had just observed in the GFE sector was precisely nil[7]. In 6th form college's, nil. Independent Specialist Colleges? Nil. There was plenty of good teaching, but even more that was declared to be only average at best. Are Ofsted judging harshly or is really that hard to get it right?

---

[7] *The report of Her Majesty's Chief Inspector of Education, Children's Services; Learning and skills* , Ofsted 2012

Chapter 2

The clients for FE and how we should relate to them

Whom do we serve, why and how?

Few statements can be made about any group entering FE
that is true about all of them. However, as an exercise in
thinking about different needs and approaches, the following
will help to clarify the changing situation and, in passing, revive
an old argument about medium and message.

The previous chapter mentioned a range of possible
activities that could be included under the term FE, or the Life
Long Learning Sector. It also warned that structural changes
continue and that wherever you are working in the next few
years you may find old cohorts disappearing and new ones
appearing or increasing. One trend will make a particularly large
difference. The 2006 White Paper stated:

> The economic mission will not be the sector's sole purpose.
> Education and training for personal fulfilment, community
> development and the love of learning all have an important
> place and will be sustained, though the pattern of
> institutions specialising in such programmes is likely to
> change. As general FE colleges increasingly focus on the
> core economic mission, local authority and voluntary
> providers may focus on wider personal fulfilment and
> community programmes, with funding targeted on securing
> high quality provision which meets local community
> priorities.   DfES (2006) forward 20

That could mean that a great deal of adult participation in
the local college may in future be run elsewhere, or at best run
by others on the same premises. The percentage of mature
students compared to 14-19 year olds adults will alter, which
may also alter the atmosphere of the institution.

The same white paper emphasised new ways to combine, so that consortia might include colleges with schools and private providers, local businesses and universities. Each will have their own special talents and thus market share. This combines with promises to strengthen sixth form colleges as they offer more vocational options. What is the specific talent of an FE provider that marks out its market?

> FE is particularly effective in providing HE for learners from more disadvantaged groups, backgrounds and communities. Many FE colleges offer flexible, local opportunities which make HE accessible to people who might otherwise face significant barriers to participation. The sector is well placed to promote wider participation in HE.
> DfES (2006) 2.42.

There is also an emphasis on continuing work on the 14-19 spectrum, with more contribution to the 14-16 groups who are now used to school for FE in increasing numbers, and for longer periods.

So, along with an economic function to provide skilled workers, FE has a social function to promote equality by encouraging the disengaged and then developing the disadvantaged to the point they can also take up a productive place in the working community. This could imply that the students in FE over the next few decades will become in, general terms, younger and more disadvantaged than was previously the case. What would this mean for teachers? This is not an easy question, and many easy assumptions may need to be examined. Consider, for example, the growth of the pre-16 market.

Pre-16

School teachers were always able to teach in FE if they wished, although they would not always be qualified to run vocational appraisal systems. Since April 2012, FE teachers with QTLS are able to teach in schools. At the time of writing it looks as if just about anyone can teach in academies, but that is under discussion.

The old cut off point of 16 became link courses 14-16 and that is evolving into a more permeable barrier. Discussion continues - endlessly - about how vocational qualifications might gain parity of esteem with academic courses. What is clear is that, one way or another, increasing numbers of under 16 years olds will be using FE. This involves FE teachers in legal responsibilities and levels of pastoral care that many of them are not used to and some had to be 'trained' for their new roles.

Unsurprisingly, almost everything offered as good advice for 14-16 year olds is equally true of 16-19 year olds. That does not mean there are not important differences, but they need to be stated carefully. Here, for example, are some often repeated claims:

14-16 students cannot cope with longer periods of study?

Lessons in school may be shorter than lessons in FE, but they are largely classroom-based. Practical workshop sessions might have to be longer but might equally be easier for students to accept, although the concentration span at any age will vary enormously from the more to the less able. Longer periods in a classroom might be more difficult for them, but for how long can you expect anyone, of any age, to sit in a classroom without developing an urgent need to escape? Many post 16 classes might usefully be shorter, more varied and more succinct. See chapter 3 on differentiation.

14-16 students are likely to have more behavioural and learning difficulties?

That depends who chose them and for what purpose. Historically, students on Work Related Learning programmes were sent away from school because they were not engaging, and FE was supposed to offer vocational pathways to try to repair the damage. These students, by definition, would be the more difficult cases. Some colleges managed to change their attitudes and had great success, but some departments, asked to supply staff for WRL, sent the least able teachers, reserving the more able for the 'better' students. Even their best teachers, used to a less challenging class, sometimes could not relate to them and were not always trained to do so before trying.

Increase Flexibility (IF) was supposed to offer parity of esteem and attract more able students to vocational pathways. In some colleges, the first cohorts were just more WRL students using IF funding, but others were more selective and the average effect was to increase in the level of ability among 14 -16 year olds in FE, so that the range was wider. Not all teachers in FE realised early enough that they had to raise their expectations for this new intake.

As more students from this wider range continue to enrol, and sixth form colleges increase their vocational links with schools, what used to define a client group will now misrepresent them, but can still act as a self-fulfilling prophecy. On the other hand, research to date indicates that the greatest improvement under IF was made by those with the lowest prior achievement, so it may be tempting for planners in future to target funds at the lower achievers to get maximum results for the investment.

14-16 students do not like change and react badly if you change routines often or without warning?

This is true of many classes regardless of age. It may be more obviously true of the fragile learner, but a general assumption that change upsets students, especially when it carries signals about a lack of care or consideration, is always recommended, regardless of age.

14-16 students come from a much more protected environment?

The original WRL intakes were often from socially deprived backgrounds, so in that sense they were sometime woefully unprotected. However, legally, the *loco parentis* expectations in schools are such that many FE teachers had some difficulty adjusting. There are legal obligations in knowing where a student is under 16, and safe routines for passing them between adults who are legally responsible for them[8]. Some schools will provide materials, notebooks and pens but FE usually doesn't, so students could be blamed for being irresponsible when the problem lies with the staff who did not understand the problems of transition.

There is a case to be made for increasing the protection offered to FE post 16 students, especially at the lower levels of ability, so we can learn from schools how to look after our more vulnerable intake. Widening participation increases the ratio of fragile learners. Students from a small school will often find it very intimidating to enter a large college building, and FE staff can under-estimate the psychological problems inherent in that physical transition, but that can also be true of many post-16 students, especially those from disadvantaged backgrounds with damaged confidence levels, and is still true of many adults, especially if they have been out of education for some years and have lingering memories of a previous failure or rejection. A large college can be a brutally impersonal environment and those who have grown used to it easily underestimate the courage required to enter it.

Mature students

The term refers to funding rules, not a psychological state. If everyone over 19 has to pay for their education, then everyone over 19 is an adult student, however immature they

---

[8] Note this does not depend on a student's birthday but on the official end date for year 11, so they could be legally entitled to pre-16 levels of care if they are over 16 but still in year 11.

may appear in terms of emotional or intellectual development. If fees are paid until 23, then 'adult' rules begin at 23. There are general assumptions made about 'adult' learners that assume they have been in work and that their 'life-experience' has altered their attitude to learning and/or the way they should be treated. These are also worth examining.

The adult leaner tends to "seek out learning experiences in order to cope with specific life-changing events – e.g. marriage, divorce, a new job, a promotion, being fired, retiring, losing a loved one …" Zemke (1984).

There are several ways we may meet adult learners in FE, and changes in funding following changes in government priorities will affect the learning context. When evening classes were reasonably priced and formed a major element of FE enrolment, it was common to find adults enrolling for classes as a means of breaking out of old habits and establishing a new self-image. The material being covered in the class was secondary to the experience of being seen as a learner, making new friends and gaining confidence. Passing the course may not have any direct vocational relevance, but the idea of succeeding might be vital to the process of re-shaping their lives. It is in this context that the OECD took a wide view in their 2003 review of provision:

> The justifications for increasing participation in adult learning (2.3 page 26-32) are extended beyond the obvious economic benefits (for example, increased employability and greater productivity) to include social benefits (for instance, individual wellbeing and increased social returns such as better health) as well as political benefits (including improved civic participation and a strengthening of the foundations of democracy)

In the 1980s I ran a class for mature students (over 21) who took O Level English as an evening class. There were usually several newly-separated or divorced members. Often, there would be women who had been at home looking after families who had now left. They saw this as an opportunity to get out of the empty space and re-establish themselves in ways they had not yet fully defined. They might have abilities considerably in excess of those needed for the qualification. Once their confidence was restored, the might go on to more advanced levels.

Now the emphasis is changing, with more focus on skills that are useful to the economy in a direct and short-term sense. Trades unions are being approached to bring more of their members into the certificating process, often with an emphasis on basic skills. There is an expectation that the proportion of college income provided by its 'customers' will rise. The wider, self-exploratory, self-validating purpose of FE may be reduced by this movement. But it may not. We cannot tell in advance how many people who appear to be satisfying short-term economic goals are also gaining in other, more complex ways. That is a useful caveat when approaching the next common assumption.

Adult learners tend to be instrumental in their approach?

It is often assumed that adults will be less interested in subjects than problems, more interested in immediate application of what is learned to a task or context. They want to know how to do something and want to learn as quickly as they can. The archetype here might be someone who wants to know how to do their own plumbing, manipulate a sound-recoding system or make their own clothes or web site. If the college sets up a course leading to a qualification, many of those who enrol may have left before the portfolio is handed in, having earned what they needed, used the facilities and got their money's worth. What do they want with some piece of paper that, if you are honest, only really exists to justify the course to funding agency, who use pass-rates to monitor 'quality' The formal syllabus and bureaucracy of certification limit an otherwise efficient exchange between student and teacher, where the latter is the gatekeeper to learning opportunities.

It would seem pointless putting anyone through a certification process they do not need, and then being labelled as poor quality, if you could instead just offer modules and equipment on a daily basis with a fee based on speed of learning. Private contractors have this freedom. Colleges would have it if they negotiated with their funding agencies, and more of them may use it in future. But this problem is not confined to adults. Many fourteen year olds might be happier learning how to use a lathe if they didn't have to pass an exam in it later. Teachers sometimes complain that students won't learn something for the sheer pleasure of learning. What they really mean is that student won't learn what they want them to learn for pleasure, and even take pleasure in the certification process that dictates much of the classroom experience. Students might willingly learn many things if we just let them get on with it, instead of imposing our syllabus and certificates on them. Fee-paying adult customers can demand that right; 14-19 year olds cannot.

This may sound like a hopelessly unrealistic abrogation of responsibility. After all, the public purse pays for FE to exist and those who pay demand a means of measuring quality. Someone has to control what happens in the classroom to ensure fairness, consistency, responsibility etc. Yes, perhaps, but step back for a few moments and consider that what is learned in any exchange between student and FE is more than a few facts, concepts or techniques. How people are taught may matter more than what they are taught, and it is worth asking whether control of the educational process ought properly to be in the hands of its clients.

Ivan Illich, over 40 years ago, argued cogently but, it appears, ineffectually, for the de-schooling of society. His argument was that educational bureaucracy, like all bureaucracies, develops a dynamic that is more interested in perpetuating itself than serving its original purpose and clients. But even if it did not, its original purpose would be antidemocratic because what schools teach people is that schools know best. Wisdom is defined by teachers and apportioned to the student, who passively accepts his or her role as a consumer.

> Poverty then refers to those who have fallen behind an advertised ideal of consumption in some important respect. In Mexico the poor are those who lack three years of schooling, and in New York they are those who lack twelve. (p11)

Kierkegaard thought education was the process you had to run through to catch up with yourself, but Illich points out that once it is 'commodified' it becomes something you have to consume for a given length of time. Once schools have taken control, education is not liberating because it does not consist of a free transaction between those who wish to know and those who help them find out or develop. They acquire a monopoly and abuse it, deciding what learning will look like and how long it will take. The process is ritualised so we pass through it without thinking to question it.

He makes an interesting distinction between institutions that exist to produce something and those that exist to be used, between manipulative institutions (gaols, nursing homes, orphanages) and convivial institutions (sewage systems, drinking water companies). This distinction is rather naïve, when you consider the effects of privatising railways and water supplies. The customers have not acquired more rights over the things they want and have little say on how they are manipulated. Nonetheless, it is a useful starting point in considering the problem of the hidden curriculum. Illich argues that the US school system teaches its students to become dependent consumers:

> Schools are designed on the assumption that there is a secret to everything in life; that the quality of life depends on knowing that secret; that secrets can be

known only in orderly succession; and that only
teachers can properly reveal those secrets. An individual
with a schooled mind conceives of the world as a
pyramid of classified packages accessible only to those
who carry the proper tags (p78)

The job market depends upon making skills scarce and
keeping them scarce (91).

The latter logic is that it takes longer and longer to qualify,
so the poor are kept out of the system. In Illich's ideal world,
anyone wanting to learn Spanish would be linked to a Spanish
speaker and encouraged to get on with it. Learning webs would
link people together to learn from each other, liberated by a
system that linked those who possess with those who desire to
possess, those who can with those who wish to. He made these
points in the days before the internet revolution. Now, if you
can overcome a natural reluctance to engage in idealism that
has been ignored as impractical, you can imagine an interesting
business concept here. Push the self-serving bureaucracy out of
the way, encourage and facilitate a free exchange of knowledge
and abilities within the population, and you are a learning web
instead of a seller of courses. Money has to change hands and
quality has to be controlled, but does that mean exams have to
be taken and courses have to be time-bound in unimaginative
ways? What is necessary and what is only assumed to be so?
Illich approaches the problem from a political viewpoint,
looking for ways to put citizens in charge of their own fate.
From a commercial point of view, we might consider a
customer seeking to use FE for service and being hampered
because they can't find what they want when they want it. To
suit the convenience of the provider, they are forced to follow
an extensive course with an exam they don't need that won't
start until September. Finding ways to provide roll-on-roll-off
education, on demand, suited to the client's needs, has proved a
major challenge to larger providers. It takes a lot of pressure to
persuade an oil tanker to change course, just to avoid a few

dinghies in its way.

Adults bring a life-history to the class which is complex and may be used positively.

Yes, there is the obvious fact that adults have lived longer, and their experience may be a resource. But

> (a) some of those experiences may be negative, especially those related to education

> (b) their ideas of what learning entails, at least in a formal context, may not have changed since they left school

> (c) they have had longer to get stuck in their ways

so that introducing new ideas may be difficult because they have to accommodate them into a mental framework that could be older than the teacher and backed by years of habit.

No matter how much status they may have at work, or at home as parents, in the classroom they suffer old memories of the class where Miss can tell you off and make you feel small. In this sense they have more to lose than younger students, so may be less willing to experiment until you have established a safe, trusting environment. But such an environment is also required for younger students. Many of the points made about adult learner also apply to 14-19 year olds.

For example, advice to teachers at the University of Hawaii carefully points out that:

> Long lectures, periods of interminable sitting and the absence of practice opportunities are high on the irritation scale

> Self-esteem and ego are on the line when they are asked

to risk trying new behaviour in front of peers

Feelings about authority and pre-occupations with
events outside the classroom affect in-class experience.
- Zemke (1984)

Well, yes, but that is also true of all other students. In fact,
adults may at first be more tolerant of poor teaching because
they have learned restraint as a function of good manners,
whereas bored adolescents have fewer reasons not to respond
with obvious rejection.

Although there are clearly differences in the way one might
approach different groups, there are not many principles of
good teaching that do not apply equally to all ages – any
adjustments should be a matter of degree rather than kind. At
the same time Illich was trying to free learners from school,
Malcolm Knowles (1968) was distinguishing pedagogy from
andragogy. The former involves learners who are dependent,
bringing little of worth to the learning process, who learn
subjects in an agreed time limit. The latter involves adults who
are motivated to learn and bring valuable experiences with a
desire to experiment and apply. They are learning because they
feel a need to learn, and have volunteered.

Kidd (1975) develops the idea and stresses that

> the deepest need an adult has is to be treated as an
> adult; to be treated as a self-directing person, to be
> treated with respect. Andragogy is student-centred and
> problem-orientated (p36)

But of whom is that not true? Who would not prefer it that
way? A summary of research into the needs of 14-16 year olds
published by the LSDA was entitled *Behaving Like Adults*
(Harkin 2006) and stressed that a major motivating factor for
them was the more adult environment, being treated with more
respect and consideration and, interestingly:

asking students how they would like to learn instead of telling them how to learn (p23)

Now there's a thought, and the next chapter explores some of its implications. Meanwhile, any argument about education that assumes adults should be treated with more respect and consideration that non-adults has missed the point of education. Chapter 4 also considers the problem that the medium is the message – what we learn is how we learn and vice versa.

The previously or improperly excluded

FE is particularly successful at educating those whom others would normally exclude. They may be whole groups, like the NEET cohorts who, under a strong economy we used to ignore but now we seek to enrol, partly as a means of social control. It might be individuals from PRUs who need to be re-introduced to mainstream systems. It might be groups or individuals with a particular mental health issue that previously we thought might debar them, but under recent legislation are obliged to accommodate.

This can pose problems of socialisation in the sense that we have to ensure that people who were previously loud, aggressive, uncontrolled and physically violent learn to behave in ways that make them acceptable outside their ghettos or protected environments.

The student experience

Andrew's parents and social worker were desperate to get him into some kind of educational experience. Aged 16, he had been excluded for the last year and just moped about at home, with no future. His history was of sexual predation on younger students and the school (a private boarder) had been allowed to

---

exclude him as 'unsafe'. The post-16 college was asked to find ways to include him. It was agreed that he could attend a certain class to try to re-integrate on condition that:

He was closely supervised by a tutor who was told in confidence some details of his history.

The courses did not require that he attend on days when pre-16 link courses were running in that area.

He was not permitted in areas where students with special needs attended classes, as they were especially vulnerable to his kind of predation and attractive to him as they often seemed young for their age.

There were regular reviews of his progress and behaviour.

Nobody else knew of his history.

He achieved a series of A* GCSEs within nine months and, more importantly, proved that he had managed to control his behaviour within college. Counselling had been arranged, despite initial objections from his father.

Colin was 19, without any qualifications, tall, loud and had a habit of staring at you which was disconcerting if you didn't know him. He hated being told he was wrong and tended to argue his case forcefully. His probation worker didn't know what to do to find him a future or a place within society; Colin thought he might want to work in the travel business, relating to clients. He was given a place on low level course to see if he could cope with its demands.

Intellectually, he coped, although he needed learning support to catch up on key skills. He argued with teachers, who sometimes found themselves scared of him, and was eventually expelled for aggressively shouting at a student for 'staring' at him.

Counselling and PA support had failed to address his emotional difficulties, some of which were chemically enhanced.

Kevin had no qualifications, a shy demeanour and a withered hand. His father shouted at him loudly in public. He wanted to be a chef. His Personal Adviser met him in a café and talked about coming to college. She found him a special glove that allowed him to manipulate the knives and food. She introduced him personally to the teachers and met him at regular intervals to build his confidence. He enjoyed the course, gained confidence and was capable of full-time work.

Deirdre was an adult student enrolled in Graphic Design. She had a weak heart and a disabled sticker for her car. The college arranged a special parking place near to her building so she could avoid stress and long walk to get to her class. Then it moved the class to a room at the top of three flights of stairs with no lift.

Andrew, Colin and Kevin are the sort of students who pass through Student support regularly, but sometimes just turn up at an enrolment centre and are processed without suitable conversation and assistance. Deirdre's was a simple case of a large organisation not talking to itself. Adjusting to the needs of individuals is a complex process, but in some cases we just need the large bureaucracy to act more efficiently and with more humanity. Sometimes it needs to act as the agent of wider society, imposing standards of behaviour and facilitating the student's growth into them so they can then move freely in the wider world.

In the latter role, we have a special problem. Schools are microcosms of their local society. You have 'rough' schools and mixed schools depending on location. FE is a microcosm of wider society. There is no social-economic or cultural group who does not access the service, often using the same building at the same time. There are very few other circumstances in which such a wide range of social groups meet in such intimate proximity. This forces people to interact in ways that are not natural to them, and not necessary outside of the FE environment.

The social mix

The clients for the hairdressing salon in X College tended to be retired people treating themselves to a special day on their pension. They sometimes went into the canteen for a coffee. Students on the animation course were usually adults, often postgraduates. They also liked a coffee before class. On Tuesdays, they all were subjected to student radio, with avant-garde music and jokes from the 16-19 media group, which the animation students found easier to tolerate than the hairdressing clients.

On other tables, they could overhear conversations about sexual adventures during the previous weekend and, from time to time, observe rows breaking out among the level one care course, which on one occasion led to abusive language and a fist fight between two girls.

Mr Smith brought his son for an interview for a level 3 Diploma course. Passing through reception, he heard a lower level group gathering for the afternoon session. They were excited, talking loudly, using language that they considered normal. Mr. Smith took his son away again, and they withdrew his application. He did not expect to encounter such behaviour as his introduction to his son's potential future, and was shocked.

In our ordinary daily lives we limit the kind of social interaction we have with people from widely different social groups. In FE, where all groups are enrolled then use the facilities closely together, they might run into 'alien cultures' more often and more closely than normal. Management of a social environment under such circumstances is an under-appreciated art.

Also under-appreciated is the extent to which how we teach is also what we teach – the medium, is the message. In fact, the whole experience of being in FE is laden with messages, and sometimes teachers try to control only the least important of them. Chapter 4 assumes that the manner in which the learning experience is organised, managed and assessed is itself a series of messages about what learning means and how educated people behave. Chapter five looks at how we manage behaviour. Both need to be considered in the context of an organisation that forces upon each other a wide variety of social groups with considerable differences in what they want from FE, how they think they should be treated by it and how they think it is reasonable to treat the teacher. We should start by considering in more detail some differences in how people learn

Chapter 3

Differences and how we respond to them

Sherry Turkle is professor at MIT and author of *The Second Self: computers and the human spirit*. She took her 14 year old daughter to see an exhibition on Darwinism which included live turtles. One was very still and the other even less than active, in dirty water. Her daughter decided a robot would be better and other children in the queue agreed - "For what the turtles do, you don't have to have live ones".
London Review of Books, Diary, page 36, Vol 28 Number 8, 20th April 2006

Can that be applied to teachers? If not, why not?

Differentiation

It is stating the obvious to insist that students are different to each other in various ways, and that any of those differences might affect the way they learn. But to apply that glaringly obvious statement to your teaching, you need to decide

what kinds of differences matter

how you get to know about them

what they imply for your teaching methods and

what you can realistically do about it.

'Differentiation' is a good example of a simple idea rendered complex by the number of ways it has been misrepresented. It is sometimes seen as something new, even as a passing fashion, when in fact the idea behind it has always been basic to good teaching. It is also particularly difficult to achieve in the FE context.

Before we spoke of 'differentiation' there was the term 'inclusive learning'. That was misunderstood in two ways. One of the arguments was about including in mainstream classes students with various kinds of physical disability or learning difficulties, a process that could be seen either as a socially responsible act or an unfair demand on staff. That particular issue is dealt with in chapter 7. For now, we need to focus on the second kind of misunderstanding, which is more general.

The client base for FE expanded and new students appeared who had more difficulty with written and theoretical work. As the FE system became more socially inclusive, it started to cater for groups who had traditionally avoided it, including the unemployed and those who, to some staff, seemed unemployable. Because unskilled jobs were becoming more difficult to obtain, there was an increase of young students who had done badly at school, had often not attended well, and may even have been moved to Pupil Referral Units (PRU) or other non-school schemes. Instead of refusing them entry, the system was asked to take them in and make them employable. It was to be more inclusive in that social sense and had to learn how to teach people with fewer study skills and more negative attitudes to learning. Some teachers felt this social role was justified, and tried to rise to it, but many also found they had been asked to teach groups they could not cope with, as their previous experience did not prepare them for it. "This wasn't why I came into FE" was a common complaint, and 'inclusivity' was sometimes seen as an imposition, an unfair demand on the workforce.

But, in the classroom context, there had always been students who could not cope with the demands of the course. Many did not know how to learn, how to respond to the kinds of teaching that were available. Drop out and failure rates were high. It was increasingly argued that they were excluded from the learning process because the way they were taught did not

suit them – too much teacher-talk that they couldn't cope with
and too much written work without adequate support. In that
sense, inclusive learning meant teaching in such a way that
every student in the class was included in the learning process.
It was a matter of varying techniques to serve better that
element of the traditional student body who did not normally
succeed. Achieving this aim required some thinking about how
we taught, and some new ideas to become more flexible.
Instead of blaming students for failing, we had to blame
ourselves to failing them.

It was in this context that FE started to talk about the
differences between students. Differentiation can be explained
as the means to reduce barriers to learning by managing the
process to allow for significant differences.

There are three ways in which a teacher might come across
'differentiation' in practice.

1) The minority or 'problem student' version

A small minority in your class suffer a particular disability or
learning problem. You make certain adjustments to help them,
treating them differently. The process of re-examining your
material and methods then benefits the majority.
For example, some years ago I taught a class of part-time adults
taking A Level English Literature. They had 34 weeks at 2
hours a week minus tea breaks to cover 8 books and then pass
three written papers, including analysis of an unseen text.
Worried that they would not cover all the material in class time,
I provided copious notes in written handouts. Acres of paper
were provided for them to read at home. Then we enrolled a
student who was completely blind. All the texts had to be
provided in braille. So did all the notes.
This took time to produce and had to be sent off two or
three weeks in advance to be ready for the class. To reduce the
load on both of us, I had to think carefully about whether a

particular set of notes was really necessary. Suddenly, the notes were more concise. The rest of the class, also receiving the more concise version, were duly grateful. They were all busy people and found the new version easier to follow. Without that 'problem' student I might have imposed too many words on the sighted for years, wasting their time and mine.

2) The new client version

You find the nature of your students has changed, or a certain kind of class is very different. The college takes in more level 1 classes and fewer level 3, or more 14-16 year olds. Your timetable changes. You have to adjust your material and methods to get through to them. You teach them differently. The process of adjustment means re-examining how you teach to widen your range of potential beneficiaries. Again, changes you make can be invigorating and benefit all students.

> Conflicts can arise between meeting individual needs and the efficient education of other children.... the most effective teaching for the learners with the most difficult behaviour is little different to the most successful teaching for others.   Ofsted, MCB (2005)

Students in more advanced classes can sometime learn despite the teacher. The teaching methods are demanding and even tedious. They expect students to be good listeners and note-takers and to cope with a lot of information presented in not very dynamic ways. Good students come to be defined as those who can cope with this and learn anyway. The rest fail or drop out quietly. With new cohorts, the majority fail to cope. They object more noisily to such demands. Seeking ways to get through to the new cohorts, you find the old cohorts are also grateful for the change. Success rates rise in both cases.

Note, this is not the same as suddenly finding that your level 2 class contains a lot of level 1 students. For financial reasons, small classes are sometimes amalgamated in ways that are not defensible in pedagogic terms. This is poor management and terms like 'differentiation' are not an answer to it. The introduction of *New Ways of Measuring Success* in 2005/6 was intended to reduce this habit but using 'chances charts' and measuring added value so that such actions were discouraged. Objections to the concept of differentiating were sometimes objections to that kind of unjustified financial management and need to be separated.

3) the diversity of humanity version

You know that people take in, process and apply information in very different ways. So you know that teaching them in exactly the same way all day every day will only appeal to a portion of them. Therefore you use a variety of methods to ensure all sub-groups get something of what they prefer. In this context, it is clear that a lesson is differentiated if

All students, however their minds work, whatever their previous experience, can find a way to make sense of what is happening.

Each student has negotiated a goal they can realistically aim for through this experience. In the short term, this may be below the minimum competence for passing that course.

The kinds of activity, the skills and intellectual abilities required for them and developed by them, are varied. They may be asked to listen or speak, to work alone or in groups, to make or analyse or write about or illustrate- but they won't do the same thing all the time, because that one thing – whatever you choose - will only suit some of the group.

You only move on when you have checked that learning has taken place and they are ready. You don't assume they will all be ready at the same time or that you have to move on now because that is what it says in your carefully typed lesson plan.

This returns us to the original questions.

What kinds of difference are significant?

How do you know about them?

How does a single teacher, with their own natural limitations and preferred style, manage to allow for them?

What do you do if you cannot?

Significant differences might include the following:

Previous notions of what 'learning' means' and expectations of how to behave. They may be learned at school or in PRUs or, with mature students, learned in another era.

The ability to understand and accept what you are asking of them. This may include attention to the way information is presented, including questions of 'readability'. It will also include the ability to perform the tasks you set, including skills you might have assumed as basic underpinning – finding information, making notes, preparing reports and handling projects or essays.

Learning styles – are they left or right brained, kinaesthetic, aural or visual? Are those questions valid? If not what should replace them?

Gender. You may have a lone girl in an engineering class or a lone boy in hairdressing. You may have equal numbers but discover, perhaps because of previous conditioning, they prefer different kinds of learning. You might move from all male to all female classes or vice versa and find the same lesson won't work with both.

Various levels of support needs, e.g. for dyslexia, dyspraxia, OCD, ADHD, or limitations on, for example, hearing, sight or mobility.

Depending on what you mean by the expression, you may wish to include cultural differences and/or social background. There will also be differences in the degree of support received at home, in confidence and self-esteem. It is worth looking in detail at issues and examples under each heading.

Previous ideas about learning and suitable behaviour

Behavioural problems are dealt with more fully in chapter 5, but a useful place to start here would be notions of 'readiness'. The term was popularised by Lewisham who, as a beacon college, made available on-line publications and ran Beacon Days, partly to explain their 'readiness curriculum'. They developed seven stages of "readiness" – classroom, learning, work, job, university, role and success. Their handbook *Students who challenge the system – a handbook for frontline staff,* explained that classroom readiness has to be achieved before there is any point putting a student into a formal group, and includes the ability to enter and leave responsibly and on time, to sit still etc. Learning readiness is more complex, and has to come after they are classroom ready. To try to achieve both at once in a single induction session would be a very difficult challenge.

As long ago as 1999 the RSA was developing a competence framework that referred to competences for relating to people, managing situations and managing information. The tutorial process is usually supposed to address these. But what happens if a student is placed in a situation where competences are required which they simply don't have? How long, and how flexible, is the period of adjustment? Who is involved in that process? If a student fails to conform to a disciplinary code within the first few days, do you allow them time to adjust to the new environment? Is that period consistent across all classes in all departments? Should it be?

'Executive functioning'[9] is the ability of the brain to process information so it can act - not to act well or badly, but to be able to act at all. Students may or may not be able to do as you ask and, in the early stages, you may not realise you are asking them to approach a task they will find impossible and may not even comprehend.

If you have read their files, and they were properly prepared with honest appraisals and references, you may find warning signals that tell you they will not be able to complete the induction task you set, or feel confident to attempt the first graded assignment. This does not necessarily mean they won't be able to do it eventually, or that they don't want to. It might mean that, because they can't do it yet, they would rather be evicted from the class than to have to try it. They may engineer a means of being rescued from the situation by being thrown out. That is the extreme end of the scale, and Chapter 5 returns to it in more detail. For most students, it may be that they quietly try to do as you ask, but privately know they can't so just hand in whatever product they can manage. 'Learning' consist of getting through the day by keeping the teacher quiet - hand them something to mark and they will, for now at least, go away and leave you alone. Confidence and self-esteem are considered below, with appropriate use of Bloom and Maslow in that context.

---

[9] See a web site devoted to Executive Function at www.personalisedlearningforum.eu. You can log on with username provided in the Introduction.

It is not unusual to find that students are classroom ready but not learning ready. The have learned how to behave in a group. They may have been socialised but they are still not used to reading and writing under the pressure of a graded response. Then how can you adapt your activities so that one group is pursuing the task whilst another has to learn what it means to carry out such actions? Such questions do not always have to be solved in advance by teachers acting like magicians, always pulling another pre-prepared worksheet out of the hat. Sometimes it is more productive to discuss the problem of learning with those who are supposed to be doing it – see below under meta-cognition.

When students start learning about your subject, do they know what kind of thinking is involved? How would you introduce them to it? Bruner's notion of discovery learning and Ausubel's advanced organisers both help here.
In very broad terms, suppose you wanted to introduce new students to the study of history. Following Bruner (1967), you might start by looking at a local object or place. For example, a bridge, a building or headstone. You can then

see what kind of questions it generates

ask what kind of records might supply the answers

start to look at them and see how answers emerge and suggest new questions

This can be done at many levels of sophistication, from primary to A level, but the principle would be the same. Motivated by **curiosity** they can experience **uncertainty** not as fearful (backing away from difficult subjects when they are explained) but as a reason to explore further.

He also stressed the importance of the way knowledge is **structured** and suggested three ways in which students can understand how an idea or a subject makes sense. It can be enacted, represented by images or graphics or explained symbolically (with statements). How many basic concepts in your subject could be represented in all three ways? Do these options represent an ascending order of difficulty for all students or do different students have different preferences? Examples are considered below (under learning styles), but note that Bruner stressed **sequencing.** His preferred sequence to encourage students to "grasp, transform and transfer" ideas was to move from enacting (hands-on exploration) to iconic (visual) and finally to symbolic (words or equations). A final element of his theory involves maximising **motivation** by trying to move from extrinsic (e.g. praise) to intrinsic (satisfying a desire to know, the satisfaction of gaining clarity). The idea of learning by discovery is hardly new.

> They should be told as little as possible and induced to discover as much as possible. Humanity has progressed solely by self-instruction; and that to achieve the best results, each mind must progress somewhat after the same fashion, is continually proved by the marked success of self-made men. - Spencer (1893) p 69

Ausubel (1963 & 1978) stressed the importance of logical structure. What kinds of connection exist between the various elements of new information and how does it connect to what is already known? He expressed his ideas about 'organisers' in a language one would not normally inflict on students:

> These organizers are introduced in advance of learning itself, and are also presented at a higher level of abstraction, generality, and inclusiveness; and since the substantive content of a given organizer or series of organizers is selected on the basis of its suitability for explaining, integrating, and interrelating the material they precede, this strategy simultaneously satisfies the substantive as well as the programming criteria for enhancing the organization strength of cognitive

structure. (1963, p. 81).

You should not therefore start any explanation until you have explained what you are about to explain, how and why. That sounds at one level like the old dictum

Tell them what you are going to tell them

Tell them

Tell them what you have just told them

Rehearse it

Apply it

except that it lays stress upon the way the information hangs together, the logical components that make sense of the individual elements.

Before you get in to any detailed explanation about the ideas, you need to sketch out in more general terms the way it all hangs together, a simple route map of where you are going that shows the major elements and their relationship in very general terms. This may often involve a diagram or mind-map, with blanks they can come back to later to fill in details. However, this image implies that all structure and connections are somehow given by a teacher and shared by all students, which is not, of course true.

A new fact or idea can only be accommodated in the student mind if it finds a way to attach itself to what is already there. You don't actually know what is already there, and it may be a mess.

You need a preview of the lesson, an overall picture of what is about to be learned - what are the ideas, principles and methods involved? What is it all about and why should they care? But the process of attaching that preview to their existing ideas has to be more than co-operative. You only know your half of the equations. You don't know what they are about to attach it to, or how they might reshape it, because you don't know what kinds of ideas and connections already exist in their minds. Finding that out is necessarily co-operative and can be chaotic.

Learning can only take place when students make the effort to reach out for your new material. You started the lesson by justifying it in their terms, so it is more likely to keep them actively engaged, and thus learning. However, although you control the formal purpose and direction, they control all the starting points. You need to negotiate a connection before you begin.

Having been simply stated, the purpose and direction must be open to question, so students can seek to make sense of it in their own terms. It is difficult for you to know in detail what each student already knows and how they think. You can try to find out by using various techniques:

> Brainstorming will empty their minds on to the board and allow you to sift through the results to ask them for connections and explanations.

> Mind maps will organise their thoughts into a structure you can then discuss.

> Venn diagrams will establish relationships and differences between groups.

You can ask them to list on post-its what they already know about the subject and what they want to know. These can be ordered and classified to identify what is relevant and accurate, and what has been misunderstood in the past. That usually involves physical movement about the room, which is usually welcome.

This will allow them to reach out from what they know to seek ways to connect. The most important principle is that the first connections have to be made by them, not by you. Once you know what they think they know, you may have to address misunderstandings from a previous context. I was once asked a question that implied total confusion between what is believed by Hindus and Muslims. Responding to this by outlining the differences and similarities between some major religions, I was then asked "What is the difference between Catholics and Christians?" which implied a need to start much further back and to simplify the whole process. Explaining how to use commas, I often have to undo the confusion left in their minds by previous teachers who spoke loosely about "when you need a pause for breath". You may discover a total misunderstanding of your last lesson, which they have creatively misremembered.

If there is a scheme of work, which was carefully explained at the beginning of the term, and you keep to it, then it will be easier for students to follow the logic from one class to the next. Of course, you may have to alter timings and re-order it as you discover new misunderstanding and find they cannot cope with the pace you had planned, but have you gone back to it and explained those changes. Is it a contract you all refer to as you negotiate the learning experience or just a list in the front of a file somewhere? Who owns this scheme? What is its status in the group? Likewise, how carefully has the marking scheme been discussed, so they know and have been able to comment on the criteria for success?

The ability to understand and accept what you are asking of them.

Assuming that students now understand what they are supposed to be doing and why, that they can connect their own previous knowledge to your new information and that their ways of thinking can somehow connect to yours, we can now consider ways of delivering the new information. Under pressure of time in a crowded syllabus, many tutors use written handouts. This may be one handout for all students in the group, assuming a common ability to read it. But how would you know in advance whether it is likely to be understood by these students?

Generalised complaints about student literacy are common enough. More interesting is the fact that the agency running initial training for school teachers advertised in 2005 for someone to run classes for applicants to the Cert Ed to raise their levels of literacy and numeracy to a level that enabled them to cope with the course. Running staff development sessions that involved teachers filling in questionnaires about learning styles, I always had to allow for the staff who could not understand the question or add up the scores and, left to their own devices, would be nervously racing to catch up with the group to avoid embarrassment. The session was redesigned to avoid that source of embarrassment, allowing a more flexible and relaxed means of handing in the final result. If some potential teachers cannot be assumed to cope easily with reading texts, why should we assume all students can read the handouts they subsequently write?

At the other end of the scale, graduates who are used to churning out academic essays simply continue on their familiar style, when the style they need for their new audience is quite different. Joseph Conrad advised that words can get in the way of what we are trying to say. How carefully created are the handouts new students are expected to process? Many use too many words with too little editing.

To begin with some simple facts that are universally acknowledged, certain physical characteristics make a difference to the readability of any text.

> Lower case is easier to read than upper case. Students may recognise words by their shape and USING CAPITALS will change the shape they are used to.

> If you want emphasis, **bold** is easier to read than *italic or* <u>underlining</u> for the same reason.

Sans-serif fonts are easier to read[10] - without the little fiddly bits on the end of letters, such as you find with Times Roman. Comic sans or Arial fonts are easiest to follow, and 14 or 12 point easier than 10 or 8.

Unjustified right margins are better than straight-edged justified text. The contours offer a set of signals for finding your way around the page.

Use white space between paragraphs, to aid navigation. Pictures and white space in general break up text and make it less intimidating.

Matt paper is easier than shiny, and buff easier than white. On whiteboards, avoid glossy surfaces under strong lights.

Obviously, clean copies which are well-produced are easier to read than poor photocopies made as the toner ran out. Shoddy or poorly printed materials carry signals to the reader about how much you care about them, and how much effort you have put in to your side of the exchange.

Sentence length and structure are important. The Sun is popular because it is easy to read. To write about complex subjects as clearly and simply as a Sun journalist is an under-appreciated skill, but you don't need to be a particularly skilled writer to improve matters – just attentive to obvious facts. In general terms, use short sentences with short words and no passive sentences. That means:

---

[10] This text is in a serifed font (Garamond) for technical reasons connected with the book trade. It is harder to sell books in sans serifed fonts and those who buy whole books are assumed to prefer it, or at least be able to cope with it. But handouts are not books and ought to be in something like Calibri, or Arial, even Comic Sans. And in a bigger font size.

The spanner should be carried to the car by the student

is more difficult than

You should carry the spanner to the car

If a new technical term has to be introduced for the first time, it might be highlighted to separate it from the text. Then, students who worry about long words, can be reassured that it will be explained to them and not feel they are unable to read the rest of the text until they have processed it. It puts the monsters in a cage so the reader feels safer.
But how do you know if you have done enough to simplify it to the point where students have a reasonable chance of understanding it? You need a measure of student ability matched to a measure of text complexity.

Like Learning Styles, references to 'readability' or 'reading age' are not an exact science, but a means to an end. Systems vary and give varying results, It is not a matter of getting some perfectly accurate measure of what a student 'is', but of finding out quickly and easily what a student can use. A system is more likely to be used if it is simple. Fortunately, several are now automated and free on line.

Most systems claim to measure the number of years of schooling required to understand a text. American systems offer a grade score, meaning what year of American schooling one needs to be in, and you have to translate to English school years. If you add to that the age at which someone starts school, you have a 'reading age'.

The reading age required for the Financial Times and the Times Educational Supplement is 17-18 years. Lord of the Flies requires an age of 11. That does not mean every 17-18 year old you meet can read the Financial Times. The interest level of the material also contributes to the experience. In theory, a 16 year old would have a reading age of 16 and be handed a text that demands only a reading age of 16. In practice, a 16 year old might have a reading age of 10 or 12 or 14. They are then asked to cope with texts that have a reading age of 18-20.

Most use a variation on two simple factors. They measure the number of words in a sentence and the number of long words within that total, defining 'long' as three or more syllables. Sophisticated versions make special allowance for abbreviations, numbers or initials or lists with semi-colons. For example, if the text includes numbers or initials then you can count every single number or letter as a syllable, so that "14" = 2 syllables and "GFE" = 3 syllables. Standard abbreviations like a.m. or p.m. are only one syllable. In some versions, standard suffixes like -ed and -ing can be ignored when counting syllables.

Obviously, some short words are harder than some long words - eon is harder than marmalade, adze is harder than computer - so any such system is only a rough guide. On the other hand, technical terms tend to be polysyllabic, but might they be very familiar to second year students and thus not need to be counted when measuring difficulty.

Most measure the limits of comprehension. That means, if a text it deemed 'suitable' for a student with a reading age of 9 then it may still test their ability to the limits. A good match between student and text may still only give you a reasonable percentage of comprehension, not necessarily 100%. On the other hand, some nine year olds have a very sophisticated vocabulary and need a greater challenge.

Also, while they work well enough for a rough guide to some prose, they are less useful for literary texts, where imagery, rhythm and even stanza forms play an important part in determining accessibility.

I shall now introduce briefly how a few alternative ways to measure readability but DO NOT PANIC. Not only are they all easier than they seem once you get used to it, but at the end I shall show you how to use your edition of Microsoft Word so the computer does it for you anyway. That only takes a few seconds. You will also find useful sites for measuring hand-outs online, with more details, on bpfe.org.uk/links

The FOG index, developed by Robert Gunning in 1952, uses sentence and word length to measure the years of schooling required. The formulae is:

> average number or words per sentence plus average number of words of three or more syllables x 0.4 = FOG grade

You can apply it to a sample of 100 words and any grade over 12 might challenge the majority of the population. You can easily create an Excel page to do the sums and there is a web site where you can submit a page for automatic screening. FOG is not suitable for very young (early primary) cohorts. The Power-Summers-Kearl index measures all syllables and is best used to ages 7-10. This is also a good source for the Fry Graph, which uses the standard criteria to offer a reading age fairly quickly.

SMOG is similar to FOG but claims to measure "100% comprehension" so it will give you a higher value (= poorer result) when you measure a text. The sample has to be 30 consecutive sentences. This is favoured by The Literacy Trust, Basic Skills Agency and NIACE.

An easy way to test a text on a class is to use a **cloze test.** Select a passage from your teaching material, leave out every nth word and ask students to supply it.

> If n = 5 then expect a score of at least 50%
> If they score less than 50% they will need guidance.
> If they score less than 30% the passage is simply too hard for them.

> If n = 7 then you could expect 80% scores.
> Between 65 – 80% expect to give some guidance
> Less than 65% and it is too hard.

This kind of testing can be used for screening for Learning Support, which is usually a part of induction. If your handouts are badly written it will reveal that most of your students require learning support. If they are well written, fewer will require it.

There are several others systems available - see, for example, but for most busy practitioners, perhaps the easiest to use is the Flesch-Kincaid, if only because it is built in to every computer as part of Word and can be used at the press of a button. It has two measures.

Reading ease is measured on a scale of 0-100. Higher scores indicate material that is easier to read; lower numbers mark harder-to-read passages.

Grade Level relates to the American system. A score of 6.1 would indicate that the text is understandable by an average student in 6th grade. This is six years after kindergarten, so 11-12 years old. In other words, grade level plus five is a rough guide to reading age. If you put that together in a table:

0-29 **Very Difficult**	Post Graduate	
30-49 **Difficult**	US college level	Or, in the UK, an **able** A2 student. Note that American 'freshmen' are in secondary not university level.
50-59 **Fairly Difficult**	US High School.	A grade score of 10 = tenth grade = an American about 15-16 years old. UK at GCSE level, with **theoretical** reading age of 15.
60-69 **Standard**	8th to 9th grade.	Ninth grade is aged 14-15, early GCSE age in the UK (year 10). Some FE entrants aged 16 **may not** understand texts pitched at this level.
70-79 **Fairly Easy**	7th grade,	i.e. the seventh year after kindergarten, so about 12-13 years old.
80-89 **Easy**	5th to 6th grade.	Fifth grade is the American fifth year of school after kindergarten, at around 10-11 years old. Sixth grade is six years after

		kindergarten, so 11-12 years old.
90-100 **Very Easy**	US 4th to 5th grade.	Of course, "very easy" is a relative term.

You can download a simple chart for understanding educational 'levels' from bpfe.org.uk/materials
All most people need is a page above their desk that tells them what grade score and readability range they need to be within range of the average student in a given class that year. You can then run all your written material through Word before you use it to see whether the demands you are about to make are unusual or excessive. For example, you may find it looks roughly like this:

> BTEC Diploma second years Monday morning start at 59-50?
>
> GCSE/level 2 Monday afternoon up to 9th 60-69 (start 70=79 term 1?)
>
> Level 1 Tuesday morning try 5th? 90-100
> A.S. Tuesday afternoon 9th plus start at 60-69?

The figures may change year by year and, perhaps, through the year. They are only, remember, rough guides, but a rough guide is better than getting lost, or not even asking the way.

But let's make it all easy and automatic.

Go to a page of text in Word.

On your top menu bar click on File. Then On the left side bar click on Options.

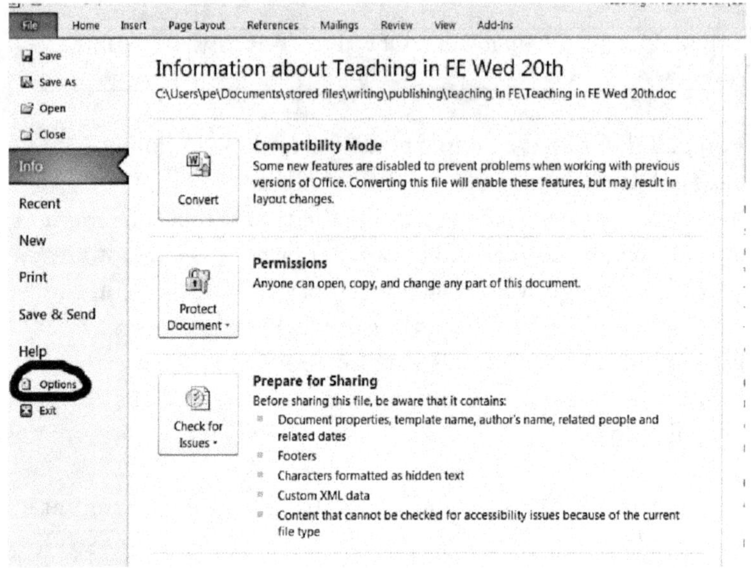

In the next menu click on Proofing.

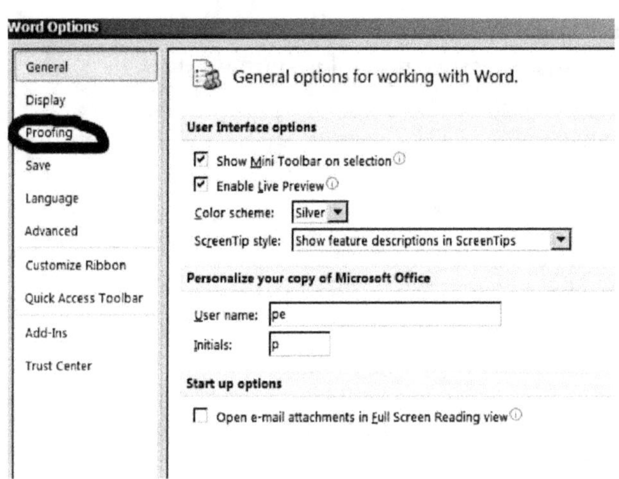

Under Spelling and Grammar tick "display readability stats".

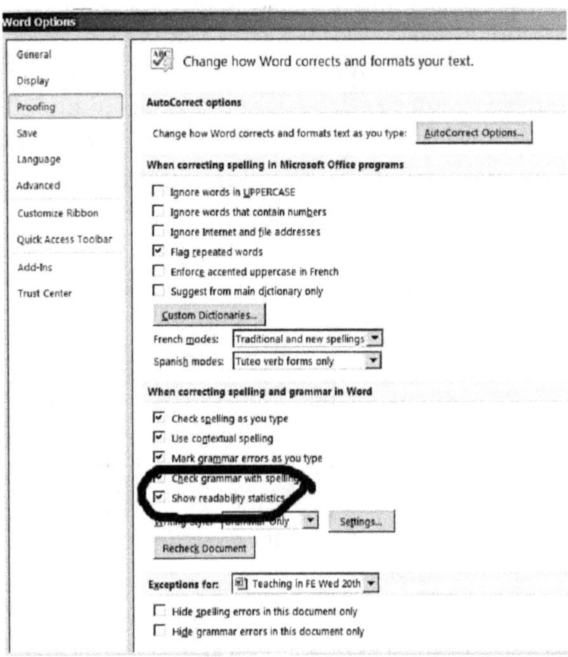

Use your tool bar (Spelling and Grammar) or just press f7 to turn on 'spell-check' in the usual way. When Word has finished checking it will also display the percentage of passive sentences you have used and the reading score and grade level.

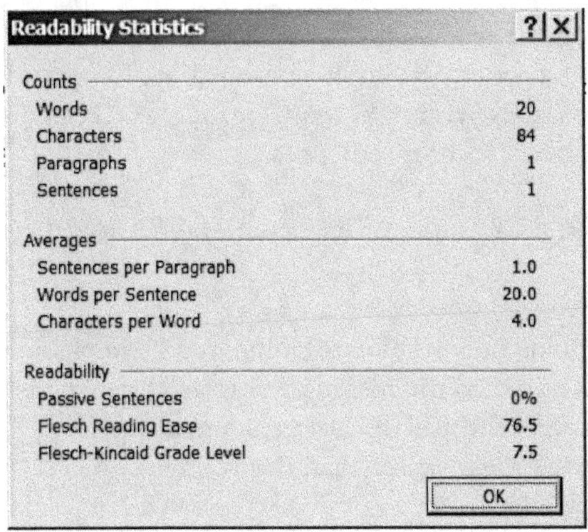

If you want it done quickly just click on "ignore" for every question to get the stats printed at once.

Once you have them, you can adapt the handout by checking quickly how far along the scale it has to move - how much rewriting might you need. If, after several attempts, you cannot make it simple enough, you may need someone in Learning Support to help. That is, after all, what some of them could be doing in student sessions anyway - helping them to simplify your handouts one student at a time.

> If in doubt, simplify again. Aim for the lowest ability, not the highest. To simplify is not to condescend. You can make it easier without insulting brighter students by using adult language but fewer syllables. If you have to use technical language or longer words, use simple sentences to contain them.

That last paragraph had a FK readability score of 60.4, grade level 7.3. That means it requires at least an intelligent 12 -13 old. We could make small changes:

> If you have any doubts, then reduce. Aim for the lowest ability, not the highest. To make it simple does not insult the reader. If you make it easy bright students will not be upset. Use adult language but short words. If you have to use technical terms or long words, put them in simple, short sentences.

That version was 84.3 - more readable - at grade 3.8 - OK for 8-9 year olds.

This rough guide only takes care of the middle range of any class. If you have studied the files and/or tested a few texts as a cloze test, then you may well discover students who are significantly more or less skilled than the average.

The former will need more challenging work to stretch them, and you may feel it your duty to offer them more complex texts as part of their education. There is, of course, an argument that literacy levels –whatever we mean by that term - are too low and require remedial action, including the integration of skills teaching within all subjects. But attempts to improve literacy are quite separate from the lazy and alienating habit of depending for learning upon levels of ability that simply do not exist.

The latter will need more help or a simpler text. In an ideal world, you will be able to offer several versions of each handout. In practice, in the short term, you probably don't have time. But then, in a sensibly arranged plan for learning, the written handout is only a small part of the package anyway. That is why we are moving on to learning styles. In that context, you may need to ask if you need so many written handouts. Would another form of information processing be better received and more effective?

In doing so, you may also wish to dwell on the way media change over time. In 1970, when chalk was still commonly used, it was rare for a teacher to type handouts. If they were duplicated for circulation it might be by photocopier, but was equally likely to be by Gestetner or Banda - processes that involved chemical aromas in confined spaces, took forever and allowed little margin for error. Since then, personal computers have become so commonplace we forget how recently they arrived in education[11]. Handouts can be word-processed, fonts

---

[11] The first email was sent in 1971, the same year as decimal coinage arrived and Swiss women got the vote. Many UK teachers considered it quite impractical to use computers in class and it was a year before Bill Gates sold his first programme (a timetabling system for the school he attended). Microsoft was established four years later. The first Apple was 1977, the year Steve Biko and Elvis Presley died. 1982, the year of the first cd player, saw the first use of the word 'internet'. In 1987 flogging was abolished in Harrow and in 1990 web browsers were invented, so the public might start to join the 'world wide web', a term coined in 1991 at CERN in Switzerland. A student born that year was only be able to leave school legally in 2007. If they went on to a higher degree they might just have started their fist job very recently.

and colours altered, interactive white boards used to display materials. By the time the majority of teachers have become used to this freedom and started to use it routinely, it will already be outdated. The new standard might include animations and interactive web sites, routinely prepared by young teachers on their mobile systems whilst older colleagues decry what they see as difficult and unnecessary fads.

Another thought process worth pursuing is that of the TLRP project led by Ivanič et al (2005), which claimed that

> students who appear to have low levels of literacy in educational settings are highly literate in other domains of life: in their domestic, community and leisure activities.

In other words, the problem is not with their abilities, but with their abilities as evidenced in the educational context.

Learning styles and metacognition

> There is **no** scientific justification for teaching or learning strategies based on VAKT and tutors should **stop** using learning style instruments based on them. There is **no** theory of VAKT from which to draw **any** conclusions for practice. It should be a dead parrot. It should have ceased to function.   Coffield 2008 p32.

Fashions in education come and go. Learning is a fashion that had reached its peak at the end of the 20thC and is now being attacked by a new wave of sceptics. However, arguments against one set of 'solutions' do not remove the real problem that prompted their introduction. The problem, put simply, is how teachers and students actually discuss the way in which students learn, so that students can take more responsibility for their own learning. This process does not automatically require a learning styles inventory, but the reality of inspection regimes will sometimes seem to.

In the late twentieth century, Ofsted increasingly came to insist upon a reference to learning styles. Ignoring them was seen as bad practice. Government-funded bodies provided material and training in their use[12] and university sites published inventories for students to work out their own styles. They were a part of the establishment:

> A feature of many of the effective lessons is appropriately detailed planning that takes full account of the individual needs and preferred learning styles of the students.
>   Ofsted WCS November 2004

ALI also took for granted that good practice would include a reference to learning styles:

> Barnsley College has given a high priority to developing students' study skills – a move that met with some resistance at first from adults who did not think they could be 'taught' how to learn, but which is now a well-regarded aspect of the course. Once students' preferred learning styles have been established, teachers then reflect these styles in their lesson plans.   ALI 2004 (b)

Meanwhile, public funds also supported research that shows most inventories are unsound and dangerously naive, and in the early 21st century articles appeared in the press decrying this educational fad[13]. This is a good example of research disabling practice – so much information that a practitioner has no time to weigh the arguments and cannot decide which authority to follow, the inspectors or the researchers. In 2009, anyone

---

[12] A good example of a positive view is in *Learning Styles: into the future* by Bill Lockitt, published by FEDA in 1997 and supported by QUILT and NCET. ALI included examples of using LS on its good practice database Excalibur
[13] e.g. TES 14th January 2005, p28 and Guardian educational supplement 4th April 2004 p16, Independent education supplement 8th December 2005 p3, Education Guardian 21st Feb 2006 p6.

putting 'learning style' into the DCSF search engine could download a publication dated 2004 *(Pedagogy and Practice: Teaching and Learning in Secondary Schools Unit 19: Learning styles)* telling school teachers how to use 'important ideas' that should inform their practice – the very ideas Coffield says we should ignore, and mocks mercilessly with a cod version (Coffield 2008 App 2).

There is a beginner's guide to learning styles in the Learning Suite at www.bpfe.org.uk but, put very simply, the ideas are as follows: Not everybody will process information the same way. Some like an overview first and some like to get straight down to detail. Some like to listen to an explanation, some prefer to look at a drawing or diagram and others want to take something apart and examine it. Some like to be given an overall idea of the lesson before they start and others prefer you to work slowly through a list of points. There are many such differences.

Any differences in how people import, understand and apply information will affect how you plan to teach them. You wouldn't plan to lecture for an hour to an audience whose attention span was known to be about 20 minutes. Should you provide overviews, diagrams, activities? Which would offer the most effective route to their understanding?

To find that out you need to analyse the differences. Various people set themselves up as authorities to explain what they claimed were the most important differences. They devised schemes and offered inventories that were then sold as a means to increase learning. A full history of their development may be seen in Coffield et al (2004a) and an argument about whether we should be using them at all is expounded in Coffield et al (2004b). A summary of both can be found in LSRC 2004b.

You may recognise some leading brand names. Honey and Mumford often appear in Cert Ed courses, with their activists, pragmatists, reflectors and theorists. Gardener's 'types of intelligence' seem to turn up in commercial systems, lurking

beneath ideas about 'active learning'. Bodies such as the DCFS
or Ofsted might refer to VAK (visual, active and kinaesthetic)
and there is no shortage of printed material about left and right
brain learning. Other oft-cited names include Kolb, Gregorc,
Pask, Dun and Dun. There are said to be differences between
convergers and divergers, serialists and holists, random and
sequential learners and so on and so on (see Coffield et al
2004b p54).

In a market where you can make a lot of money selling your
system, brand names started to compete for the right to be the
most popular form of measurement. They often began as
academic research which was complex and time consuming,
but were then simplified for the market place. Teachers, as
customers for the goods, bought the ideas and applied them.
They didn't have time to check the original research, or weigh
one system carefully against another. They used whatever
system was popular locally, or mentioned in their Cert Ed
course notes, or filed in the staff room resource cupboard.
They took the system on trust.

Of course, some colleges enforce a standard practice, so you
have no choice about which system or terminology to use. But
even if you did, what systems have authority, or a suitable track
record for your classes. In the study by Coffield et al, several of
the more popular brand names met few of the criteria set by
researchers, but the authors of the report carefully conclude
that more research is required before it would be possible to
recommend any single inventory for practical use in the
classroom, and that it would need to vary according to context.
Meanwhile, teachers continued to feel obliged to use some
system or other. But what did they do with it? Had they
increased learning with these systems, nobody would have
objected. As Deng Xiao Ping used to remark, what does it
matter if a cat is black or white, so long as it catches mice. If it
works, use it. Unfortunately, there were too many examples of
teachers making two fundamental mistakes:

measuring a preference and then telling the student they were a type – as if they might be somehow permanently incapable of certain kinds of learning

measuring the students then doing nothing about it at all.

Thus, students would be told they were kinaesthetic learners, who preferred to learn through practical sessions, and then use that fact as an excuse not to try reading notes or listening to lectures. Nobody explained to them that they were supposed to develop all kinds of learning, and the teacher didn't tell them how they could do so, probably because nobody explained to the teacher how that could be done. Measurements were taken but nothing changed as a result. This was sometimes because teachers did not understand the system they were using, sometimes because they did not know how to continue the discussion they had started, and sometimes because the whole exercise was only ever intended to decorate some files prior to inspection – use the trendy words and gain tick points from Ofsted. The poor practice recorded in Coffield et al (2004b p1 and 4) can be found across the country. But is there real, potential change being wasted by poor practice, or should we just give it all up, despite Ofsted's preference?
Coffield et al make allowance for an opinion that learning style awareness is only "a cog in the wheel of the learning process" and that

It is not very likely that the self-concept of a student, once he or she has reached a certain age, will drastically develop by learning about his or her learning style.
cited Coffield et al (2004b) p 50
referring to Desmedt et al (2003 147-148)

but they do recommend that

consideration be given to developing for schools,
colleges and universities and firms new programmes of
study focused on human learning and how it can be
fostered (p51)

and they cite work by Marzano (1998) in which

approaches that were directed at the meta-cognitive
level of setting goals, choosing appropriate strategies
and monitoring progress are more effective in
improving knowledge outcomes than those which
simply engage learners at the level of presenting
information for understanding and use. Interventions
targeted at improving meta-cognition produced an
average gain of 26 percentile points (across 556 studies).
This is about 5 points higher than the mean gain
calculated for studies in which attempts were made to
improve cognition without an explicit meta-cognitive
component.   Coffield 2004b p53

Research on the development of adult literacy also supports the
importance of an awareness of how we learn

.. it is not easy to predict precisely the body of
knowledge and skills that learners will learn from any
learning teaching event, however carefully it is planned.
..... through developing understanding of things that
may accelerate or interfere with learning, learners
become more explicitly aware of how they learn in
educational contexts and in life
Classroom discourse has been researched widely to
suggest that, when classroom interaction works in
tandem with explicit awareness-raising about what is
being learned, it exerts strong influences on language,
academic and social development. Learners learn to
construct knowledge from talk. - Ivanič and Seng
(2005) 5.3

Students learn better if they know more about how they learn, and take responsibility for the process. Learning styles inventories provide a starting point and they work if used as part of an overall strategy. Using them on their own is like paying for a dietary product on the internet without also having a calorie controlled diet. It would be kind to Ofsted to assume what they mean by a reference to learning styles is a serious dialogue between students and teachers about how learning takes place. That is what is recommended here. The argument is that students might be relying on a means of studying that relies upon their weaknesses, not their strengths. You might be teaching them in ways that demand the very abilities they least possess. Both sides of the relationship need to explore those possibilities.

First, you will need to engage students during induction in a conversation about how they learned before. What worked and what did not? Why? What strategies did they use to try to cope with the problems of learning? Whose job is it to bring about learning? If they agree that the problem is equally shared between student and tutor, then you will need a language to use when discussing the matter. Learning style inventories provide a useful set of shorthand terms which, controlled in context, can do this. Instead of talking about good students, boring teachers or hard subjects, they can speak about tendencies and styles that can be analysed and changed or allowed for. If this is the beginning of a dialogue, then throughout the year you can continue to check on what they are doing about trying to learn more efficiently and how you can adapt material and techniques to make it easier for them. Learning and teaching become something you discuss and try to encourage as a team. Learning styles provides us with a vocabulary that might serve a serious purpose so long as we do not take too seriously or misuse the inventories is offers.

If you go www.bpfe.org.uk you can use The Learning Suite to download materials that help teachers and/or students make rational decisions about what ideas would actually help them

They are differentiated at levels 1, 2 and 3. They should be used
to discuss, in a neutral language, problems such as sitting still
for long periods, not knowing what the lesson is going to be
about, having no context for new ideas and not being able to
learn in the way teachers expect. The student's part of the
contract is to think about how they learn and try to adapt
consciously an effective series of strategies.

> It is the mark of the educated man to look for precision is
> each class of things just so far as the nature of the subject
> permits. - *Aristotle, Ethics IB*

Gender

For the purposes of this text, sexual differences are
biological and gender refers to roles assigned or adopted within
society. In a simple world, we could then say that sex means
matters to do with organs and reproduction, which do not
really concern us, and gender is to do with matters of
behaviour, role and expectation, which probably do. This can
be complicated in several ways.

Science can explore the brain and find that a woman's
frontal lobe, used for decision making and problem solving, is
usually larger, as is her limbic cortex, used for emotional
response. In men the amygdala, used for emotional memory,
and the parietal cortex, used for spatial awareness, are usually
larger than in women. But so what? What does this does this
tell us about organising learning in classrooms?

When we speak of differences in ways of learning, there will
be those who argue they are caused by biological differences
and others who prefer to see it as a socially created difference,
albeit at an early stage of development. Science is not so
advanced or so simple that we can settle such matters finally on
every occasion, and nor do we need to for this purpose. For the
moment, what matters is not what causes a difference but how
we identify and respond to it.

The recommendation is not to teach people on the basis that sex or gender limits them to a particular kind of learning, but to allow for differences in how they *might* prefer to learn at least some of the time. This may vary, and preferences do not always have to be treated as limitations.

By the age of seven we find girls doing better at tests for reading than boys. We know from statistical returns that boys and girls by the age 16 have been achieving GCSE results that are significantly different. The problem was sufficiently serious to warrant a 'gender and achievement' page on the Standards Site from which to download a 'toolkit' to 'Raise Boys' Achievement (DFES 2003). This repeats the familiar idea that the ways boys and girls learn are quite different, the answer to which is said to include 'a range of teaching styles' so that no students is excluded by a style they consistently find unsympathetic. For example, they argued that many schools tend to underplay kinaesthetic learning can be particularly significant for many boys.

The general consensus in most literature is that boys prefer active and varied lessons. They like to work on their own or in pairs. They don't collaborate well and tend to dominate discussion. They enjoy challenges, will speculate and take risks, but may rush in unprepared. A rejection of learning may be underpinned by a lack of role models and learned behaviour that includes 'defensive aggression' towards testing environments. They will turn off more quickly than girls. They are probably more kinaesthetic, they need to be challenged, to be able to speculate and experiment, before being tied down to your formal outcomes.

Girls, despite their potential for violence at times, are said to prefer small groups and more passive activity. They are better at multi-tasking, more likely to accept homework and value reflection. They may feel the environment is too 'masculine' and feel inadequate, undermined or undervalued in certain subject areas or occupational cultures. Thus, girls will probably be stronger in communication skills, reflective thinking, collaborating, attention to detail and linear processes. They may lack confidence and be averse to taking risks, prone to overwork and worry, blame themselves for what goes wrong. They may work in too much detail and avoid speculative thinking.

In a mixed class, if you are using a range of techniques and learning experiences, and if you are encouraging feedback on how students feel about the problem of learning, such differences in what boys and girls prefer will already be catered for. Or, at least, you have a system for exploring and adjusting the way you organise their experience. In FE, and increasingly on link courses 14-16, where vocational choices tend to be gendered, problems of a different order may arise. Vocational areas have an occupational culture which tends to affect the atmosphere and behaviour norms in a vocational dept. What is considered normal and acceptable may vary in classes for, say, motor vehicle, care, hairdressing, engineering and media. Individuals who find themselves on the receiving end of a culture which is only comfortable for one gender will feel uncomfortable and may be unable to learn well. They may feel threatened. This issue, and a possible response, is considered in chapter 7 on equal opportunities.

Finally, of course, one has to remember that causes are often masked. In 2009 we celebrated the fact that boys finally outperformed girls in maths GCSE. The reason suggested was that maths GCSE had reduced the coursework element. Will reduced coursework in other subjects see boys do better on future? Would they test better at reading if we used motorcycle magazines? Figures are easy to read but often complex to comprehend.

Support needs

It is in this area where differentiation tends to be seen as the issue of the problem student. Teachers have expectations as to what students should be able to do in order for the teacher to

offer them work in a coherent class. If one student is less able
to cope with written handouts or making notes from the board,
then to 'differentiate' is understood to mean 'making special
allowances'. Applicants have been rejected on the grounds that
they will be 'unable to cope with the demands of the course'
when, in fact, they are intellectually capable of learning but
disadvantaged by an inappropriate dominant and rigid style that
is incorrectly considered to be necessary. The fact that
sometimes a large percentage of the class have support needs,
some of which are complex, does not always encourage a more
flexible or sympathetic view. There are several obvious
responses to this.

Chapter 6 considers the problem of transition, including the
difficulty of knowing in advance what support needs exist and
how to respond to them. There are issues to be explored
elsewhere about how teachers relate to tutorials and to learning
support staff. It is useful to consider at least a brief
introduction to some of the labels that are bandied about,
sometimes carelessly, and wonder what they might mean for a
teacher seeking an inclusive or differentiated learning
experience. Chapter 5 lists some of the more common and
suggests initial responses.

If you have simplified written material in line with previous
suggestions, and varied the learning styles required in your
classes, you have already reduced the problem significantly.
Learning support tutors should not have to spend time
simplifying complex reading matter or helping students
produce complex written responses if they are not logically
required by the nature of the subject or context. That is not an
argument for what is sometimes called 'dumbing down', but for
what should really be called intelligent marketing. You don't sell
ideas to a complex market by insisting they all read long,
tedious advertisements. Educating students should not be a less
subtle and sophisticated process than selling them IPods and
burgers. Unfortunately, only ad agencies can afford such an
array of good writers and designers. That is why the DfE laid

such emphasis on producing sample material for general release.

On bpfe.org.uk/links you will find sources for material that may be more suitable for a wider range of students. Intranets and internet sources are encouraging a free exchange of material, so that one individual, with limited time and expertise, can call upon a wider pool, and respond more flexibly. Of course, material made by someone else is not necessarily suitable for your style of teaching and may not feel 'right in the hand' until you have adapted it to some extent. Can you deliver someone else's material with as much conviction as you do your own?

cultural differences and socio-economic background

This is a particularly difficult area because of the danger of self-fulfilling prophecies through stereotypes. Some of the issues will be explored again in chapter 7 on equal opportunities. It presents itself in various ways.
I have listened to tutors explaining that young Japanese students, enrolling in significant numbers for an Art Foundation course, are less willing to disagree with tutors because their culture teaches them that disagreement is bad manners, and this causes difficulties to their detriment. In essence, it is not so different to arguing that girls in a male-dominated class don't take part in discussion, except that the latter can be met with an exhortation to manage the process better when the former needs a serious discussion about how much truth resides in the statement and, if it were true (how would you know?) whether learning in a British college really requires Japanese behavioural norms to be somehow 'anglicised'.

It is still not uncommon to hear arguments about black male students achieving less well than Asian or Chinese males, and less well than black females. Even if it were still true in all areas, it would not mean all black males will under-achieve, but it does warn us to respond to whatever has caused under-achievement in some cases. Would it mean you have to react or plan differently when faced with a black male applicant or new entrant? The implications of the data will be discussed in chapter 7, with suitable caveats, and we can carefully separate issues to do with country of origin, ethnicity, gender and social class. Does progression in our education system require 'British' middle-class behaviour? To what extent is education also socialisation in that sense?

Now we have opened access to education and encouraged students from all social groups to stay with us for longer, teachers are subject to norms of behaviours that are acceptable in certain socio-economic groups but shocking to teachers unused to their presence. Issues of behavioural norms and our response to them are discussed in chapter 5, where we have to consider what is largely a social transition for some. For the moment, it is worth recording a conversation that occurred when a group of local employers and dignitaries visited a youth club on a notorious local estate. Nervously wondering if their hubcaps would still be there when they came out, they spoke with the 'clients' and asked one of them what he wanted to do when he left school, fully expecting him to say "plumber". His ambition, easily explicable in that context, was to be a criminal lawyer, and he had been carefully planning his school career to that end. The visitors spoke excitedly about this for several days afterwards. Had they been planning a class, or careers evening, for such people, would they have made allowance for the ambitious, gifted and talented end of the market?

Notwithstanding the dangers of stereotyping, we also need to differentiate between those who have or lack all manner of basic requirements, including the bus fare to get to college, breakfast before they arrive, a place to work when they get back, support from parent(s) or guardian and a need to work long hours to fund the course. This raises problems when setting extensive project work. A lack of previous academic success, not only of their own but among their extended family, will also be disabling.

Students learn best when they feel secure and confident. Most, although not all, respond positively to praise. It is therefore reasonable to assume that before you ask them to attempt difficult learning experiences you should ensure provide a secure environment in which they can attempt easier feats, succeed and receive praise. The two conceptual models traditionally used in this context are Bloom and Maslow. In 1956, Benjamin Bloom headed a group of educational psychologists who developed a classification of levels of intellectual behaviour important in learning. They identified three domains of educational activities; cognitive – affective - psychomotor.

They then analysed the cognitive and affective domains, but not psychomotor. They identified six levels within the cognitive domain which were, starting with the least demanding kind of activity:

Knowledge – state, remember, define, label, list, memorise, describe.
Comprehension – state the problem in your own words, explain, classify, organise and interpret
Application – use the information in a new situation, apply, employ and practise
Analysis – separate into component parts and see organisational structure; compare, contrast, discriminate; give reasons, cause and effect
Synthesis – bring parts together into a pattern, crate a structure, write an essay about it, design a poster.
Evaluation- make judgements about value or fitness for purpose; consider evidence.

If you start too far up the scale you are asking too much too soon. Students may become frightened and react by behaving badly. If you start low but stay low you are not stretching them so they get bored and may react by behaving badly. If you start with low order skills so they all get it right, you can praise them, build up their confidence, then move to the next stage while they still feel positive. This is often called the medal and mission method. Good lesson design in therefore effective manipulation of their emotional condition – the proper organisation of intellectual progress is also the proper organisation of emotional condition – they are inseparable. The role of feedback through formative assessment, and a recent revision of Bloom's ideas, are considered in the next chapter.

Maslow's ideas are discussed more fully in chapter 5 on behaviour, which considers implications for managing the learning environment. Briefly, his starting point was that individuals were basically trustworthy and self-governing. They would react badly only if certain needs were not met. His hierarchy of needs included physiological (are they cold or hungry), safety, belonging, esteem, cognitive, aesthetic and self-actualisation. They are "pre-potent", meaning you have to satisfy all the lower levels before you can make demands at the higher levels. So if you want students to think about ideas you need to make sure first they are physically comfortable, secure and confident. Medal and mission techniques can increase a feeling of confidence and security, and that in turn increases the sense of belonging in that group.

Some students will need this more than others. If you begin by using simple questions so you can allow them to get the answers right and praise them, then you can direct the questions accordingly and vary their difficulty according to the ability of the student in question. If they are revision questions about prior learning, they may also help to shape the advance organiser and inform new connections.

In the wider context, of course, one also has to consider a difference in what level of challenge to set for any student. Praising successful colleges, Ofsted claims that in the best practice

> The system identifies a minimum level to
> which students should aspire, based on an

> analysis of their abilities, and monitors their
> progress against this. Students understand
> that these are minimum targets and are
> motivated to exceed them. - WCS

If, after analysing ability, you decide some students will
struggle to a D whilst others will easily obtain an A, then
obviously you may wish to set different missions. Individual
Learning Plans (or Programmes) and the use of information for
setting targets are part of Chapter 6, but for now we can turn
our attention to a general consideration of which teaching
techniques allow you to differentiate most easily, and how you
can do so by input or outcome. The latter is often
misunderstood.

So which teaching techniques differentiate?

> A class is not differentiated when assignments are the
> same for all learners and the adjustments consist of
> varying the level of difficulty of questions for certain
> students, grading some students harder than others, or
> letting students who finish early play games for
> enrichment. It is not appropriate to have more
> advanced learners do extra maths problems, extra book
> reports, or after completing their "regular" work be
> given extension assignments. Asking students to do
> more of what they already know is hollow. Asking them
> to do "the regular work, plus" inevitably seems punitive
> to them. -   Tomlinson (1995)

If you want students to do different things because they have
different learning rates and potentials, then you have to design
the tasks accordingly. To solve the problem of the early finisher
by asking them to help the slower students is not mentoring, it
is abrogation of your own responsibility. On the other hand,
you probably haven't the time to develop a dozen different
assignments for each class or topic. Even if you did, the

psychological damage done to a student who was always
handed the least challenging task by the teacher might be
considerable. Instead, it is safer and more efficient to have one
task but with three possible ways to approach it. Thus, for
example, your task sheet might offer the options:

You **must** (all of you must to Pass)

You **could** (some of you might = Merit)

You **might** (a few of you might = Distinction)

Students will then negotiate their own choice of target. You can
subtly encourage the able but lazy and help to instill realism in
the overambitious. Background information can be made
available to all, perhaps in both simple and extended versions.
It will be more used by those aiming at higher levels of
outcome. Then you are designing a single task but a range of
background material and help sheets.

Likewise, of course, task sheets which are mainly questions
would logically require simple questions first, to increase
confidence, with the more complex at the end, where only
more able students may ever get to see them.

Some tasks are so open in themselves that a wide range of
effort and ability can be bought to bear on them. "Designing a
flyer" might involve some students in advanced graphic design
and a level of creativity you had not imagined possible. Some
will give an oral delivery with fluency and, panache, informing
and entertaining at a level that surprises you. If you are lucky,
the best designer will be the poorest speaker, so you have
provided parity. In any event, they need grading on the same
scale as those who struggle to convey a minimum of
information in acceptable form.

If your barriers are criterion referenced, that is less of a
problem, except that you cannot reward the student who is
better than a Distinction. Most students tend to feel

instinctively that rewards are norm referenced, and need evidence in the form of printed criteria as the start of the process.

You might have allowed them an open choice as to how they present their material. Some will use the traditional written report or poster, because they can imagine (or manage) nothing else. Some may create a stunning multi-media display, or write a song. That differentiates well, but did your criteria make it clear how you would grade such disparate results on the same scale? Will a Distinction poster slip to Merit because a multi-media display made it look tired by comparison? If not, what is the reward for the latter's effort? Sometimes, in pushing the gifted and talented, we have to argue that such work is its own reward.

Other tasks are open to different applications and contexts. After careful preparation and examples, you might ask a media class to investigate news values without specifying whether they use newspapers, radio or t.v., UK or international sources. Group work has its own dynamics. Mixing students with different learning styles, and doing so as part of a publicly shared plan, allows them to provide for each other's weaknesses. Of course, you will always need a record of who did what. On the positive side, the record allows you to show how differently people work, and how effective teams are formed. On the negative side, it allows you to spot the passengers who are trying to pass through the efforts others. When trying to differentiate by input, some methods seem to have a natural advantage, although even the best won't work if used badly and even the 'worst' methods can be improved easily. Geoff Petty has published much useful material on this topic, freely available from his web site[14] and what follows was informed by his work. As he points out, you are not encouraging yourself to differentiate if you constantly employ

Uninterrupted teacher talk

---

[14] Linked from bpfe.org.uk/links and worth bookmarking.

Closed questions or questions answered only by volunteers

The same style of written feedback (e.g. always the essay or formal report)

The routine experience – teacher talk followed by a task to repeat what was said in their own words.

Assessment tasks where criteria are not clear, or where feedback only occurs after it is too late to alter the product or process.

However, as Petty also points out, you can drastically improve even the least promising technique:

Talking from the front = no differentiation.

Talk, but vary the complexity of your explanation from advanced to very simple – could work, but how would you know?

Talk but ask questions to check understanding – what if the least able never answer?

Talk but use directed questions, with the easiest questions aimed at the least confident and more complex questions aimed at the most able – differentiates to a degree. But how long are you talking for?

Talk with varying levels of complexity, with directed and varying levels of question, and after a maximum of 20 minutes switch to another activity to apply what was said – becoming sophisticated class management.

Ditto but with handouts provided in advance for dyslexic students, and/or a copy in to their learning support tutors – sophisticated class management. You could also put it on line so they can vary font size.

It will be clear by now that to allow for a range of learning styles and ability levels might involve a teacher in creating material and attempting exchanges that are far from their own comfort zone. Whilst it is good to develop professional flexibility, but there will be ideas, styles and techniques so far from your own natural personality and experience that you do not feel comfortable doing it, or competent to do it well. In which case, don't. Nobody wants to be part of a failed experiment. Something less adventurous but done really well might be more productive.

An engineer of my acquaintance finds it difficult to do mind mapping at all. I find it easy to create organic maps to record a creative process, but he considers my results unusable until he has set them into tables and lists to control them. Between us, we create good material, compensating for each other's weaknesses. Some students will prefer his style of teaching, some prefer mine. What both of us can do is monitor what they need and try to reach out to all elements of the class within our limited abilities. There will never be a perfect match or teacher to all students, but all of us can be more professional analysing what they need and how we can try to provide it.

One answer to personal limitations is to use more than one individual. Many students feel uncomfortable when familiar faces are replaced, but when a colleague and I tried team-teaching an A level evening class for the whole year, results were better compared to the norm for our individual classes. If timetabling problems do not allow it, then at least you can share material and ideas, so that colleagues from other areas provide insights that might not otherwise occur to you. Subject Learning Coaches were provided partly for that purpose and Virtual Teacher Centres are useful. Inevitably, someone else's material will need to be adapted to your own idiosyncrasies, strengths and limitations.

Another route is to create multi-authored on-line material. A community college in Hampshire decided in 2006 to offer internet learning through the night on the grounds that truants might prefer that method and this tune back in. This allowed for another differences we have not considered – the way body clocks operate, with some people preferring to learn outside the hours convenient to providers. Future options might include on-line operations 24/7, with many authors offering different styles to try, so we are released from the tyranny of the individual teacher and plugged into a 'market economy'?

There is no point using any technique if it has no effect. An interesting strand of academic research it to measure the 'effect size' of various interventions. Petty's site has some interesting material on this, drawing on Hattie, explaining that:

> An effect size of 1.0 is enormous and would advance a student by one whole year or increase the rate of learning by 50%. Anything above 0.4 is above average in educational research

The inaugural lecture of John Hattie, Professor of Education at the University of Auckland explored this area and argued that the greatest effect on learning is created by reinforcement, with an effect size of 1.13, whereas extrinsic rewards only achieve 0.37. Programmed instruction has an effect of 0.18 whilst questioning has 0.41, mastery learning 0.5, remediation and feedback 0.65. Figures given by Coffield et al (2004b p 52), include reinforcement 1.13, direct instruction 0.82, student's disposition to learn 0.61, class environment 0.56, peer tutoring 0.50.

So, in summary,

> A differentiated classroom offers a variety of learning options designed to tap into different readiness levels,

interests, and learning profiles. In a differentiated class, the teacher uses

(1) a variety of ways for students to explore curriculum content,

(2) a variety of sense-making activities or processes through which students can come to understand and 'own' information and ideas, and

(3) a variety of options through which students can demonstrate or exhibit what they have learned.

Tomlinson (1995)

You can't be all things to all people, and that is not what is required to differentiate. What you can be is mindful of their differences and professional in the way you plan the learning experience, which means including students in a dialogue about how they learn, and what each of you can do to assist the process. It may help, when seeking alternative ways to communicate ideas and encourage participation, to peruse this list of alternatives styles and media. Are there any you could feel comfortable using but usually do not use?

Peer assessment in pairs or groups, buzz groups, individual or group research, worksheet, students make presentation or deliver lesson in turn, formative tests and quizzes, hands-on experiments, case studies, visits or visitors, animation, group emails for revision questions (cheaper than text messaging), web sites for homework tasks and backup material, teacher-led question and answers sessions (directed or undirected), writing frames, making demonstration video, watching video with question sheet (different sheets for different groups?) making their own textbook, past papers (taken or analysed), revision in groups with teacher as prompt, guide and resource; students revise by addressing class on topic, making flash cards or mind maps to share; students make songs or rhymes to recall information; students make diagrams or web sites to

organise new ideas, computer-based, demonstration,
debate, brainstorming, gapped handouts, guided
discovery, directed reading, discussion
(controlled/free/cross-over/fishbowl), field work,
games and simulation, open or distance learning
packages, mentoring, role-play, seminars, tutorials (of
various kinds), work shadowing, work experience, team
teaching, workshops, mini-enterprise .....

More sites and texts you might wish to explore are shown
below. The next chapter explores the related but different
question of how we can teach students to learn, and how that
process relates to the wider question of their role in society, and
therefore to the purpose of FE. It extends the motion of meta-
cognition, looking at what we mean by 'skills' and 'learning'.
But the final word here may be given to Miriam, a young
student on work experience within a GFE. She had to be kept
busy in the office so she was asked to write an open letter to
teachers. This is her unprompted response:

"Dear Teachers

Learning exercises

I am writing to explain ways of easy learning to help you with
your students. If you are having difficulties with your learning
skills and finding it hard to teach your class, here are a few
pointers:

Make lessons more active, interesting and fun.

If you have a class that does not seem to be paying much
attention, maybe it is because you are explaining it in a way that
the students are not interested and can't not be bothered to do
their work.

By making it more active, you could choose activities to make it more interesting; for example, put your students in little groups and set an activity. That way they get talking and discuss their opinions and also get more ideas for their work. You could also draw pictures and graphs and use words that are more fulfilling, that make your work more interesting.

Helping out

Most students find it hard to get on with their work. This is maybe to do with them not understanding the way you have explained the work, that's why they might feel embarrassed to ask you or even afraid to ask. To make your students feel more comfortable with you and your teaching skills, always tell them to ask you if they do not understand and also to ask, if they need any help with their work, either to improve or just to make them understand it more clearly.

Here are few suggestions to do if they do not understand the work you have set out:

Get them to write on a piece paper a list of things they did not understand in the lesson, but tell them they need not to write their name. After the lesson look at the pieces of paper with their problems and try to solve and improve ways of making it more understandable and easier for them.

Always go around the class and see if anyone needs any help in their work.

If you see that a student is struggling with their work, ask them what part they do not understand and what part they need help on, always give advice on how to improve and how to achieve better grades.

Tell your students that if they need any tips or have any concerns about their work, then just to see you after a lesson, after school or to make an appointment with you.

It is important to be positive with your students, and help them in every way you can.

I hope that this information will be quite helpful for you and that it improves your skills and approaches for your teachings techniques, and that your students will feel more comfortable in your classes and feel to learn more.

Yours sincerely

Miriam J******* Student (aged 15)

So what, then, is personalised learning?

This phrase has seeped into the language of education to the point where everyone uses it but few people can agree on its precise meaning. The summary below is taken from the site devoted to Executive Function.[15]
Buzz-words can be interchangeable. In some conversations, 'personalised learning' sounds very like 'student-centred', so it can degenerate into a vague term of approval that has as many meanings as it does users. Also, once a phrase it is officially approved, it has market currency and is immediately associated with new products or services, so that marketing speak takes over from rational discourse. If the phrase is to be meaningful, it has to be used with precision.
So what do government documents mean by it? Is that how you understand the term? How might it change according to time and place?

---

[15] www.personalisedlearningforum.eu and sign in with the password and username from the Introduction.

As early as 2004, the TLRP referred to personalised learning as The Big Idea and in January 2007, *the Teaching and Learning in 2020 Review* described the hallmarks of personalised learning and made the case for why all schools need to work towards this vision:

> Personalising learning is learner-centred and knowledge-centred .... close attention is paid to learners' knowledge, skills, understanding and attitudes. Learners are active and curious: they create their own hypotheses, ask their own questions, coach one another, set goals for themselves, monitor their progress and experiment with ideas for taking risks, knowing that mistakes and 'being stuck' are part of learning. Work is sufficiently varied and challenging to maintain their engagement but not so difficult as to discourage them. This engagement allows learners of all abilities to succeed, and it avoids the disaffection and attention-seeking that give rise to problems with behaviour." It is also "assessment-centred" using both formative and summative systems to encourage learners to "take an active role in their learning" and to encourage them to reflect and review. DFES (2007) p6.

In this context, personalisation can sound like just another word for good teaching, but expressed as a Platonic ideal. Personalisation is also said to be a "matter of moral purpose and social justice" (p7) and change-drivers include an expectation of greater social diversity, increased mental health disorders and changing work patterns (p9). In that context, it can sometimes look like a term for coping with Armageddon, where teachers are responsible for changing human behaviour on a massive scale whilst dealing with social and economic chaos. It can also sound like something used in a remedial sense, to deal with the less able to put right a problem, as opposed to something positive that defines a rational approach in any context.

The term becomes so packed with meaning it means everything, and thus nothing. One could choose a particular theme, for example, the role of feedback in learning and thus the need to use assessment methods that encourage self-evaluation, but a colleague with different problems might focus elsewhere, such as the use of small group work to overcome ESL difficulties.

Can "personalised learning" mean something concrete in opposition to, say, "non-personalised learning" without just meaning "good teaching" as expressed by idealists? Is it just a convenient title for a larger and complex reformation. The answer to both is probably 'yes'.

Teaching and Learning 2020 Review defines the "skills for personalising learning" as:

> analysing and using data, with a specific focus on assessment for learning
> understanding how children learn and develop
>
> working with other adults (including parents and other children's services professionals)
>
> engaging pupils as active participants in learning (p31).

This has implications for ITT and CPD, and provides an outline of what 'personalisation' means in most government documents. Much of the content for 20:20 is taken directly from *Personalised Learning – A Practical Guide* which was launched in October 2008. The Practical Guide starts by defining personalised learning as "taking a highly structured and responsive approach to each child's and young person's learning, in order that all are able to progress, achieve and participate. It means strengthening the link between learning and teaching by engaging pupils – and their parents – as partners in learning". (p5)

The idea that a connection should exist between teaching and learning ought not to sound radical. If the government think they are presently disconnected, they are asking for more than a new technique. The term is clearly a useful label for an overall approach to education, and is explained under 9 subheadings.

Key elements are high expectations and careful planning which were again discussed under the nine headings:

High quality teaching	Includes the ideal that students will be involved, engaged, accept responsibility for their own learning and work independently. Raises the question of how to teach weaker students in a group without lowering expectations. *Was that not part of all previous teaching? Why not?*
Target setting and tracking	Insists that targets setting should be ambitious and based on precise data, detailing some of the potential sources. *This begs the question of how reliable any data set might be and how skilled you are at knowing what you need to know, interpreting it when you get it and applying the conclusions. Assumes more autonomy than some teachers have? Or think they have?*
Focused assessment	Measures whether the expected progress has been made. It is important that "every child knows how they are doing and understands what they need to do to improve.... it

	is rarely enough to simply set a pupil a numeric or curricular target ... They need to understand not just what to improve but how to improve". There are three kinds of assessment for learning. Day to Day includes sharing lesson objectives and getting feedback. Periodic includes planning with reference to national standards. Transitional might involve external tests to recognise achievement. There is a recognition of spiky profiles. *The importance of feedback cannot be overstressed, tied to discussion about metacognition – how do you (can you) teach people to learn? Is that an addition to teaching them history or part of doing it properly?*
Intervention	The documents refer to three waves. Wave 1 is class based teaching. Wave 2 is small group work, often used to accelerate progress or for 'catch-up' learning. Wave 3 is the individualised approach, perhaps intensive 1-1, both for the weaker student and for the gifted and talented. *Does this encourage a view that personalised learning is always something you do from temporarily and often as an emergency solution to a problem? A positive view would include the idea of differentiating projects and support materials from the start, to avoid rather than solve problems? Is this easier to*

	achieve with older students, e.g. in FE, or with certain kinds of teaching?
Grouping	Might be by "age, ability, friendship groups or gender".....guided learning is an instructional sequence for small groups which is integrated into lessons to provide a bridge between whole-class teaching and independent work" *Flexibility within an organisation assumes a professional's ability to organise the experience of their own students, making whatever changes they think right.*
The learning environment	Includes all aspects of the environment, including resources, and the key term is flexibility. *How much authority does a fully qualified and experienced teacher have over the wider environment? Do we need to encourage more awareness of their discretionary powers?*
Curriculum Organisation	Stresses the flexibility of the National Curriculum, the idea of stage not age and cooperation (e.g. school and college 14-19) to offer more choices to suit students' needs. *Which could mean "don't do what you think you have been told – do what you know to be right. You have their permission to serve the interests of the student by deviating as required'.*
The	Cooperation with "a range of local

Extended Curriculum	providers, agencies and other schools" makes it easier to deliver ECM goals. *Ask not for whom the bell tolls. Localism in 2010-11 is just the latest of a series of moves to involve other agencies and motives for doing so vary widely.*
Supporting wider needs	Stresses relationship with families and the multi-agency team with a lead professional (LP) *More discretion within a classroom is matched with far more connection outside.*

In 2004, David Milliband was Minister for School Standards and Professor David Hargreaves was Associate Director of the Specialist Schools, a senior Demos Associate and a Fellow of Wolfson College, Cambridge, a major influence on the development of personalised learning. Interviewed by Futurelab, Hargreaves described it as "a complex and continuing professional process of education', emphasising the notion of process over product. At an OECD conference, Milliband had referred to "building the organisation of schooling around the needs, interests and aptitudes of individual pupils" whilst Hargreaves warned that "teachers have generally responded well to the pressures on them to improve, but unless they are willing to reconsider the structure of the profession in a more radical way, the transition will be far more painful that it need be." So it was never just about a new technique we can apply but about a new way of being professional, with new relationships and structures. Certainly, the notion of consulting students about their learning had powerful advocates. The TRLP research sheet No. 5 June 2003 argued that "how to listen and learn, as well as to teach and lead, is the challenge for teachers, schools and their communities".

Hargreaves' influence may also be seen through iNet and Special Schools and Academies Trust (SSAT), where nine 'gateways' were identified:

> Assessment for learning
> Learning to learn
> Student voice
> Curriculum
> New technologies
> School design and organisation
> Advice and guidance
> Mentoring and coaching
> Workforce development

By 2007, a report entitled *Personalised Learning Approaches used by Schools (ref RR843)* was able to look at how this was working out in practice. It concluded:

> Many of the factors that seem to facilitate progress in the case study schools are not specific to personalised learning, for example a strong focus on learning, effective staff development and successful leadership ... personalised learning ... seemed to have multiple meanings across the school ... (p68)

But is also pointed out:

> One contrast that has emerged from this work, relates to the established practice in public services of fitting individuals to the services offered, whereas all the case study schools had adopted approaches based on the premise of adapting the service to meet the needs of the pupils. (p69)

citing with approval Hargreaves' statement that:

> ... instead of expecting students to adapt to the pre-ordained structures, practices and routines of the school, these could all be questioned and if necessary adapted better to meet the needs of learners. Instead of students being expected to fit into the school, the school was being changed to fit the learning demands of students. (p69)

They asked whether personalised learning approaches offered anything new and concluded that:

> schools which might be characterised as strong on personalised learning see learners as co-investors in education, not in the financial sense, but in terms of their aspirations and commitment to learning. They maintain the focus on learning and all other activities are seen as contributing to this. However, the learning on which they focus goes beyond the school to future employment, health and citizenship. It is exemplary in lifelong learning, by giving pupils the skills to learn and motivating them to succeed in their own interests and aspirations and hence in their own terms. (p72)

Another route through National Strategies emphasised the need to plan interventions carefully. The idea of 'provision maps' was to offer an "at-a-glance way of showing the range of provision the school makes for children with additional needs, through additional staffing or peer support."

This does not mean personalised learning is an idea only relevant to people with special needs, but it does encourage the view that it is somehow more relevant, or perhaps especially relevant. This is probably not deliberate and is certainly not the case, but could good teaching as defined by the documentation prevent some students from developing special needs?

There is also room for confusion when an apparently new idea seems to describe something that is already being done. For example, Connexions staff could have spoken with authority about CAF, a standardised approach to conducting an assessment of a child's additional needs and deciding how those needs should be met, used by practitioners across the country, or about APIR, the Assessment, Planning, Implementation and Review which is the assessment tool Personal Advisers use for recording sessions and work with young people. Successful practitioners sometimes find that new thinking is only their old thinking being more widely shared, but now top down instead of bottom up.

So, after all that, what is personalised learning, and what is it not?

It is not a product or a single technique. It is a process founded on a philosophy. It is an attitude and methodology rather than a set of dogmas. But it insists that even though a class is a group, and may have to be taught as such some of the time, the education of each individual within that group must be based on:

A clear understanding, accurately recorded, of the personal strengths, weaknesses and potential of the individual learner

A relationship in school or college where the individual learner is able to discuss rationally with responsible adults how they are learning, what to do if they are not and how to improve. Note - it is not necessary to accept any current theories about learning styles or metacognition to do this. The conversation can take place without buying in expensive questionnaires of subscribing to the latest fad.

The use by that adult of research summaries as well as data to inform these conversations, so that they know how to manage the learning process for each individual. This does not contradict the previous point. You can reject whatever you find unconvincing, so long as you have thought about how learning actually works.

A concept of learning that stresses the responsibility of the learner for their own development, then listens to its own propaganda by allowing the learner an active part in that process, helping them to understand how learning works in their individual case.

An open attitude within the school or college that welcomes informed debate with and, if necessary, organises assistance from a number of other parties, including other schools and colleges, voluntary agencies, employers and parents.

What this means for the organisation of a school, college, curriculum or lesson depends on who you are teaching and how you normally do it at the moment. But it is not is not something you bolt on, apply, mug up on or pay lip service to. In essence, it is really something you are. Or are willing to become.

Chapter 4

Skills and metacognition

We are not as good as we used to be at building ships, making steel or mining coal, but we are world class in broadcasting, the advertising industry, architecture, art and design.   Andy Duncan, CEO C4, Jan 2007

I question the propriety of raising the awareness and aspiration of learner who then cannot find jobs worthy of a human being. .... paying close attention to misunderstandings is an intrinsic part of Teaching and Learning   Coffield (2008) pp 15, 17

In English at school we study a grammar book by a man called Ronald Ridout, read Cider with Rosie, do debates on fox-hunting and memorise 'I Must Go Down To The Seas Again' by John Masefield. We don't actually have to think about stuff.

David Mitchell, *Black Swan Green* (2006)

Thinking involves self-monitoring; dialogue involves critique and respectful disagreement. The ability to master both is a definition of educated discourse. How does a student learn to engage in educated discourse with a teacher?

The ability to learn is more than a set of cognitive skills. It requires the willingness to develop those skills and the intention to deploy them. Learning is an emotional experience. Moreover, the term 'skills' has become so widely used in so many ways that it is in danger of turning into Nasruddin's donkey.

The story concerns a crafty smuggler who, every week passed by a customs post with his donkeys laden with various goods. The officials knew he was smuggling, and they delved deeply into his panniers to find out what. They could see nothing illegal and had to let him go. This continued for many months, until he announced he had made so much money he was going to retire. Desperate, the officials who had searched him so many times begged to be told what it was he had so cleverly smuggled under their very noses. "Donkeys", he told them.

Sometimes it is the very obvious we need to question.

In a general FE college, and increasingly in sixth form colleges, the context for learning tends to be broadly vocational.

> We agree with Sir Andrew Foster that the key strategic role for the sector, the role in which the contribution of FE to learners' lives, to society and the economy can exceed that of any other part of the education and training system, is to help people gain the skills and qualifications for employability, so that they are equipped for productive, sustainable and fulfilling employment in a modern economy.   DfES (2006) 2.4

The key term in that paragraph is 'fulfilling'. There is more to education than the need for employment. There is more to employment than the need to earn money. Both, however, are usually required to empower students.

Chapter 2 outlined the way that clients for FE may be defined and how its role is changing. A great deal of the argument about purpose is informed by notions of 'skill'. There are said the be skills that are 'basic' or 'key' skills which every student must have in order to be fit for the employment market. For many years there has been much loose talk about employability and skills and, in a poll of CBI members in 2005, it seemed that 41% of them were concerned at the lack of English or Maths skills among applicants and the same number were concerned with their "attitude to work", whilst 72% were unimpressed with "their business awareness" . A 2011 CBI /EDI survey of 566 employers showed 42% were "not satisfied

with the basic use of English by school and college leavers" and
"o address the weaknesses in basic skills, almost half (44%) of
employers have had to invest in remedial training for school
and college leavers".[16] In 2006 the Leitch Review, found that
more than five million adults lack functional literacy. The
National Literacy Trust produces an annual survey with some
very interesting data. Their 2012 report claims, for example,
that:

> one in six people in the UK struggle with literacy ....this
> means their literacy is below the level expected of an
> eleven year old NLT (2012 (1)) p2

In 2007, only 35% of five year olds in the most deprived areas
reached the expected level of attainment, compared to 51% of
pupils in other areas. (ibid) p5
There are significant differences in gender and social
backgrounds, with young white boys receiving free school
meals being less likely to enjoy (and therefore to develop well)
in reading and writing, but the general picture shows some
improvement:

> At Key Stage 2 (age eleven) the percentage of young
> people achieving the expected levels for reading increased
> by 8 percentage points over ten years, from 78% in 1999
> to 86% in 2009. In 2010, there was a slight drop of 2
> percentage points. Overall levels remained the same in
> 2011. The percentage of young people reaching expected
> levels for writing increased from 54% in 1999 to 67% in
> 2006. However, from 2006 to 2009 levels plateaued and
> the percentage remained the same (67%) three years later.
> The percentage of young people reaching expected levels
> for writing increased by 4 percentage points in 2010, and
> further increased by 4 percentage points in 2011.
>
> NLT (2012 - 1) p3

---

[16] NLT 2012 (1) page 5

Meanwhile, the number of jobs classified as elementary and operative continues to fall, so that literacy demands made upon the workforce to get any job at all will increase. Additionally, a report from the IPPR (Margo et al, 2006) looked carefully at "the current conception of what need in order to succeed in life" and argued that our "increasingly service-orientated economy" placed increasing emphasis on social skills, making them 33 times more important than they were a decade ago and thus disadvantaging prospective employees from particular social groups.

The employer's perspective

Interviewed by FET&C in 2005 about what makes people employable, an estate agent talked about morality. Although he required a certain degree of literacy and numeracy from his employees, his greatest worry was that they didn't seem to enjoy it. The worked only for money, not for the pleasure of doing a job well. Having spent the money, they were left unsatisfied. His problem was not with a lack of basic skills but with a merely instrumental attitude to work. He imagined many people swapping vocational sectors throughout a working lifetime, seeking the right kind of satisfaction.

A senior executive in a Sector Skills Council, asked the same question also emphasised the need to 'engage' with work, to have a 'positive attitude' and be 'willing to take part', to be 'motivated' and 'persistent'. The lack of such qualities had nothing to do with level of qualification, and was missing from graduates as often as from unqualified school leavers.
A builder, willing to take on an apprentice and teach them on the job, found it difficult to hire one that was willing to turn up every day on time.

Visited by a member of the LEA, a travel agent complained that her new employee lacked "numeracy skills". By this she meant that the young girl had booked someone's holiday on the wrong date.

Travelling between colleges late at night, looking for a hotel in heavy rain, I recently became lost and tired within a mile of the destination. The map provided by the hotel's web site was not clear. I rang reception, told them where I was and asked how to get to the hotel. They offered to tell me the route from the M1. I explained that I was not on the M1 but very much closer. They started to read out the route from the M1. Who was lacking what kind of skill here? How could a previous teacher have avoided the problem?

One useful distinction circulating at present is between three kinds of skill[17]

Transient skills are very specific and useful for a while. They would include the ability to use a particular software package. Quite soon, that package will be outdated and you have to master another version, or another kind of package altogether (upgrade your version of Microsoft Office or Dreamweaver or switch to an Apple Mac). These skills tend to offered by private companies and enterprising colleges because they are quick and easy to package and sell and relatively easy to teach.

Enduring skills are the underpinning concepts that make proper use of transient skills, such as design skills or the basis of good programming. There is no point learning how to use a software package to make web sites unless you understand what makes a good design and how people really process information. These enduring, underpinning ideas are more complex and more difficult to develop. Without them, transient skills are of no real use. Employers might complain that students know how to use many kinds of software but can't make anything useful with them.

---

[17] Explained to an audience at Sussex University in 2006 by Jonathon Hirsch of Hirschworks during a seminar on employability, but already current within DfES.

Transferable skills include the kind of murky concepts referred to as life skills or work skills or business skills. At one level they include the ability to turn up on time in the right clothes and form the right professional relationships. At another level, they include the ability to learn and to apply that learning. If you have the right transferable skills, you will be able to teach yourself the new software package and may not need to attend a course. It is in this area we explore how people feel about learning and working, what kinds of attitude make good students and employees, or useful citizens. These are the most difficult to define and to foster, and it is here that most complaints arise from both teachers (they can't learn) and employers (they are no use to me).

In addition to this we have: **Basic skills** in what we call literacy and numeracy. If you can't read and write at all you are said to lack them. Once you start the process, you can progress to the next stage. The number of adults deemed to lack them is said to have risen dramatically, but is that because adults are more illiterate or because we are looking harder for cases? Or have we changed the definition?

Key skills were supposed to be fundamental to the process of learning and becoming employable. They are more advanced than 'basic', at levels 1, 2 and 3. Now we have to decide what makes someone numerate or literate or competent in ICT at each level. How do you define, teach and assess such skills? The CBI complains that too few people pass GCSE English and Maths at grade C or above. But then it will be argued that the GCSE syllabus and the teaching styles associated with it are not suitable for the majority of the population. Failure does not imply illiteracy or innumeracy in some permanent and universal sense but a mismatch of qualification with cohort. Key skills are more practical and vocational and this kind of teaching should be used instead. Then you find there are very high failure rates among key skills classes. Students do not like attending and teachers do not like the assessment regime. So now we have something else.

Functional Skills then arrived to become a component of

the new 14-19 qualifications and of GCSEs. The concept was similar to key skills but differently defined and assessed. The idea was that students cannot obtain the full diploma without passing them but (b) they should not be denied the diploma for lack of some skills they don't really need.

Coffield ((2008 p 25) recommends attention to three distinctions made by Michael Young: specialist disciplinary knowledge, context-specific knowledge (learned at work) and trans-sectoral knowledge (general education rather than core skills). The debate goes on about what 'they' need and why, and how we can make them want it. Many teachers become upset when students arrive without the necessary skills to learn efficiently from their teaching style, and blame previous teachers for not preparing them adequately.

It is important to book a holiday on the right day, but failure to do so is not caused by the lack of a mathematical key skill. It is important to turn up on time, to gain personal satisfaction from your job, to feel you can learn from it and develop personally within it. It is important throughout your life to be able to learn. Transferable skills contribute to all these things. They also contribute to literacy and numeracy.

Study skills are, logically, skills you need to study. But do we mean by that the ability to learn (which includes affective elements like an intention and some confidence) or the ability to churn out what teachers want for assessment (like essays with good spelling?). You can learn how to write essays. You don't always need to write essays to learn.

Thinking skills are what we require to establish the truth and relevance of a proposition. They might tell us that what we are asked to do at college is pointless or inefficient.

Agenda for Change reflected the government's concern that "last year 300,000 young people left school with fewer than 5 GCSEs" (DfES 2006 p. i) but the 14-19 White Paper was concerned that

> Those who progress further through the system, into A
> levels and higher education, are very much less

criticised for lacking functional skills. Nonetheless, some universities are concerned that they do not have these skills at high enough levels - for example, they may be able to read and write well, but may be less strong at writing extended, analytical prose. It is sometimes argued that because the so-called 'compensatory' assessment system at GCSE means that a good grade can be achieved because strengths in one area compensate for weaknesses in another, GCSEs do not fully secure achievement in the functional core of maths and English.   DfES 2005 (2.26)

It is also possible to pass a GCSE with an A-C grade but be unable to spell or punctuate to a level that some FE teachers would consider minimal, causing them to argue that standards are too low, or that students are coached for the exam rather than educated so they have permanent abilities.
There is an obvious difference between

worrying that too few people leave school with any qualifications

arguing that too few people are fit for work because of failure at school

arguing that academic results pre-HE do not fit students for progress within HE

arguing that graduates lack skills valued by employers

agreeing on definitions of literacy that suits all purposes and audiences

Terminology and careless thinking can confuse the issues. It is sometimes useful to pause and consider whether our conversation confuses study skills and a version of 'literacy', and how much meta-cognition may contribute to employability and academic progress.

It is traditional to find confusion here. In 1976 over a quarter of boys leaving school in Coventry entered engineering apprenticeships. Other popular destinations were clerical, retail and public services. The LEA set out to find what young people had to read and write within those areas, and what kind of conversations they had. They found that engineering demanded more reading than was anticipated, but across all areas there was a tendency to complain that new employees did not read properly, or at all, material that was, in fact, very badly written. There was a mismatch between the kinds of writing demanded by the job and the kind required to be qualified through the college. Managers complained about the illiteracy of apprentices but researchers found that many of the skills they were said to lack they did not, in fact, use on the job. In some cases, noise levels were so high that "very few job-related conversations took place" but "sign language and gesture played an important part in the communication" (report to the steering committee, November 1978)

It is nearly half a century since Venables (1967) suggested we test vocational ability with non-verbal methods, also pointing out that young workers wanted to learn a job (with limited things to learn) rather than be prepared for work in a general, more flexible sense (with lots more to learn), although modern research complains that our focus on employability will limit our aims to preparing people for contributing to economic effectiveness rather than developing 'social purposes' (Coffield 2008 p59).

There is the additional confusion caused by a recent insistence on entrepreneurial skills. It is easy to accept that students need to learn about personal finance – how to manage credit cards, savings, loans and mortgages. Some teachers, especially in schools, find it harder to accept that they also need to take part in a mini-enterprise, setting up small businesses as part of the learning process. These have included a wide range from selling stationery in the foyer to shining shoes - forgetting that most people wear trainers. Some teachers find that a useful way to encourage foresight and responsibility, as well as teaching applied numeracy. Others have seen it as an insidious way of teaching that market forces are the dominant force in our lives and, politically, that this is right and proper, which is begging too many questions for them. They also argue that whilst the economy needs entrepreneurs, it needs workers employed by them in much larger numbers. Should we be encouraging risk-taking by this means? Do risk-takers make good employees?

Certain caveats suggest themselves:

Never assume that employers know what they need, as opposed to what they want.

Never assume that employers, or even most teachers, are familiar with the illogicalities of assessment regimes, with their complex relationship to what they claim to measure.

Never assume that employers or teachers possess in abundance those skills the lack of which they lament in their students.

Never assume that students know how to learn just because they have somehow washed up in your classroom, perhaps with some qualifications that allowed them entry.

We need to distinguish very carefully between other people's ideas of what skills are basic or key or necessary for employment and our own identification of what skills are required to benefit from the course we are teaching. That is not the same question, although they may be related.

It is possible that a drive to increase employability that focuses only on narrowly defined vocational skills will have missed the point, especially if they are often transient. Being able to carry out certain tasks with a degree of accuracy or speed is not the same as being willing to do so with an appropriate attitude. Nor does it guarantee that the employee will be able quickly to learn new tasks as their role or the nature of the industry develops.

Whilst government papers refer mostly to skills, employers talk more often about attitudes and flexibility. Employers can teach skills on the job and buy in trainers for certain key areas. What they can't teach is the ability and willingness to learn and to apply learning. Listening to 21st century debate, one is reminded of William Cory, the 19th century lyric poet and master at Eton:

You go to a great school not so much for knowledge as for arts and habits.

> For the habit of attention and the art of expression
> For the art of entering quickly into another person's thoughts
> For the art of indicating assent or dissent in graduated terms
> For the art or working out what is possible in a given time
> For taste, for discrimination, for mental courage and mental soberness

Stripped of its antique elegance, that could be the syllabus for what was later called a Wider Key Skill.

Subject tutors, trying to instil the basic vocational or academic skills, also complain that students do not know 'how to learn', and lack the skills and attitudes required to benefit from the course. There are many ways to interpret that complaint, but it is notable that what tends to frustrate both teachers and employers most is not so much a lack of knowledge, which is relatively easy to provide, as an unwillingness to engage. Perhaps the problem is in the affective domain? What kind of people are we making?

Some teachers have an image of an educated person, with

certain basic skills and qualities inherent in that definition, and wish to teach the student those skills and encourage in them those qualities so that, whatever their vocational choice and academic pathway, they are in some broad and general way 'educated'. They are then concerning themselves with all possible futures for that individual and, in wider terms, with the evolution of a civilised society.

It is not uncommon to assume that educated people are reflective and rational, believing in logical debate and careful weighing of evidence. Those qualities might be built in to a syllabus and assessment scheme and demanded of students to qualify for something called Communication or Working with Others or Critical Thinking. Then we meet individuals with successful careers and degrees who seem, on the face of it, to behave irrationally, immorally and with less concern for the facts or for others than for naked self-advancement or some bigoted set of beliefs we find obnoxious. Should we ensure that a young student is somehow 'better' than such people, and refuse them a certificate if they are not? It is not unknown for a pleasant, well-meaning student to fail the course whilst a deeply unpleasant neighbour slides though with ease.

This may not be the place to spend time on the vexed question of what we mean by 'educated'. It is, however, the place to spend time on asking what skills we intend to foster, why and how. The 'how question really ought to come last.

For most teachers, the matter of 'what' is settled by syllabus. It could be argued that, for the most part, students come to FE to gain a qualification to get work. Our duty is to make sure they pass. The result of passing is that they gain confidence and a more positive view of the educational system. Then they take up a productive role in society and feel valued and independent. The difference to their lives, and perhaps to their personal philosophy and value system may be immense, although largely outside your direct control. You haven't taught them to be better people, but you have improved their life-chances. They may or may not be better people as a result. It is not mere co-incidence that the most violent prejudices are often manifest among the dispossessed. Economic progress can moderate opinion where rational debate was ineffectual.

Some students will come to take academic qualifications that lead to HE. You may feel that part of the preparation for academic life is the ability to weigh arguments and deliver the conclusions in measured, elegant prose. You may feel a dedication to notions of objectivity or truth is important. Notwithstanding some of the internal politics of HE institutions, you may be right. But before they enter such places they need to jump through hoops set at a certain height and diameter by people who want to maintain 'standards' by keeping out the unsuitable. So study skills may mean learning how to behave when you arrive at university, or it may mean learning how to pass the exam to get you in. The difference can be considerable – university tutors often complain that the kind of thinking encouraged by A level is dysfunctional at degree level and new students have to be 'decontaminated' in their first fresher term. Moreover, if each academic discipline has its own culture and way of thinking[18], then 'study skills' might need to be very subject specific.

Ecclestone (2002) found a sample of GNVQ students to be "cheerfully instrumental" in the way they approached the course, putting most effort in to easy units where they would do well (p119) and increasingly putting most value on their teachers' command of the assessment regime (p145). Learning for its own sake, enjoyment of subject, becoming autonomous learners or educated people – none of this matters if you are afraid you will fail and be rejected. If teachers find it frustrating

---

[18] Paul H Hirst , in texts such as *The Logical and Psychological Aspects of Teaching a Subject*, argued that teaching a subject is about helping a students to think mathematically or historically or scientifically – that there are forms or fields of knowledge with their own rules of discourse The idea is not without its detractors, but if allied to the notion of vocational cultures and thus differing needs of employment sectors, it reminds us not to assume too easily any generalised curriculum that covers all forms of 'studying'.

to be limited by a badly designed syllabus, forced to coach narrow exam-passing skills rather than explore issues more widely, then they may feel morally obliged to take on the assessment boards and change the system. It would, however, be ironic if the result of any reform were to give teachers more job satisfaction and students a higher failure rate, or a set of skills they never use outside the classroom.

Another problem exists with the idea that perhaps our job is to teach students how to learn in some abstract way. Coffield et al (2004b) take issue with a suggestion, made at a Learning Styles Information Network, that we should be teaching "attitudes, skills and knowledge" instead of "knowledge, skills and attitudes", an idea condemned as a

> fashionable platitude which, if put into operation, would result in the modish but vacuous notion of a content-free curriculum, all learning style and little or no subject knowledge (p60).

Support for this idea comes from the TLRP

> Our enquiries led us to the conclusion that learning how to learn is highly contextualised and cannot easily be separated from learning 'something'. It is not profitable to plan, teach or assess Learning How to Learn separately from planning, teaching or assessing learning in a specific subject - TLRP 2006

and from the 'infusion' approach of their Thinking Skills Project. The Welsh Government set up a Thinking and Assessment for Learning Programme and issued a revised guidance document in June 2010 entitled "Why develop thinking and assessment for learning in the classroom? (Guidance document No: 037/2010).[19]

An increasing number of commercial web sites and texts

---

[19] Guidance document No: 037/2010

have for some years been promoting the idea that we can teach thinking skills and, as a result, get better subject learning It is not uncommon to see claims for what can be achieved by learning to think as opposed to thinking more carefully about how you learn. Certainly, any student would benefit from an awareness of what is meant by intelligent thought, the criteria by which the college judges their thinking and its product and increased self-monitoring, but does that mean a single keen teacher can run a few quick classes, divorced from the way the rest of the college operates, and expect it to make any immediate and significant contribution to overall success rates?

Bearing in mind all those caveats, how do we link the problems of study skills to the previous arguments about meta-learning, and to the practical problems of bringing about student success?

Moseley et al (2004) have explored in depth a range of conceptual models and frameworks for 'thinking skills'. They claim that:

> Thinking skill approaches with children and young people are usually very effective, especially if they are directed at meta-cognition, self-regulation and what we have called 'value-grounded thinking'. Their effectiveness is likely to be greater if they are used for learner self-regulation rather than coming fully under teacher control. (p11)

They are aware throughout that

> thinking is a human activity which involves cognition (knowing), affect (feeling) and conation (wanting and willing) (1.2)

and that the Qualifications and Curriculum Authority (QCA) conceptualised thinking skills as
> information processing
> reasoning

enquiry
creativity
evaluation

They note that in post-16 education,

> although there are many opportunities for developing
> thinking (notably in key skills as well as in subject areas)
> relatively little has been done to embed thinking skills in
> pedagogy and assessment (1.5)

and refer to a lack of "critical thinking" to be lamented, especially in FE colleges that also offer HE. However, that does not mean they assume that all 'thinking' in FE ought to be a high order critical process. On the contrary.

They trace the first use of the term 'metacognition' by Flavell in 1976 (2.4), who explained that students would be engaging in metacognition if, for example, they:

Noticed they were having more trouble learning A than B

Decided to check something before accepting it as a fact

Decided to make a note of something in case they forgot it

Actively monitored and orchestrated such processes to gain an objective

That is not so different from the conversation in the preceding chapter, where the language of learning styles was used to enable students to think about how they processed information and became more consciously responsible for the process. However, in analysing what they mean by 'self-regulation' Moseley et al stress that there are affective components – students have to feel able to and wish to try (2.5). In this context, they later explore a taxonomy of educational objectives from Marzano which also stresses the emotions associated with gaining knowledge (3.2.2).

For Marzano, there are three levels. The cognitive system processes relevant information, but this is controlled by a metacognitive system that "sets goals and strategies". This in turn is controlled by a "self-esteem system" to do with attention and motivation that "monitors discrepancies between perceived and desired states".

Any debate about 'study skills' ought properly to be a debate about metacognition, about how students work out what they want and why, work out what they can't do in order to get what they want and why not, then set about trying to do it better. Formative assessment is part of the process by which they do so, but another part might include a discussion in class about what 'thinking' means to them in the context of the course, the assessment regime, their ambitions and fears.

Another interesting framework in Moseley et al is a revision by Anderson and Krathwohl of Bloom's taxonomy (3.3.2). In the previous chapter it was argued that the proper planning of the learning process manipulates the emotional condition of the student by facilitating success. This is done by working in order through a hierarchy of skills, awarding 'medals' at the lower end before setting a 'mission' in the higher orders. Anderson and Krathwohl offer six categories for the cognitive process which, in ascending order, are:

remember - understand - apply - analyse - evaluate - create

Just as the teacher is consciously using this progressive structure to plan the learning experience, the student might use it to make conscious what they are doing, seeking ways to be better at each of the skills and discussing the criteria for success.

Moseley et al offer an integrated framework for understanding thinking and learning (4.3):

Strategic and Reflective thinking
Engagement with and management of thinking/learning,
supported by value-grounded thinking (including critically
reflective thinking)

Cognitive skills		
Information gathering	**Building understanding**	**Productive thinking**
Experiencing, recognising and recalling Comprehending messages and recorded information	Development of meaning (e.g. by elaborating, representing or sharing ideas) Working with patterns and rules. Concept formation Organising ideas	Reasoning Understanding causal relationships Systematic enquiry Problem solving Creative thinking

Again, this may be useful not only for teachers to plan an experience but for students to plan their own journey. In 5.1 they chart the percentage of each type of thinking found within each of the key skills areas. The formal context for certification will change over time, but in any context it would be fair to argue that a systematic charting of the kind of skills required to succeed, with examples of what each means, is the minimum of information to offer the students if they are to have any chance of managing their own futures.

Moseley et al offer a number of statements as "supported by

research findings" (6.2) which include:

Learners have different preferences, needs, backgrounds and skills.

Most learners think of teaching as the transmission of knowledge.

Many learners have had negative experiences at school.

Thinking and learning are active processes.

Learning often involves a re-conceptualisation of information.

Motivation is the key to active learning.

Students need to have appropriate, specific and challenging goals.

The quantity and quality of instruction make a big difference.

Learners can benefit from thinking skills interventions irrespective of age.

Learners can benefit from thinking skills interventions irrespective of ability.

Teaching for critical, creative and caring thinking is rare in FE colleges.

Many teachers and employers want compliant thinkers and learners.

Learning is affected by contextual factors.

Progress is facilitated by constructive formative assessment.

It is such assumptions that help to explain the original design of the so-called 'soft' key skills. The 'hard' skills were

> Application of Number (AoN)
> Information Technology (IT)
> Communication (Comm)

'Hard' refers to the nature of the evidence for qualification – they included an external test. The 'wider' or 'soft' skills were

> Working with Others (WWO)
> Improving Own Learning and Performance (IOLP)
> Problem Solving (PS)

They could be gained with just a moderated portfolio. There are, however, internal matters of organisation to be addressed when trying to teach people how to learn as a separate 'subject'.

The student and teacher experience

Staff in college X generally agreed that students did not know how to study. They lacked the skills and attitudes that would allow them to carry out tasks and create portfolios to a required standard. Because the syllabus was long and the lesson time short, nobody felt they had time to teach the students how to learn before they started learning.

Because the key skill IOLP was all about learning how to monitor, evaluate and improve your own ability to learn, it seemed a useful addition to the curriculum. Because it was funded by load banding, it could attract additional income to pay for more teaching time on top of existing commitments. Because it looked difficult to manage, and involved putting together a portfolio of evidence, existing tutors did not wish to introduce it in tutorial time, so a small number of staff,

---

centrally located, agreed to try to introduce it as a pilot scheme by offering additional lessons which they taught on behalf of the departments.

Some students responded well to the idea of examining how they learned, but major problems included:

1) The teacher for study skills and metacognition was not formally connected to any subject content or departmental course team, so students often felt it was an additional call on their which they could ignore.

2) Targets for improvement had to be set in the context of work given by subject teachers, whose co-operation was varied as they had no evidence the project would be worth their time.

3) Even when co-operation from student and teacher was forthcoming, the time taken to organise the portfolio grew alarmingly. Seeking evidence from disparate sources and organising its display\eventually pushed out the improvement of learning to which that evidence was supposed to refer.

The idea was dropped.

In college Y, IOLP was integrated into tutorial times. The extra funding allowed tutors to have more time available for group or individual consultations. Collection of evidence for portfolios was better organised and the IOLP requirements provided a structure for the tutorial programme. It remained the case that learning how to learn was largely additional to, not fundamental to, the process of attending subject-based classes.

If learning how to learn becomes just another subject, or a slot on the tutorial programme, then many points have been entirely missed. Study skills are about more than just three different ways to remember a list, and metacognition requires a certain co-operative, exploratory frame of mind in both staff and students, a new institutional culture. Which is not to say an individual, perhaps working in an unreconstructed wilderness, cannot make a significant contribution. Consider, for example, the use of writing frames.

Presented with a mass of facts or ideas, students often do not know how to organise them to structure a response. They will benefit from a pre-ordered framework into which their response may be fitted. This can be a simple visual organiser like the one below:

Which one to buy?	Product A	Product B	Product C	Product D
Under £50?	Yes	No	Yes	?
Guarantee for at least 12 months?	No	Yes	No	?
Delivery included in price?	No	Yes	Yes	?
Passed UK safety tests?	No	Yes	Yes	?

Another way to organise their response is to use writing frames. These give them a framework to build on – step by-step instruction on what good writers would do. Geoff Petty has written interestingly about them, and offers examples on his web site[20]. There is a good essay planning pro-forma from Solihull and the same page has material from the National Literacy Trust to provide frames for a maths investigation, an IT project and writing about Art.

Below is a simple frame for completing a project or report:

---

[20] All links to web sites updated through bpfe.org.uk/links

How to carry out this work

clarify your purpose

Read carefully and discuss exactly what you are supposed to be doing, and why.
What are you supposed to be proving with this work? What criteria will be used to judge it? Who will read it and what will they hope to gain from it? (N.B. most work has two kinds of audience – the person it pretends to be for and the person who grades it. Do not confuse them)

brainstorm and mind map

You can start by letting your mind run wild and thinking all kinds of wild ideas to get you started. The most crazy idea may turn out to be the most useful and really original. Once you have some useful ideas, make sure you use mind maps to organise them and turn them into sub-headings. Make sure the sub-headings closely relate to your purpose in writing it.

clarify your time frame

Make a note on a large poster and in your diary of the final date for handing it in. If at all possible, move back a week and aim for an earlier deadline to play safe. Work out roughly how long you think you can spend on each of the following stages, and keep track of your progress.

control information

Once you are clear what you need to produce, then decide what kind of information you will need to produce it. List possible sources (libraries, internet, friends, hand-outs and old notes from previous lessons).

Beware of three major problems:

1) Gathering so much you don't know what to do with it. As it comes in, start to keep ideas and information under separate headings, or in separate folders (e.g. with Word) so it has some kind of organisation from the very beginning. In fact, you may start by analysing the best headings, then seeking information to go under them, and maybe add and subtract headings as information comes in.

2) Forgetting where you found it, so you can quote a reference in your bibliography. Write it down at once and keep it safe.

3) Not being sure how it is relevant to the assignment brief. It may look very interesting and maybe you can find a purpose for it later. But if your "odds and ends" folder is bigger than the rest you are doing it wrong so go back and re-think what kind of information/sub-headings you are using.

check relevance and time spent 

Re-read the assignment brief often to make sure you are doing what you are supposed to be doing.

Check your time allowance and don't go over it.

Once all the information is under a suitable sub-heading, and all sub-headings have enough information, you can think about a conclusion and, finally, an introduction. (How can you introduce something that doesn't exist yet?)

gain critical distance

Put it away for a few days. If you planned your time well you have included time to have a break and come back later. Read it later and see if it still makes sense to you. Was it as good as you remember it? Does anything need improving? How can it be improved in the time you have left?

proof read it

Use spell check (f7 - watch out for homophones) and be especially careful of technical terms. Look for sentences that don't read clearly and simplify them if necessary.

Have you answered the question and fulfilled the purpose? Does it meet the criteria?

hand it in on time

and congratulate yourself for being well organised.

evaluate your own process

What was easy and what was difficult? Why?

You will notice this general advice will encourage self-control but also provided checkpoints for teachers to monitor the process. You can encourage them to manage their own time whilst talking to them about how they do so. Conversations might include how they form groups and whether those groups worked efficiently; what kind of allowance they made for their own learning preference; how they made us of learning support etc. If they had a checklist of such questions before they started they could use it as a basis for self-monitoring as well as for reporting back and writing up their self-assessment for submission.

All of this encourages students to examine how they process information and to talk it through with their teachers, but their motivation in doing so is to learn something specific in their subject area. Moreover, as Petty points out, it is important that frames should not be just handed to students as blanks for them to fill in, but developed with them as a group exercise and issued as a summary of debate. Only then have they engaged in the process of discussing how they think, as opposed to merely trying to follow instructions.

One of the issues under transition (chapter 6) is the way students and teachers agree on what constitutes learning, and one of the greatest problems will be with the definition of plagiarism, especially with project work. Students who have been used to teacher talk will expect to sit and be talked to, or at. To them, learning may mean making notes, responding to questions or perhaps just being in the room, but it will be a led by an adult who sets the pace. Asked to go and find information, they will not know how, or why. The weakest end of the scale involves what used to be called FOFO learning, politely translated as 'go away and find out'. It sets students some questions and then empties the classroom. It gives the teacher a breathing space, and that's about all. The stronger end will involve explanations of how to define the task, prepare the search, use resources, and probably involve library inductions, lessons on use of the catalogues and the internet etc., with the teacher supervising and process

Some students will have spent many happy hours in previous classes gathering chunks of information and sticking them together with coloured titles and pictures to make a 'portfolio'. They have learned how to cut and paste, how to colour in and even how to make an index, but not necessarily how to analyse and synthesise. It may be that their last teacher, under pressure from an assessment regime that demanded large number of portfolios to be handed in early with extensive documentation, emphasised presentation over process, and had no time to allow them to explore creatively, or to discuss what they were learning from all that gathering and sticking together.

The student experience

A class of level 2 motor mechanics had been looking at the four stroke cycle in petrol engines. They looked at a real engine that had been cut away so they could see its parts move. They looked at diagrams on the board while a teacher explained about sucking in vapour, compressing it, exploding it and expelling the gasses. Then they had to produce something for their portfolio to prove to a moderator that they had learned something. They were not skilled in writing things down neatly (or at all) and many could not draw well. Universally, guided by heavy hints from the teacher, they went to the same web site, downloaded a rather complex diagram and then carefully pasted it in, without acknowledgement.

There are two issues here. Of course it does not prove they

have learned, so is not suitable evidence. They would have been better answering questions on cloze sheets, taking photographs of the model in four positions and labelling it, or being recorded making an oral explanation.

Equally important was the fact they had presented as their 'work' something that was not theirs, and which they had not actually worked on. They did not think of this as cheating, but as required behaviour – they found a nice neat diagram and used it to make a nice neat portfolio to keep the teacher and moderator happy, then got back to the serious business of messing about with greasy engines in order to learn about them. As far as 'assessment' was concerned, the fact they had seen the diagram was considered enough, and the evidence that they had seen it was in the fact they had filed what they looked at. This had nothing to do with fixing broken cars.

This is a more innocent kind of plagiarism than that of a student who chases up essays on the internet and steals them, but between the extremes is a large grey area where those who have been bought up on project work and internet based FOFO learning have always thought of learning as gathering and sticking together, not as analysing, discussing, selecting and synthesising. They are not cheating, but doing what they have always been asked to do, so on cannot suddenly condemn or even punish them for it. That is why any regulations on plagiarism should be issued with a handbook, differentiated by level, to explain to students the difference between using and stealing, between 'gathering' and 'learning from'. Annex 3 contains samples, with useful links for detection.

Assessment, feedback and self-improvement

> The only legitimate purpose of an examination is to permit the teacher and learner to work together to decide how to improve the educational process of the student. In other words, for the teacher and leaner to decide what to do next - Tribus (undated) p12

We have grown used to the idea that exams exist to sort sheep from goats and to hold teachers accountable. If there are only ten places or jobs available and fifty applicants, exam grades save you having to interview everybody. If more than half a class fails a test, the teacher will be hauled in to explain. Also, we have been used to the idea that assessments, or qualifications through assessment regimes, are what matter, so that the final assessment process should be allowed to dictate what is taught and how.

The whole process of succeeding in an institution can easily become a game of knowing how to gain grades by knowing the rules that govern them (Ecclestone 2002, Miller and Parlett 1974, Becker 1968). But there are more sophisticated attitudes to the notion of assessment. We want students to become responsible for their own learning, to learn how to improve. Tribus hyphenates this to remind us that they need to be *response-able*.

> The Assessment Reform Group[21] argues that:
> Assessment is one of the most powerful educational tools for promoting effective learning. But it must be used in the right way. There is no evidence that increasing the amount of testing will enhance learning. Instead the focus needs to be on helping teachers use assessment, as part of teaching and learning, in ways that will raise pupils' achievement.
> *Beyond the Black Box* – pamphlet issued in 1999

They continue with a number of statements that have to be taken into account when considering 'study skills'.

> research indicates that improving learning through assessment depends on five, deceptively simple, key factors:

---

[21] Association for Achievement and Improvement through Assessment

the provision of effective feedback to pupils;

the active involvement of pupils in their own learning;

adjusting teaching to take account of the results of assessment;

a recognition of the profound influence assessment has on the motivation and self-esteem of pupils, both of which are crucial influences on learning;

the need for pupils to be able to assess themselves and understand how to improve.

These requirements are undermined when teachers "assess the quantity of work and presentation rather than the quality of learning." Using moderated coursework as a means to gain accreditation in a crowded syllabus can tend to discourage experiment and encourage neatly presented, 'safe' but quite pointless portfolios. This might not be the case if it were normal for all work to include a self-assessment, although simply asking for a paragraph at the end of the process is often less useful than it appears.

The student experience

Asked to take part in a group discussion on a matter of importance to the syllabus, a level 2 class did so with varying degrees of finesse and preparation. Evidence for their portfolio included a sheet signed by themselves and their tutor that recorded the time, date and title of the discussion with a brief assessment of their own performance, to be followed by that of the tutor.

One of the least successful but most confident students recorded the fact he had made "massive" contributions, when in fact he had not really begun to fulfil his potential. His

---

performance, like his assessment, was mainly good-natured bluff. He expected to smile his way to a pass grade.

A shy and hesitant student, for whom the process had been a personal trial for which had carefully prepared, wrote that he had been disappointed with his performance. Although it was a considerable achievement by his original standard, he felt he could have done much more. He would have failed himself for a thoughtful, brave attempt.

To learn from that experience, the students needed to do it at least twice. Starting with the criteria that would make a contribution 'useful', they would then need to discuss their own assessment in terms of (a) how they met the criteria (b) how honestly and accurately they could assess their own performance. Learning about discussion means not only research, logic and verbal skills but also the social skills of monitoring and altering one's effect upon others, the intellectual honesty required for self-analysis and the confidence to know when something has been achieved.

As the Assessment Reform Group points out, confidence is often reduced by assessment, which is more often used to label and control than as a co-operative means to take stock and discuss progress. If assessment is to be used to help students learn, they will need clear criteria, individual goals, and individual feedback on progress towards those goals. They need to reach agreement with external authorities on what makes good work, and how it is to be done. Self-assessment is part of the process of doing good work at all stages of that work, not something to be tacked on the end when it is too late. It may be useful to add a paragraph to each major project to ask for a written self-assessment, but that should not send the message that self-assessment only happens once and is always summative or retrospective, rather than formative as a conditioned reflex.

More fundamentally, in the context of academic study, Barnes (1975) pointed out some time ago that what students need to develop is a language of exploration, a world where essays are related to *essayer* – to try. If the teacher asks only for a final draft for approval, then an important shift takes place in the kind of language a student tries to use, even at the start.

There are serious time-management issues involved with formative assessment. If work is to be exploratory, drafted and redrafted, guidance given and progress reviewed, then more class hours need to be given over to making the finished product. However, accepting poor work quickly is a pointless process with a quite different goal. Working more carefully avoids wasted time and muddled repetitive actions, so the overall time taken to achieve appropriate standards will be less.

And what is 'work' anyway? Using what you already knew to gather and stick together some facts, or learning through experiment how to gather and analyse new information in a more productive way? Do the criteria and grading schemes allow both teacher and student to differentiate between the two?

It is in this context we can solve the problem of standards for feedback. When goals are set, especially for new students in term one, it may be necessary to set them well below any level of ability that will ultimately be required to pass the course. Nervous about 'standards' and pass rates, teachers can also be nervous about giving students an initially easy target to encourage them. Medal and mission systems require some early success, so you can offer praise before offering a further mission to improve. If students receive 'realistic' grades that tell them they have failed, they may stop trying. If they receive praise and encouragement, they may try harder and get closer to the target level. This is another example where a teacher needs courage as well as patience. If they can avoid being bullied too early by external factors (pass rates and standards) they can bring about more real progress within the class. Feedback is then neither norm referenced (the class) nor criterion referenced (the external standard) but ipsatic – referenced to the individual's short term potential. It may ultimately be helpful that strong government pressure on schools links a drive to personalised learning to more detailed personal assessment.

To summarise, it might be argued that:

> Whatever vocational skills or academic knowledge students might acquire, they also need the ability and willingness to apply it and to learn more later, which is actually more fundamental.

> Students are more likely to learn if they feel confident, and if they know how to monitor and regulate a process for self-improvement. This requires a particular openness from the teacher, who needs to be very clear about what kinds of skill are being demanded and the criteria for success.

> This requires a discussion between student and teacher concerning the kinds of skills and attitudes that define educated behaviour, which students will reasonably, if sometimes incorrectly, translate as behaviour required to gain the qualification.

> Feedback from an external authority, usually the teacher, is necessary to assist students with self-evaluation, but should never replace it.

> The kinds of task set and the way they are managed carry important messages about the personal and intellectual qualities a college wants them to develop.

> The most important things – transferable skills and affective development such as how to learn independently, monitor our own learning process and enjoy applying what we have learned – cannot be taught in isolation but are rarely discussed explicitly by

those teaching 'subjects'.

The Learning Suite[22] offers differentiated material to apply
what students learned about learning styles to their self-
development and advice sheets on some basic techniques such
as note taking. These can be used as part of a class activity or
placed on the intranet for part-time students to help
themselves.

Medium and Message

If we want students to be self-reliant, interrogating the
world and reaching independent conclusions, we need to teach
them in such a way that we appear to desire that outcome. If
study skills require those abilities but the way we teach demands
passive obedience, there is dissonance between the medium and
the message.

Postman and Weingartner (1969) laid stress on the
importance of questions – encouraging students to want to ask,
to know which ones to ask and how. Their argument ought by
now to be so widely accepted that it doesn't need repeating, but
it is still sometimes the case that

> what students do in class is to guess what the teacher
> wants them to say" and sometimes "just about the only
> learning that occurs in classrooms is that which is
> communicated by the structure of the classroom itself
> (p31).

In other words, they learn to please authority to get a quiet life.
They consume and obey.

If we teach them to ask how they learn, to exchange in
dialogue with the teacher about how learning can be mastered,

---

[22] www.bpfe.org.uk/materials - use password and user name from
Introduction

we are teaching them to accept responsibility for their own fate
and to be confident in learning independently.

> Once you have learned how to ask questions –
> relevant and appropriate and substantial questions
> – you have learned how to learn and no-one can
> keep you from learning what you need to know.
>
> ibid p34

The manner in which the learning experience is organised,
managed and assessed is itself a series of messages about what
learning means and how educated people behave. Before
turning to the problem of managing behaviour, it is useful to
consider the checklist they provide. Their definition of a good
learner stresses self-reliance and independence (chapter 3). If
teachers do not behave in the right way, the following message
may be received instead:

> Passive acceptance is a more desirable response to ideas
> than active criticism
>
> Discovering knowledge is beyond the power of
> students and is, in any case, none of their business
>
> Recall is the highest form of intellectual achievement
> and the collection of unrelated 'facts' is the goal of
> education.
>
> The voice of authority is to be trusted and valued more
> than independent judgement
>
> One's own ideas and those of one's classmates are
> inconsequential
>
> Feelings are irrelevant in education
>
> There is always a single, unambiguous, Right Answer to

a question.

English is not history, history is not science and science
is no art

And art is not music ... and a subject is something you
'take' and when you have taken it you have 'had' it, you
are immune and need not take it again- The Vaccination
Theory of Education.   ibid p32.

One may object that they speak from the privileged
viewpoint of a liberal academic institution, that they sound like
a pair of old hippies and this sort of Socratic questioning is
fine for a philosophy course but a pain when trying to get thirty
fifteen year olds to build a brick wall without making it wavy or
flinging mortar about. The answer, of course, is that all
education, especially when tied to notions of employability,
starts with learning to learn. At appropriate levels, perhaps, but
nevertheless it is an active process or it is only sabotage
sanctioned by a syllabus. Learning the art and desire for
responsible enquiry is more important than learning facts or
basic motor skills, although the latter, if only as a medium.
Nobody wants a brickie whose wall falls down. But do we want
a straight wall and nothing else? How about a brickie who asks
whether the wall is in the right place? The next chapter
considers the problem of behaviour in FE. What kind of
problem is it? But first we might want to think about what a
lesson will be in ten years' time.

What is a lesson anyway? Social networks as social judo (blogging back to happiness)

Children and young people who engage in technology
based texts, such as blogs, enjoy writing more and have
more positive attitudes towards writing – 57% express a
general enjoyment of writing vs. 40% who don't have a
blog.   NLT (2012(1)) p3

I tried to teach gas fitters about communication skills but they didn't really care. I asked what they considered to be important to learn and they said they were about to leave home and couldn't cook. I borrowed a kitchen, taught them some simple dishes that were nourishing and cheap, and, in return, they listened to the stuff I was saying about communication skills. It seemed only fair.

In the days when computers meant Amstrads and new progams came on cassettes, I was excited to get hold of some new exercises that allowed students to learn simple 'holiday' Spanish, French or Italian using a keyboard and screen. This was not because the class I had in mind needed to learn a language. They just needed to learn something, *anything*, that made them feel positive about learning. The game element of using a screen was novel and so unlike proper leaning they joined in with enthusiasm and could say hello and order a beer in three new languages. The willingness to learn proved transferable.

On a related matter, if students are reluctant readers, why not give them a pdf file to save to their desktop. Then they can go to View in the top menu and activate Read Out Loud. This allows the machine to read it to them, as many times as they like, and they can choose the sex and speed of the voice that reads. Gimmick? Yes, of course. But will it help to overcome resistance by being amusing. And by showing you are trying to help them out.

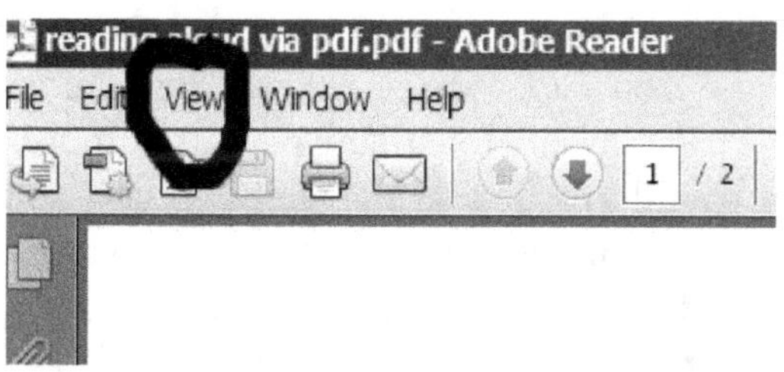

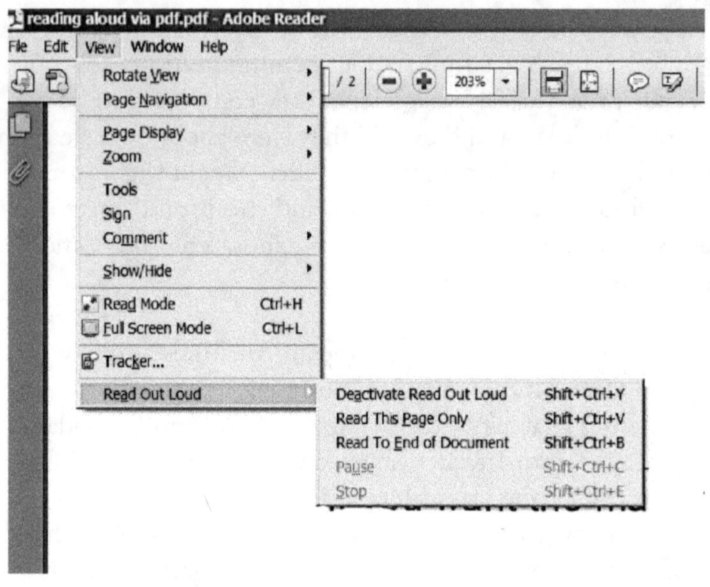

There are times when what you need is progress for its own sake, and stubbornly doing what you thought you ought to do pays decreasing dividends. That's when teachers tend to get depressed and the working relationship, even their self-image can suffer irreparable damage. On such occasions, it is worth remembering that the first rule of judo is to use the strength of your opponent against them. If a large enemy pushes against you, to push back is futile. Instead, move backwards quickly, and they fall over.

So how many times has a teacher complained that students won't turn their 'phones off in class? I have observed several lessons where a back row regular just sat quietly texting while the teacher in the front, unaware or not wanting to notice, used their up energy to no avail. How many parents complain that their offspring spend to long playing games on line, texting or using social media? Can you just reason them into reading Dickens instead? Things are what they are, and it may sometimes be worth considering alternative attitudes.

If a student is often late why not set up a system to automatically text them at 7.a.m? (Use the college system, not your private mobile, or they'll ring back at 3.a.m.). Now Facebook pages are set up for courses where students can talk to each other about a project or essay. Many colleges use Moodle and/or simple free software like Hot Potatoes to make online quizzes. E-learning is getting cheaper al the time. If it snows heavily, most classes could use simple software to stay in touch, pass on material, ask questions and get answers. Plagiarism if a major problem precisely because students are so quick to use Google, even if they rarely grace the library. For how much longer will a teacher in front of a class be the norm? What skills do students need in the next twenty years and how far will they be developed by sitting and listening? And what level of IT skills will a teacher require in 2023?

Chapter 5

Managing behaviour – theirs and yours

Three things, all of the same sort, are merciless when they get the upper hand; a water flood, a wasting fire, and the common multitude of small folk. For these will never be checked by reason or discipline.

John Gower

But whenever, as scholars sometimes do, I turned my back on books, declaring them to be the graveyards of the language, and sought contact with simple folk, I encountered the little cannibals who lived in our building, and after brief association with them, felt very glad to get back to my reading in one piece.

The Tin Drum, Gunter Grass

The most effective teaching for learners with the most difficult behaviour is little different to that which is most successful for all learners.

Ofsted, *Managing Challenging Behaviour*, March 2005

If you begin this chapter by asking how to manipulate students to make them behave, you are starting in the wrong place. You can't answer a question properly until you know exactly what kind of question it is, and what it implies about those who ask it.

It ought to be simple, really. Students usually come to you because they want something. In providing what they want, you have the upper hand. All you need to do is:

Know what it is they want, and why they haven't got it already

Enrol the right students on the right course so they can get it

Make sure you give it to them in a form they can cope with

Collect their gratitude and go home.

So what kind of problems arise under the heading of 'behaviour', and why?

There are four levels at which we might approach the question. In descending order, they might be characterised as:

A civilised society

A managed area

A managed college

Taming tigers in a cage

In a civilised society, all young students come from stable homes with loving parents or guardians who feed them properly and provide books to read. Reading with them when they are young, they also provide support for their studies through the course and monitor their consumption of alcohol and other stimulants. Teachers, meanwhile, are all fully trained and well-informed about any issues that affect the students' learning. They welcome them to a well-designed college with decent facilities and a full range of pastoral and financial support. Problems still occur, because humanity is imperfect, but they are dealt with efficiently by a system everyone recognises as fair and applies consistently. Mature students are charged a reasonable fee for a fully supported service that recognises their potential contribution to society after they qualify.

While we are working towards this situation – and every time we educate an individual out of the worse alternative we contribute to it – at least the local schools, colleges and other agencies should be working together to exchange information and advice so that we know everything necessary about the student and arrange adequate support in good time. All agencies involved in education or social support would consider it in their mutual interest to exchange information and facilities to extend choice and increase the efficiency and range of support.

Until that is true of all areas, at the very least we can make sure all tutors know what they need to know about the students before they plan the curriculum and certainly before they meet them, at which point they offer them a tailored and engaging educational experience with adequate support, employing a disciplinary process that is recognised as fair and applied consistently. When things go wrong the college managers swing into action to support both parties in any dispute, analyse the situation, act firmly for a fair response and then learn from it.

If none of the above pertains all the time, or even if they do but life happens to be unfair occasionally, you will find yourself locked in a cage with an ambush of tigers, wondering how to tame them and whether you will survive the hour. You will, but you shouldn't have to. Managing behaviour is about **managing** it, not reacting to it when it is too late. Of course, when you are in the cage, you need to know how to react, but rule number one is to reduce the need for cages.

By the end of the chapter, we shall have looked at ways in which individuals and groups may be 'managed' by teachers, and at how teachers can deal with stress when faced with dissent. However, before we start dishing out medicine to cure the effects, perhaps we should ask whether better management might minimise the disease. Drain the swamps and you get less malaria. Also, of course, what is defined as unacceptable in one area will pass unnoticed in another. This is not necessarily a bad thing. Whilst standards should be universally high, what is right may be defined in context.

Relative values

A new teacher to the school went to his Head of Year to complain that 15 year old Kirsty had told another student to "fuck off". The Head of Year explained that Kirsty's family history was complex and the pressures on her this year considerable. A few months ago she would have told the teacher to fuck off. That she had not done so was considerable progress. Tolerance was to be exercised.

Kirsty was then sent to her local FE college for a catering link course. She came up against the iron discipline of the kitchen. Gordon Ramsey notwithstanding, her language was not considered acceptable, although the first time she was sent out of the kitchen it was actually for refusing to wash up. Her background was explained and allowances were made. During a stormy relationship with her FE teachers, mediated by an LSA, she learned to accept her share of the chores. Keeping Kirsty on-side became a project and it worked for two terms, until it became clear that no employer would accept her for an apprenticeship post-16, at which point she told the college to fuck off and disappeared.

Kirtsy's problems were such that sympathy for her situation allowed most staff to make allowances because, once she let go of the college/school focus, she had nowhere to go but down. Up against the demands of employers, who had no reason to make any allowance, she finally walked away and could no longer be supported. Neither the school nor the college had made her 'work-ready'. Had they made too many allowances? Would she have responded better to more discipline, or simply have left earlier?

Swimming against the tide.

Trainee teacher A stood in front of a class of level 2 adolescent girls in a sixth form college. Being observed as part of her Cert Ed. course, she had arrived early and set up her material, warning the observer that the class were pleasant enough but tended to rowdiness. She proceeded to talk to them about revision methods, explaining in abstract terms what could be done to increase their chances of passing an exam they were about to take.

The girls in the corner, emotionally engaged with the idea of taking the exam, ignored her whilst they explained to each other what they did or did not know about the subject, how they usually behaved in exams and their methods for preparing for exams. The teacher constantly asked them to be quiet and listen to her. She also directed questions at the least confident, to try to include them, but received monosyllabic or quietly shy replies, which she sometimes interrupted to ask the noisy girls in the corner to stop talking to each other.

Had she asked the talkative girls to lead the session, she might have achieved a more coherent social dynamic. Had she asked the class to organise a collective revision course for the exam and talk about how they would allow for personal idiosyncrasies, instead of focusing on abstract notions of revision in general, she might have made the learning more relevant and thus more attractive. The students knew better than she did what they needed, but she had material to present so she presented it, blaming them for not listening quietly to it. What could have been dynamic engagement became instead just another lesson to be suffered by both sides. Her justification was that she did not teach the subject they were being examined in, but had been asked to talk about revision in general terms to apply to all subjects.

Swimming with the tide

Four young females on a care course had failed their level 2 exams twice. They were about to be removed from the course as a poor investment. They were not badly behaved but did not seem to know how to learn.

Teacher B was asked to help them revise for a third and final attempt. He knew nothing about the subject, being from Student Support and thus outside that vocational area, but he looked at the old papers and asked them to explain what they had found difficult.

It transpired that (a) that were supposed to write the answers to each question on a new sheet but did not know that (b) they had not drawn any theoretical conclusions from their wealth of work experience (c) they understood the theories of child development but not the exam questions as phrased. After some short sessions discussing exam technique and rehearsing subject knowledge in that context, they all passed. Questions could then be asked about their previous learning experience – what sort of system put them in that position?

Trainee teacher C was concerned at the constant interruption from mobile 'phones ringing in her class. She explained to students that it was annoying, discourteous, disrespectful and prevented learning. They argued that some messages were important. They seemed addicted to texting. She compromised by agreeing that five minutes in every 30 were to be given over to turning on 'phones and updating messages, if (a) the other 25 minutes were spent with phones turned off and (b) they used their 'phones find out why any missing students were not in class. The compromise worked, and it allowed them to work hard and then rest their brains regularly, but she was worried that she would be in trouble herself because college policy was to have no use of mobiles in class, on pain of punishment. Was she undermining college discipline by trying to be popular, or being realistic in the face of overwhelming odds? Or both? What freedom do teachers have to make a deal that actually brings about peace and progress?

What is unacceptable behaviour? What constitutes a problem that needs to be addressed or managed, perhaps by using formal punishment? An initial distinction can be made between:

> Ordinary classes having a bad day.

> Classes who routinely behave badly in an ordinary way – low-level disruption and lack of obvious enthusiasm.

> Classes behaving in ways that require an extra-ordinary explanation, sometimes with apparently destructive intent. They seem out to cause trouble on purpose.

> Individuals (or groups) who seem to be unable to manage their own behaviour, even if they wanted to. They are always in trouble and don't know what to do to avoid it.

When you perceive student behaviour as a problem, do you find its effect

> inefficient (they are not learning)

> uncomfortable, wearing or threatening (you don't know what to do next, don't enjoy trying anymore and feel it may be hopeless?)

When you consider it, do you assume its causes to be

> Social - they come from the 'wrong background'

> Organisational - we put them through the 'wrong process'

> Psychological - their minds don't work as you want

them to

Pedagogical - the classes you give don't work with them

or a mixture of those?

The problem with socially-based reasons for dysfunctional behaviour is that they locate the problem and therefore any potential cause outside the sphere of activity of any individual member of staff - 'If it is a problem for society it isn't mine so I don't have to change anything'. It is important to define any problem in terms that allow for action by individuals, to locate the perceived cause within a perceived sphere of influence.

What kind of behaviour is unacceptable, and why? Is it:

Students not doing what the teacher wants, how and when the teacher wants it?

Students behaving in ways that will not, in the teacher's view, bring about the result teacher wants?

Students behaving in ways that will not, in the teacher's view, bring about the result the student needs?

Students behaving in ways that will not, in the teacher's view, bring about the result the student wants?

Students behaving in ways that will not, in the student's view, bring about the result the student needs?

Students behaving in ways that will not, in the student's view, bring about the result the student wants?

In an ideal world, students and lecturers would want the same outcomes, agree on the kind of behaviour that would bring about that result and then agree on ways to obtain and manage that behaviour which accords with their desires. But how many forms of behaviour might be productive if viewed from another point of view, or responded to differently? Do we, for example, label as bullying what is only normal unpleasant behaviour, unremarkable before but not in our 'risk-averse society'? Should the 'victim' just learn to defend themselves, not run complaining to authority figures?

Research into behaviour is hampered by difficulties of definition and the focus of attention shifts. The Elton Report (1989) identified the major problem as low level disruption ('sorry' seemed to be the hardest word?) and Ofsted in 2005 (Ofsted, *MCB*) confirmed this is still their major concern. Their measurement is the number of schools in which inspection identified behaviour as an issue, and by this criterion they argue that behaviour in primary schools has been improving since 1996 (fewer concerns from inspectors) whilst

> the proportion of secondary schools in which behaviour overall has been judged good or better has declined since 1996/97 from over three quarters to over two thirds. Over the same period, the proportion where behaviour is unsatisfactory, at just under one in ten schools, has not reduced. - Ofsted *MCB* 4

They confirmed that the major problem had not altered since Elton. It was still primarily one of low level disruption, getting worse as students enter Key Stage 3, although they also recorded that

> Between 2001 and 2003 there was a 25% increase in the number of pupils educated in PRUs. Between 2001 and 2004 there was a 14% increase in the number of pupils placed by Leas in independent special schools catering solely or mainly for pupils with special educational needs (SEN). Most of the pupils admitted to these schools have EBSD or severe learning difficulties (SLD), often with associated challenging behaviour.

Problems of definition mean we cannot make international comparisons (Ofsted, *MCB* 13; Birmingham, 2003) but there is a growing tendency in all official reports to assume that schools need to concern themselves with "emotional health and wellbeing" (DfES 2005 (b) p11) or "social, emotional and behavioural skills" (DfES 2005 p5). They are to be agents of social control, and it sometimes reads as if we are reacting to a major social crisis by ascribing to teachers what used to be ascribed to parents and priests.

Manuals on how to manage behaviour tend to refer, sometimes rather breezily, to a need to keep students "engaged" Ofsted's careful language reminds us:

> ... although there is nothing as clear-cut as 'a boys' learning style', many schools have found certain approaches to be particularly helpful. For example, although many boys are willing to contribute orally, they can be helped to become more reflective in their replies. Their Motivation can be enhanced by giving them greater access to computers for interactive learning or to help them improve the presentation of their work. Boys often respond better to lessons that have a clear structure and a variety of activities, including practical and activity based learning, applications to real-life situations and an element of fun and competition. Many boys find it helpful to be given short-term targets and feedback that focuses on how they can improve – Ofsted, *MCB* (41)

and

> High staff turnover and a significant proportion of temporary teachers can lead to inconsistencies of approach towards pupils with more challenging behaviour. (ibid)

In other words, if students are subject to poor organisation and unimaginative teaching then, bored and frustrated, they will understandably hit back. Wouldn't you? Irwin Edman (1896-1954) offered ambiguous food for thought when he claimed that

> Education is the process of casting false pearls before real swine

Although low-level disruption is the most common problem, more attention tends to be focused on the headline cases of particularly challenging behaviour – the more aggressive, violent or destructive – and there is an argument that such cases are increasing.

In general terms, we know that anti-social behaviour is not new. The term yob is back slang for boy, used since at least 1859. Hooligan comes from an Irish family in London, used since at least 1898 and vandal, used in our sense since 1663, referred to a group unpopular with the Roman Empire. The term 'dysfunctional' can mean not doing what the authorities want you to do. For most of the population, there is an age at which young people tend to become more irritating. Their music, their clothes and their general manner start to seem not only different to one's own but incomprehensible and risible. One of the benefits of teaching for a living is that daily contact with young people, many of whom turn out to be quite interesting, can inoculate against that fate. Nevertheless, it is still not unknown for experienced teachers to complain that behaviour is getting worse, that widening participation or IF links brought in groups of people who don't know how to make proper use of such a valuable resource as a teacher and that managing classroom behaviour is becoming more difficult. What are the facts?

In June 2006 the BMA published a report claiming that more than one million children suffered from mental disorders requiring treatment. One in ten children between the ages of 1 and 15 had a mental health disorder, ranging from sleep problems to temper tantrums and depression. In the last 30 years, there has been a doubling of conduct disorders, including stealing, lying and provocative behaviour. This is not just a result of better reporting or change of classification, but a real decline in the mental condition of the young across all social groups, regardless of income. Among the causes discussed were rising divorce rates, increased drinking and competitive pressures. At the same time, Margo et al (2006) point out that the systems which award status to children have been increasingly commercialised. "Seven to 11 years olds are now worth nearly £20 million as consumers" and "children from the poorest social groups are the most interested in consumer and materialist concerns." Children mature earlier and have earlier sexual experiences. The "socialising capacity" of schools and parents is correspondingly decreased.

Another major element of educational debate in primary and secondary levels is the effects of diet on behaviour. Government publications concerning diet in schools have been largely focused on physical health, obesity and heart disease, but slowly the message is percolating that behaviour is a function of the brain which is fed with vitamins, minerals and fats from food. If for example, the national diet suffers a seven-fold decrease in a vital component which happens to be vital for brain development and function, it is not so surprising that the behaviour of the next generation worsens. The Mental Health Foundation reported in January 2006 that the rate of depression has increased and tends to occur at a younger age so they ran a campaign linking mental health to diet. It is worth pausing here to separate the kinds of question a teacher can usefully ask from those that only generate despair. Background knowledge without the ability to use it to generate change leads only to frustration. What is it worth knowing about, and why?

Dr. Bernard Gesch is a Senior Research Scientist at the University Lab of Physiology, Oxford. He is also Director of the research charity Natural Justice, which investigates causes of criminal anti-social behaviour. With the co-operation of the

Home Office, he conducted a clinical trial to test empirically if better nutrition could significantly improve the behaviour of 231 young offenders at a maximum-security prison. His conclusions include:

> In the future we may have a choice where we continue to lock up even more of our children, or we nourish them properly

The headline statement is that during an 18-month study on inmates, disciplinary offences fell by at least 25%. Those receiving vitamin supplements for a minimum of two weeks were involved in 37% fewer violent offences[23].

His argument is that changes in agricultural practice mean that even foods we think of as healthy, because they are fresh fruit and vegetables, may have significantly fewer trace elements than in previous generations. In addition, many people do not eat the right ratios of essential fats to nourish the body and thus the brain. Whilst we have dietary standards stating a minimum intake for bodily health, we do not lay down any standards for mental health or behavioural patterns, although there is an obvious link between nutrition, behaviour and potential criminal activity.

Often our pollutants are also neuro-toxins so nutrition has to counteract that too. And bad foods tend to be addictive foods. Yet we consider ourselves somehow 'above nature', as if how we behave is due to a decision-making process somehow divorced from our animal self. This is not so. We have to feed the animal correctly to obtain the right behaviour.

Changes in diet may be altering the composition of the human brain. The wrong kinds of fats are changing its basic

---

[23] previous research has found similar figures. Richardson (2006 p82) cites examples that changed diet to reduce antisocial behaviour by 21%, suicide by 100% and the use of physical restraints by 75%. Links for Bernard Gesch, Natural Justice and further case studies studies are in the material linked at bpfe.org.uk/materials

make-up. This could increase depression and anxiety. The
WHO recommends that we should take no more than 10% of
our calories as sugar, but some breakfast cereals are 40% sugar.
Too much sugar in rats creates nervousness and aggression.
Why would that not be true of humans? If rates of offending
in the UK have increased ten times since 1950, how much of
that could be due to changes in the way we produce and
consume our food?

Professor Michael Crawford is Director of the Institute of
Brain Chemistry and Human Nutrition at London
Metropolitan University, a consultant for WHO, FAO,
Millennium Danone Chair at the University of Gent, Chair at
the Albert Schweitzer International University in Geneva. He is
also a Member of the DoH Committee on Borderline
Substances and chair of the English branch of the McCarrison
Society. His concern is with the ecology of food production,
how the way we grow or rear it will affect our physical and
mental health, and he has advised several governments on the
difficulties we are storing up if we feed our brains on
increasingly inferior materials[24].

For example, a chicken in 2004 had a third more calories and
a third less protein that one purchased in 1940, vegetables have
lost large amounts of the minerals and trace elements they are
supposed to provide us with – potatoes lost 47% of their
copper, 45% of their iron, 35% of their calcium, all their
vitamin A and more than half their vitamin C; carrots had an
even bigger loss and broccoli lost 80% of its copper and 75%
of its calcium; tomatoes have one tenth of the copper they had
then.

Animals are reared differently becoming obese with lack of
exercise and changed diet so that we, in consuming them,
become increasingly obese. Over 8% of six year olds are
clinically obese. Having sold off the playing fields and closed
the gyms to pay for books and teachers' salaries, we feed the

---

[24] Michael Crawford's and the McCarrison Society are linked at
bpfe.org.uk/materials

inactive pupils on poisonous cheap stodge and wonder why they don't concentrate after lunch. And this is the industry charged to educate the rest of the population.

We evolved to eat wild animals that in turn ate in the wild. Now we rear them intensively and, as a result, the ratio of omega 6 to omega 3 in our diet has changed from 1:1 into 15:1, a massive imbalance. Farmed pig, fed on cereals high in omega 6, have a ratio of 20:1, whereas a wild wart hog has 3:1. That is partly why fish is still good for you – some of it, at least, is living wild. On this kind of argument, all children are, in a sense, malnourished by industrial societies. We increase the amount they can afford to eat but change the type of food to highly refined and processed forms, causing obesity, heart disease, strokes and mental illness. Crawford has shown that the population or our rich, western, developed country were actually better nourished during the last world war, because we had fewer highly refined and processed foods, more local organic crops with less sugar, fat and meat.

Dr. Alex Richardson is Senior Research Fellow, Mansfield College and the University Lab of Physiology as well as Director of the charity FAB (Food and Behaviour) Research. Dr. Richardson started to involve herself in research on diet when she realised that all her other research into behavioural and learning difficulties kept leading back to one root cause. Conditions such as ADHD, dyspraxia, dyslexia or autism affect around 20% of school age children and twenty years of research have persuaded her that changes in diet would be the single most significant response to many behavioural and learning difficulties.[25]

Dr. Richardson is concerned with the problem of 'junk fats' (trans fats and hydrogenated fats). We know that the food industry has created artificial fats to solve the problems of a long shelf-life. They're unknown to nature but occur in many

---

[25] Richardson (2006) p42. This book is a very approachable comprehensive guide, written for parents. Links to her academic output and to FAB are at bpfe.org.uk.

cheap margarines, fried and baked foods. They are so bad for our physical health that the US government fixed the safe level at zero. They increase the risk of heart disease, stroke, diabetes, and some forms of cancer; they speed up ageing and, as the brain is 60% fat, adversely affect cell-signalling systems (Richardson 2006). Junk food implies junk brain function. But junk food is cheap, easy to cook and often addictive.

You have probably read media stories about the effect of fish oils on behaviour or learning ability, suggesting that offering supplements to young children will significantly alter the way their brains operate. Dr. Richardson's work includes an experiment to test the effects of dietary supplements on 117 children between 5 and 12 years old with developmental co-ordination disorder (developmental dyspraxia). It was a randomised, double-blind placebo trial – academically impeccable – and the results included better progress in reading and spelling with significantly reduced ADHD-related symptoms.

Schools that I interviewed for a virtual conference in 2005 confirmed that their own experiments with diet had dramatic effects. They were less scientifically rigorous and subject to the objection that a change in teacher's attitudes or behaviour might also have affected behaviour, but one of the more controlled involved a psychologist who used a range of tests on 100 children. These included tests for number, spelling, reading and non-verbal reasoning. A year later, they were tested again. Findings from around 8,900 tests included an improvement of 69% in non-verbal reasoning, 50% in number, 33% in spelling and 30% in reading. The greatest improvements were in the students whose original scores were average or below average.

In a crude response to work on diet and cognition, some American schools started to boost exam results by altering student diet on critical days, knowing that "good nutrition ... improves short term cognitive ability" and that "boosting calories enhances psychological and verbal intelligence scores", they altered student intake for short term gain and "tests showed that increasing meal calorie counts by 100 boosted pass rates in maths, English and history/social studies by between 4 and 7 percent"[26].

In a post-16 environment, where you have no direct control over student eating habits or even over the contents of the refectory, it is concerning to read the dire effects of too many additives and too much sugar. Failure to learn, or even to behave within acceptable limits, may be partly or even wholly attributable to a chemical imbalance that is easily remedied. If students are tired, irritable, aggressive, depressed, confused or nervous, it may be that a simple change in diet will help them enormously. Some facts seem straightforward. The consumption of high-sugar drinks rose by 64% between 1983 and 1997. Between 1998 and 2002 the amount spent by 8-16 years olds on crisps, chocolate, gum and cigarettes on the way to school rose by 68% to £433m. If children miss breakfast and instead consume high sugar levels and nicotine, they arrive with their brains on an artificial high. Then high blood sugar levels stimulate the release of too much insulin, which reduces blood sugar, so they become confused and irritable. It is easy to make a case for providing breakfast before you try to teach them.

But altering behaviour by altering diet is not always a simple matter, and sometimes the chemistry becomes complicated. You might discover, for example, that a chemical called dopamine is essential for healthy brain function. Iron is necessary for dopamine to work. Dopamine depletion is a factor in ADHD. Students with ADHD might have abnormally low iron levels. So maybe they ought to have red meat, nuts and seeds to give them iron, unless they have nut allergies, or are vegetarians. Then you find that dark beers contain high levels of a vitamin B found in green vegetables and are a rich source

---

[26] 5 *TES Friday* magazine (15th April, page 20) article by Raj Persaud (Gresham Professor for Public Understanding of Psychiatry) *Information is taken from The Journal of Public Economics - Food for thought: the effects of school accountability plans on school nutrition* Pages 381-394, David N. Figlio and Joshua Winicki, Volume 89, Issues 2-3, Pages 157-566 (February 2005)

of anti-oxidants. Research starts to suggest that a pint of Guinness might be as good for you as a plate of spinach, improving eye sight and helping to avoid erectile dysfunction if taken in moderation. This may or may not be a subject for classroom debate.

Parents concerned at the complex chemistry of diet might turn to a source such as Sally Bunday MBE, founder/director of the Hyperactive Children's Support Group, a registered charity which has been successfully helping ADHD/Hyperactive children and their families for over 25 years. HACSG is Britain's leading proponent of a dietary approach to the problem of hyperactivity and has substantial documentary evidence, supported by scientific studies and contains information on their expert advisers with other links. They produce a number of useful publications, *including Essential Fatty Acids, Minerals and Vitamins – a collection of documents and case studies.* This is an excellent place to start for anyone who needs a layperson's guide to the science of nutrition. It will tell you, for example, that boys require a higher intake of essential fatty acids that girls, but that four fifths of all children tested seemed to be consistently thirsty, which is a cardinal sign of a lack of fatty acids. So, can we conclude that in a class of children denied water and asked to sit still for long periods, it would not be surprising that many of them played up, especially the boys? And that using a disciplinary code would make no difference to them because it doesn't tackle the cause?

So, all-in-all, it would be perverse to ignore all the evidence that dietary issues affect behaviour, and that unless something drastic is done about the nutritional habits of the country as a whole, we might expect behavioural problems to continue increasing. What can a class teacher in FE do about that? It was argued in chapter 3 that students needed to take more responsibility for their own learning, and to engage in healthy dialogue with teachers about how to learn. Part of that dialogue might include pointing out matter-of-factly how diet affects their ability to concentrate, remember and recall, suggesting that a small change in regime would make learning much easier for them. That does not mean you have to spend time weakly trying to persuade a group of 17 year old motor mechanics to swap burger for tofu, but you might be able to use key skills or tutorial time integrating basic facts about nutrition and brain growth (and erectile dysfunction?) in ways that will cause them to think. BTEC provide level 1 qualifications in Healthy Eating.

Meanwhile, breakfast clubs that are popular in schools might also be used for certain socio-economic groups in colleges, or at least a subsidy through student support offered for extreme cases of behavioural dysfunction – and free water made available in learning areas.

It will often seem that difficulties for teachers are increasing because of factors beyond their control. It would seem that children as a whole are becoming more difficult and FE is enrolling a higher percentage of the more difficult among them. Indeed, FE is rightly proud of its ability to cope with such cases. On the other hand, FE staff in the early days of IF were often rudely awakened to a level of disaffection and behavioural difficulty they had not previously imagined, and teachers whose timetables shift from level 3 to levels 1 and 2 classes suddenly realise just how privileged they had been.

This does not mean that FE will not contain a large number of very civilised students who will behave very well, and one of the more encouraging elements of working in FE is to enable those with a previously poor reputation and self-image to remake themselves with a fresh start in a different environment. Nevertheless, it would be naive to image than entering teaching of any kind would be anything other than challenging at least some of the time. It is a teacher's function to manage behaviour to bring about learning, and that management process can be challenging. On the other hand, it would also be naive to imagine the fault is entirely on the side of the student at all times. What we expect them to tolerate is sometimes too much to ask.

Consider the last time you were part of a class or audience, perhaps on a Cert Ed course, a staff development day or a conference. What was the worst element of it and how did it make you feel? How many teachers sat in the back row, failed to ask a question, murmured objections and were gone before the end of the day?

The student experience

A

Jason, aged 15, knocked on the door of the co-ordinator's office. She was busy and about to go to a class. He explained that he had been sent to her by the class teacher. She asked why and he explained angrily that he hadn't "done nuffing wrong" and it was all "that pillock's fault" because he "keeps picking on me". She sat him down and elicited details. Jason, having turned up late for a brickwork class, had been told to wait and be quiet in a way he considered rude and unfair. He expressed his irritation by slamming his trowel into his mortar and splashing his colleagues.

His behaviour was wrong and had to be dealt with, but it was also something that should have been dealt with by the teacher. This was not the first time that teacher had sent people to the co-ordinator's office, nor the first time his tone of voice had caused dissent among that cohort. The co-ordinator began by saying "Well, Jason, I'm sorry we upset you."

B

A level three media class were observed in their first year. The teacher, an experienced professional in his own media field but relatively new to teaching, ploughed through an oral delivery and elicited some half-hearted responses. A small group in the corner were talking among themselves and had to be told to stop doing so. They paused then restarted more quietly.

Homework was requested but only a portion had completed it.
They were told to get it in by next week. The oral delivery
continued. At one point a student asked a question that was
perceptive but not on the teacher's script. It was described as
"interesting" and shelved. They were then set group tasks and
started to talk about their weekend.

Example B would not be seen as a behavioural difficulty by
the teacher, who was quite happy just to get through the hour
and go home. It was, however, a waste of the students' time,
and they might have achieved a great deal more had he
bothered to challenge them with a more intellectually
demanding experience. For a good student to cruise though a C
grade is as wasteful as, if less final than, a poor student gaining
Fail when they might have gained Pass.

> He that is himself weary will soon weary the public. Let
> him therefore lay down his employment, whatever it
> may be, who can no longer exert his former activity or
> attention; let him not endeavour to struggle with
> censure or infest the stage till a general hiss commands
> him to depart.　　　　　Samuel Johnson, *The Rambler*

Example A is more difficult. The teacher is exasperated by
the student, who has probably been a nuisance for weeks. But
he is also not in control of his own class, and sees discipline as
something to be handled by a superior authority. Sometimes,
referring on is essential. That is not the same as using others as
a threat because you do not want to invoke the disciplinary
code. Reading between the lines, one suspects that his idea of
control is to speak loudly to them in an aggressive tone and,
when that fails, to send them to someone else. Invoking the
code against his students by issuing his own official warnings
would involve him in (a) filling in paperwork (b) having to
justify his tone in public if they appealed (c) probably reducing
his class size to uneconomic numbers if the appeal went his
way. Both teacher and student feel threatened and both, in their

way, may feel inadequate. Locking horns like two stags in battle, they would prefer someone to stop them fighting, but can't do it on their own. It is at times like these one might go back to basics and recall Abraham Maslow (1908-1970).

Maslow's starting point was that individuals were basically trustworthy and self-governing. They would react badly and behave violently only if certain needs were not met. You don't assume the student is faulty and needs manipulating and controlling. You assume they are capable of behaving decently if treated properly. That raises a different set of questions – do we believe in original sin or the child within?

The hierarchy is "pre-potent". That is, you have to satisfy all the lower levels before you can make demands at the higher levels. An original model had five levels but two more were added later. It starts with the most basic and works upwards:

1) Physiological

Which means

These are the most basic needs - air, water, food, sleep, sex, etc. If they are not satisfied we will feel distress (pain, irritability). We have to satisfy those needs first, then think about everything else. If you feel thirsty, you need water. If you find you can't breathe, you forget you are thirsty. But in neither case do you give a damn about homework schedules.

So in terms of student behaviour it means

Are they eating properly (the right things at the right time?) See the notes on diet and behaviour – hunger, satiety, additives, sugar rushes and thirst all affect behaviour. A Red Bull and a doughnut for breakfast will not set them up to sit still and listen carefully. A greasy burger for lunch will not feed the brain and trans fats can hinder cognition in the long term. Students do not know that.

Is the room cold or too hot and stuffy? How does it feel for a student sitting down as opposed to a teacher moving about and focusing on the subject?

And in teacher management terms it means

Managing start, finish and break times to suit the age and level. Breakfast clubs? Information and projects on nutrition (and student support for those in need?) Water freely available. More responsibility for the refectory?

There are certain conditions that benefit from close personal attention but all students behave better when nourished properly (see Gesch trials)

2) Safety

Which means

That might mean a secure home or family relationship. Or not being bullied at lunchtime. Not being threatened by the unknown. The drive is to create order out of chaos, but some forms of externally imposed order are very threatening (anyone for role play?)

So in terms of student behaviour it means

Do they know why they are entering the room, and what will happen to them when they get there? Do they have confidence in the person managing that environment to protect them? Are they feeling threatened by the subject being taught, the disorder of the class or the teacher's sarcasm? Do they have faith in the disciplinary system to treat them fairly (in their eyes)? Are they on a final warning, or about to be bullied, or going home to violence? For some students, the fear of the situation will become a physical sensation, triggering the 'fear and flight' response common to all animals and, if necessary, a physical response against anyone who increases that threat or blocks their escape route.

And in teacher management terms it means

The relationship within the class and the purposes of the experience must all be clear and not threatening. How consistent is the class experience? For younger students, a change of teacher is a major upset and they feel unsafe. An unexpected change of time, place or topic can also create insecurity. Clear plans and targets, carried out and assessed as agreed, increase secure.

Having to write or doing sums can be a threat (they expect to fail, look daft and be punished) so the best students in the workshop turn feral in theory classes, even with the same teacher. The order that works may not be an order that is imposed, but one that is negotiated and evolved in this light. What kind of support makes them feel safe? What targets would they accept?

Is the college/school disciplinary system seen to be a source of protection or of unfair decisions? Within its wider context, can they agree a set of class rules they own that allows them to feel safe with each other and with you?

Are you really in charge and can you defend them against each other (or themselves?) What process would lead to their accepting you as nominated referee (source of security) and how would it differ from merely currying favour

3) Belonging

Which means

A step up from being physically safe is being an accepted part of a group.

This might be spoken of as a need for love, applause or camaraderie but the key is acceptance and companionship. You might achieve immediate physical safety by avoiding other people, but once you feel safe enough to venture out, you can try to achieve this next stage.

Note that the original DfES approach to emotional wellbeing is to be distinguished from the fashion in FE for what is called Emotional Intelligence, defined by Goleman (1996) as "the capacity for recognising our own feelings and those of others, for motivating ourselves, and for managing emotions well in ourselves and our relationships". I have not made extensive reference to his book because the tone is so American it irritates many practitioners. Also, there is a difference between (a) knowing that emotions are part of learning, and managing the process accordingly for all students and (b) accepting that a discussion about managing their own emotions may be necessary for some students, in tutorials, or when referred onwards for professional help. This distinction needs to be maintained, although it is also worth noting the view of Camila Batmanghelidjh, the psychotherapist who founded Kids Company to work with brutalised children in south London.

> What these children want is not snazzy sports centres and computer courses. They need loving human beings that they can come into contact with. Nobody is prepared to pay for or invest in that, but this is what these children are starved of. They're starved of gentle, kind thoughtful human contact.
>
> cited in Independent, 7th June 2005

See also the report from the IPPR (Margo et al 2006), which claimed that "recent Mori polls have shown children's concerns to include parents not always being there when needed, and not making them feel loved and cared for."

So in terms of student behaviour it means

Do they feel included in the class and listened to? If they have to choose between class and teacher, would they feel they could belong to the group more obviously because they reject the lesson with noisy interference? Can they expect, as a matter of reliable routine, positive comments and praise as part of the class routine? Is the learning environment a source of comfort or stress, inclusion or rejection?

Does the class have factions? Does it work together on projects and on consultations (e.g. through student reps to unions or quality systems)?

And in teacher management terms it means

Teacher - student relationships

Do they acknowledge that you reject the behaviour but accept the person? Has this been discussed before the year started and then re-inforced? Do they feel safer in Student Support than in the class? Why? Safer when the LSA is present? Why? How well do you consciously manage the use of rewards and praise?

Tutorials are about how well they learn, but also a chance to learn more about why they are here and why they behave as they do. They can lead to personal (private) contracts which set out the limits of what is expected and what rewards/penalties follow.

student-student relationships

Do mentor systems help to build up a sense of belonging to the college or dept. in general? How far are the projects planned so that each has a role and can build on class activity to feed a sense of belonging?

4) Esteem

Which means

This might be self-esteem or the esteem of others. The former includes the need to feel competent (or avoid situations where you feel incompetent). The latter sounds like acceptance but that can be passive, whilst seeking prestige can be quite aggressive and, at times, become an attempt at dominance.

So in terms of student behaviour it means

The class clown can have self-esteem, status and power over colleagues and teachers. Was another source open to them that they believed to be attainable? Is competition within the class based on approval by the system for achievement or is that secondary to other forms of status which are seen as the only ones realistically open to them?
Is criticism or a disciplinary procedure something they can accept in a private setting or is it a public humiliation and a power struggle? Is class work competition by academic means or another kind of battle?

And in teacher management terms it means

Self-esteem

How much do you know about them? Before you started the year, did you receive adequate notes from the school or previous college tutor on what motivates and obstructs their learning? What have they done they are proud of and how does that set of skills relate to the demands of the class? Do you know enough about individual learning styles and how to use that knowledge?
Before they enter the threatening world of new material, were they reassured by reference to familiar concepts that linked and prepared (scaffolding, medal and mission) or did they have to reject it before it rejected them? How far can you turn threats to their confidence into opportunities for praise?
Was the work set based only on syllabus content or does it refer to their known strengths? If it meant to address known

weaknesses does it start out by highlighting them and thus creating negative reaction?

How flexible was the plan? Can you intervene and change if they seem to be losing the battle (or not trying to avoid failure?)

The respect of others

Does praise for successful work build esteem within the group or hinder it? How can rewards build esteem in the eyes of colleagues as well as the formal system?

Are they addressed by the formal system in ways that seem to value them individually? When taking a break, ordering lunch, using the facilities, are they treated with respect and consideration? What would that look and sound like? Relate that to the message of the physical environment, in the class and the wider context.

Do they understand the concept of emotional intelligence? Is it worth a tutorial session, introduced as a survival tool?

5) Cognitive needs

Which means

The stage when you want to understand what is happening around you to the point where you find meaning and self-awareness beyond any immediate defensive requirement. You might seek it in intellectual challenge or a in a relationship.

So in terms of student behaviour it means

What are they genuinely curious about? It may well be a host of matters apparently not relevant to the topic on the syllabus

And in teacher management terms it means

Objectives in lesson plans usually start here, a long way up the hierarchy. How do you tell the difference between deliberate disruption and genuine curiosity? How can you encourage and harness the latter when the exam is so close? Is conversation genuinely exploratory or just an obvious way to get them to say what you want?

Does the lesson actually challenge them? If they wanted to co-operate, would they find it possible but not easy? Many projects merely rehearse what they can already do. Does yours differentiate to stretch each one fully? Do they need to examine concepts and seek out relationships, or just listen and note down? Would it look more interesting approached from another angle?

6) Aesthetic needs

Which means

Seeking pleasure or satisfaction from their surroundings. This doesn't involve using a teacher's model of what is beautiful or tasteful (or not ugly).

So in terms of student behaviour it means

When was that room last decorated, by whom and how? When was it last tidied? Repaired? Or is the message – "this is what you deserve and how much we care"? Colour can affect mood and thus cognition.

And in teacher management terms it means

How much control does each tutor have over the room in which they teach – their working environment? If none, does that help them to have authority with the class and to do their job? Are displays of student work professionally managed?

7) Self-actualisation

Which means

The highest level of need. It involves growth to realise your own potential

So in terms of student behaviour it means

Are lessons in general, and is this lesson in particular, a means by which they achieve personal growth? Do student and teacher agree on what that would look like, or are their concepts antithetical? Do class experiences include genuinely open exploration or is the dominant feel one of restraint in a good cause? How often and how strongly do they connect with the world they are waiting to return to at 5pm?

And in teacher management terms it means

Are expectations for students usually high throughout the college/dept./class week?
Does the class experience each week contain opportunities for meta-cognitive exploration and reflection? Do staff compare notes in this context?
Is there agreement among staff on the kind of behaviour that characterises a successful student?

*

Of course, there is a difference between an ordinary class having a bad day, or even a notoriously difficult class, and a student who suffers from a dysfunction so severe that you cannot find a way to reach them, and perhaps start to feel you should not even be asked to try. There are arguments with logic on both sides about whether students with certain disadvantages or 'conditions' ought to be educated within the mainstream provision. Part of that argument can be saved for the chapter on equal opportunities, but for now it is worth considering what we mean by certain labels that are sometimes used carelessly.

Most of the terms below describe not a simple 'condition' but a tendency or spectrum that has a wide range of examples within it, many of whom have been professionally successful. If 20% of the school age population is said to suffer from a range of conditions, then we cannot think of them as occasional problems. They are a range of teaching questions affecting a substantial and growing minority, many of whom may not have been diagnosed. Not being a doctor or clinical psychologist, you may feel it is unwise to attempt a diagnosis on your own, and you may well be right, but if you are able to recognise the possible need for diagnosis you can call in support when necessary and react positively in the meantime.

As with the lessons of learning styles, what helps someone with a particular disorder may also be useful for the rest of the class. And before you become depressed by reading them all in one list, remember, as Richardson points out (2006, p52), that Einstein probably suffered from at least two of them, and was sacked from two teaching jobs for poor spelling.

The next chapter looks at the way information about students is processed during transition and how teachers relate to tutorial systems, including the problems of referring on for additional support. For the moment, we can focus on some basic information about the more commonly used labels and what they might imply. These include, beginning with some general 'catch-all terms,

Emotional and/or Behavioural Difficulties (EBD), sometimes ESBD (add Social)

Additional Social Needs (ASN)

Additional Learning Needs (ALN)

Dyslexia

Dyspraxia

Attention Deficit Hyperactive Disorder (ADHD)

Aspergers

Autism

Tourettes syndrome

And for each we can consider

The label

What it means

What causes it (and/or aggravates it)

What it may mean to you

How you can react usefully

Note this is only a rough guide to help you become orientated. A more complete discussion with up to date references and links may be found at www.personalisedlearningforum.eu.

Emotional and/or Behavioural Difficulties (EBD) or ESBD (add Social)

What it means

Students with EBD often provoke strong reactions in those that teach them. Students find it difficult to manage their emotions and this often manifests as inappropriate behaviour. They may find it difficult to establish and maintain relationships with peers and adults.

What causes it (and/or aggravates it)

Many and various, as this is a catch-all label.

What it may mean to you.

Traditional reprimands and sanctions will often not work with this group. If they don't understand their own condition they can't rationally react to your system. You may find controlling your own emotional reaction increasingly difficult, so that appropriate help from outside works both ways.

How you can react usefully.

Often people with EBD will have been labelled 'difficult' or 'disruptive' for many years and may suffer poor self-esteem. It is usually necessary to go back down the Maslow hierarchy to increase a sense of safety and belonging before making more challenges. In extreme cases, you may need the red card system – hand the students a red card and allow them to show it to you if they suddenly feel the need to leave the room to avoid losing control. If not abused, and properly understood by the rest of the class, it can avoid more widespread disruption that involves others who are themselves borderline but coping. If formally diagnosed as EDB, the student attracts additional funding to pay for support such as LSAs. Make sure they get it.

Additional Social Needs (ASN) is an even more general term. Probation services and the Youth Justice Board receive additional funds for the social needs of their clients, as you might expect. GFEs may decide that a student requires support for child care or emergency rent and food and fund that through Student Support. The fact somebody comes from an economically deprived background does not in itself indicate any behavioural difficulties, but some socio-economic groups may have norms and expectations which differ from yours. An example of this could be persistent swearing. This is not the same as Tourette's syndrome, which is a medical condition – it is just that this is the norm at home, along with shouting loudly and reacting physically to provocation.

Some students with ASN may have never learned organisation or communication skills. They may need support to form and maintain positive relationships with peers and adults, even in their own social group. Adam Smith argued that the greatest tragedy of the poor was the poverty of their aspirations. You may find that students with ASN have very low expectations, which affects motivation. Aim Higher was started to provides funds to encourage school students to consider university as a goal, and FE used those funds for various forms of short term motivational courses.

Additional Learning Needs (ALN)

What it means.

Another catch-all title which may usefully be replaced by a more precise term, although you may take a while and need expert help to find one that fits. The LSC funding guidance used to promise funds to support:

> any activity that provides direct support for learning to individual learners, over and above that which is normally provided in a standard learning programme that leads to their learning goal.

In 2013 the Skills Funding Agency web site expressed it thus:

> Additional Learning Support (ALS) is intended to enable Learners to achieve their learning goal by providing additional funding to help them overcome any barriers to learning. The funding is intended to be flexible and to help support Learners who have learning difficulties and/or disabilities .... there is a Costs Form that can be used to record different levels of ALS spend.

What causes it (and/or aggravates it) – see below for a selection

What it may mean to you.

Students' learning needs affect their behaviour in class. This sounds obvious, but many students' learning needs are undiagnosed – often for many years. These are sometimes referred to as hidden disabilities. They include Dyslexia, Dyspraxia, Attention Deficit Hyperactivity Disorder (ADHD), which are described briefly below

How you can react usefully.

Details below, but if statemented the student attracts additional funding to pay for support. Make sure they get it.

Dyslexia

What it means.

Dyslexics may possess an unusual curiosity and an ability to think laterally or divergently rather then follow logical or sequential patterns. They are often right-brain dominant (see chapter 3) and can sometimes solve complex problems whilst failing to manage what seem to be simpler tasks, such as reading. They may suffer, to varying degrees, from

> Confusion with direction or sequencing, affecting their ability to handle reading and writing.

> Confusion with sounds and direction, confusing words and mixing left with right.

> Poor memory for anything that has no personal meaning (e.g. the random nature of a telephone number)

Slower processing (need additional time to understand concepts and complete exams)

If poor spelling seems to include irrational clusters of letters or reversals of d and b etc then it is worth checking the personal files again and considering screening.

What causes it (and/or aggravates it).

Theories continue to develop, and include an increasing reference to dietary influence[27]. A full discussion is updated on www.personalisedlearningforum.eu.

What it may mean to you.

Dyslexics are sometimes undiagnosed until well into middle age, although other mature students may refuse formal support because they have their own coping strategies. You probably cannot make much headway teaching dyslexics to read and write more accurately, because you haven't had the training and they may not be able to respond anyway. They may have a history of underachievement, with attendant frustrations, and have learned to hide from written work as a means of coping. But you can present material in way that are better for them (see chapter 3) and others may be able to help further.

How you can react usefully.

If not already diagnosed and supported, you will need to contact learning support to ask for a diagnosis. They should also have a stack of good advice on how to present written information for such students (see chapter 3). Under the rules at the time of writing you can get extra time for any exam (apply in plenty of time).

---

[27] E.g. Richardson (2006) p247

There are usually successful dyslexics in your area who can be role models, including mentors from higher courses or from university. It is a disadvantage one can learn to cope with, and a positive attitude counts as much as learning support.

Make sure debate about meta-cognition includes frank and realistic discussion about proper coping strategies (Learning Support will advise on a personal basis) and, conversely, make sure lazy spellers don't try to abuse the term by using it inaccurately as an excuse.

There are not always quick fixes, but sometimes coloured filters or rulers can make a difference - see the links on the plf site.

Dyspraxia or developmental co-ordination disorder.

What it means.

Dyspraxics are as common as dyslexics but the term is less widely used. They are more often male than female, but not exclusively. They may be perfectly capable and intelligent in a general sense, but appear incapable or careless when rushed. They suffer from a lack of co-ordination with motor skills – anything from holding a pen to bumping in to things – and may appear generally clumsy and uncoordinated. They find it difficult to organise their time and will focus strongly on a task but are easily distracted. Also tending to holistic or intuitive thinking, they may be very creative but appear lazy.

What causes it (and/or aggravates it)

Dietary causes are indicated, but not exclusively[28]

What it may mean to you.

If you have a word to describe a series of events or

---

[28] Richardson 2006 pp251-2 but also see plf site.

frustrations then it may be useful to the student, because he or she is able to locate the cause in a sense outside themselves. They may feel more able to consider coping strategies if they can use a technical term for their general disorganised clumsiness. Meanwhile, you may find yourself in a classroom or workshop with someone you have to try hard not to find unusually frustrating in lots of small ways that mount up.

How you can react usefully.

Make sure information is laid out cleanly and is not too fussy or distracting. If something has to be bought in next time, make sure they write it down. Use meta-cognition debate to focus on realistic aims for organising time and work space. Get Learning Support to advise on a personal basis. Rehearse new terms as part of mastery tasks.

Attention Deficit Hyperactive Disorder (ADHD)

What it means.

A chemical imbalance that affects students' attention, planning, organisation and self-criticism. Extreme cases are very difficult to live with at home and very disruptive in class, but milder cases will possess a creative energy you can channel, if you can manage their tendency to forget basic equipment, their lack of sustained attention and their tendency to become distracted.

They will fidget and move around, talk and act without restraint or apparent consideration. Some will be under medication. My six year old niece managed her own Ritalin until she decided for herself to come off it, so their ability to engage intelligently with debate and to act responsibly in a wider sense are not affected. Extreme cases may be triggered to manic states, so you need to know the prognosis - what is the worst case scenario?

What causes it (and/or aggravates it).

ADHD is a chemical imbalance in the brain. Sufferers have low levels of dopamine (controls concentration and attention span) and serotonin (aids sleep and feelings of well-being) but high levels of norepinephrine (causes aggression). It is likely it can be aggravated and affected by diet but not "caused" by it, and a disposition may be inherited.

What it may mean to you.

Students may present in class as being inattentive, hyperactive and may act impulsively. A number of conditions commonly co-exist with ADHD. These include depression, anxiety and obsessions, opposition defiant disorder and Asperger's syndrome.

How you can react usefully.

You should have known about this before the student arrived. If you didn't, find out why not and make sure that doesn't happen again (see chapter 6). You may need the red card system and/or an LSA. You will certainly need to manage your own irritated reactions (see below) and those of other students, who may find the presence distracting. Allow for relaxed periods between active sessions.

Aspergers is a mild variant of autism – see below – which is easier to deal with, although anxiety states can be high if students are forced to interact with others when they are unwilling or unable to do so. The lack of precise diagnostic criteria make it difficult to say how commonly it occurs, and it may easily be confused with oppositional disorders because students simply do not understand the world around them.

Autism

What is means.

This is a term usually reserved for the more extreme cases of the behavioural disorder range, although it has its own scale from mild to severe. More common in males (three times as many), it is increasing in both males and females and may affect 1% of the population[29]. It includes an inability to react socially. They simply won't understand your point of view, or even wish to engage with it, and avoid physical connection, preferring objects to people, an ordered and even obsessional routine to ordinary eye contact or conversation. They may possess a high IQ but you may have trouble getting them to use it for purposes of which you approve.

What causes it (and/or aggravates it).

A controversial question - research is under way at Stirling and Edinburgh into a causal relationship with fatty acid deficiency, although it is often argued that there is a strong genetic component. See the plf site for updates.

What it may mean to you.

You will find it difficult to relate to such students, because they do not wish to relate to you. They may have verbal skills but have no wish to converse or explain just because you think they ought to. They may avoid eye contact, have a limited range of expressions and exhibit repetitive movements. Put simply, they have their world and it is not yours. At the mild (Aspergers) end, you can establish contact and make progress, but may need specialist help to get through to new students. A rare form of Asperger's is savant syndrome. An 'autistic savant' might be brilliant at passing exams, memorising lists or name

---

[29] 10 - Lancet July 5th 2006

and dates in ways others can learn from, but unaware of how to make eye contact or laugh at a joke. Their memory might be exceptional but their anxiety and lack of social skills require allowances from other students as well as teachers.

How you can react usefully.

Explain yourself clearly and mean every word that you say. Don't waste words and don't try to use humour as a controlling mechanism.

Any effect will be harder than normal to achieve and, depending on the profundity of the case, you may have to limit your expectations. That does not mean progress in some direction cannot be made, but it does mean you need to be realistic and well-informed in order to make it, offering achievable aims within both your ability ranges. I have known students with Asperger's pass a National Diploma whilst serving on the Union Committee, and enter university. It required only moderate consideration from the teaching staff. I have also known students with mild autism to be sent on a link course without adequate warning or training for the staff, causing considerable stress.

One autistic student was sent on a media course for radio interviewing. An experience less appropriate would be hard to imagine. The answer always lies in adequate analysis and preparation.

Tourette's Syndrome

What it means.

Symptoms can include facial tics, repeated movements and sounds, which can include sniffing and throat clearing. There may be anything between 199,000 and 331,000 sufferers in the UK, affecting up to 1% of school children, and is 3 to 4 time more common in males than females (is there any learning difficulty that works the other way round?).

What causes it (and/or aggravates it).

TS may be inherited, but the cause is not known. It can be treated but not cured.

What it may mean to you.

Although IQ range is not different, there may be a need for learning support with reading and writing, arithmetic and perceptual problems. The movements may disturb others at first, although they can often be accommodated. Only 10-15% of TS suffers have involuntary swearing among their symptoms.

How you can react usefully.

As with any learning difficulty, you may find it helpful to try tape recorders, typewriters, or computers for reading and writing problems. You may have to get extra time or help for exams, and a private room. If tics become overwhelming the TS student may need to leave the room (use the red card system?). LSAs may be necessary for some cases.

Cantering through this introductory information is not the same as being an informed professional in educational psychology, or even a member of Student Support. You are not expected to replace them, and they exist so you can refer on or ask for help. Nor should a list of labels lead you to suppose that only students with a label attached may cause behavioural difficulties. If badly handled, any class can cause trouble. It is part of your professional responsibility to manage the energy levels of a group and the emotional temperature.

We can now consider techniques for managing energy levels, the question of emotional reaction and, if all else fails, handling a crisis and using a disciplinary procedure.

Motivation and persona

Fear of failure is a strong motivator. Conditioned by years of poor SAT tests, mockery or public slights from others, or even, originally, a genuine desire to please that is overwhelmed by a fear of not doing so, some students expect to fail. The best way is not to try. And the best route to not having to try is to be expelled, or sent home, or left alone in the back row. If they can persuade you they are hopeless, you won't ask them to risk failure. This emotional conundrum is sometimes beyond ordinary learning support issues, although a good relationship with an LSA can provide a route in the long run, because students can accept praise for small successes and slowly prepare to try again for something larger. Praise from a teacher in public might carry too large an implication of expectations that frighten them, not to mention the need for street cred. Meanwhile, they will be conditioned to defend themselves in advance by attacking you before you 'expose' or 'humiliate' them.

Some students may need attention to validate their existence. The need is emotional and being punished is better than being ignored, so punishing them for their transgression only increases the incidence. They may not show an obviously disruptive pattern. An excessive desire to help, or to contribute can also be wearing and ultimately destructive.

If a student is obviously looking for a fight, asserting their power over the teacher, then obviously fighting back is the best way to lose. You have descended to their level, proved that stags lock antlers, and even if you win you can look ridiculous. You are no different to them, only better at it. The bigger stag, for the moment. Worse, it is possible to achieve a partial victory – they stop that particular act for the moment – which masks an underlying failure – the classic dumb insolence betrays a knowledge that they have dragged you in, and the obvious sneer behind their co-operation can be even more undermining.

Again, remember all this is being played out to an audience, who are also actors in the final result. To offer help to the combatant, even to find a reason to apologise, may bring you more real authority in the long run. That may be what the rest of the class may really expect of you, until you disappoint them, but not what the difficult student expects, until you wrong-foot them.

Of course, it is probably not you they want to harm anyway. You just happen to be there, exerting authority. Their motivation may lie in other slights from years ago, or a lack of love and respect at home. If your persona deals with that professionally, it doesn't matter. If the real you gets involved then, win or lose, you lose. That is why it is important to make it plain that you condemn the act – always – but not the actor. Standards need to be maintained but bridges built where possible. Giving in is wrong, but so is 'winning' the wrong way.

Lecturers and students both benefit from increased self-awareness. As a minor example, both can avoid those irritating habits that they didn't know they had. That is why Cert Ed courses need video cameras. Both may realise they have behavioural habits that undermine their consciously avowed intentions. That is why we have mentored class observations and tutorials.

But who do we mean by tutor and student? Students may adopt a pose or persona, often acting less concerned than they really are as a defence mechanism, or to gain status in a context where learning is not cool. But that is probably not their real self. We need to be sure when we are dealing with a persona, and how to manage the difference. In the same way, tutors may find it useful, often necessary, to adopt a professional stance, a persona, which they use when managing classes but not (if they are well advised) at home. So any social interaction should be between:

the real student, the one behind the mask

and

the professional version of the tutor,

the one who is in control of any emotional reaction

Thus, for example, if a student is seeking conflict then teacher knows it is best to withdraw or rise above it. This will involve conciliatory moves. Chapter 6 considers the techniques of motivational interviewing, and the concept of 'social judo'. When a large strong person pushes against you, to push back is to lose. If you wait for a moment and then pull, they fall over. Likewise, a student trying to provoke an argument can best be wrong-footed by a refusal to engage which, being considerate and well-mannered, will cause them to withdraw from unfamiliar territory.

For a tutor to become emotionally involved, or react emotionally, is ineffective and could be damaging to the member of staff. If, on the other hand, they have adopted a professional stance, a persona, which they use when managing classes, any social interaction is easier to manage and easier to leave at work when you go home.

It is difficult, and sometimes facile, to list the rules that would seem to apply to all classes in all conditions, but in very general terms, the persona of a successful class manager would be:

1) Positive, with high expectations both academically and in terms of how people are expected to treat each other in class. Tone of voice and non-verbal communication need to be measured, never aggressive. Rewards and sanctions need to be applied consistently and in ways that all parties can see to be fair. This would include any observers, who are watching how you deal with it, but remember that neither praise nor criticism is always easy to accept in public. You may need to choose a quiet moment later on.

2) Seen as supportive for all students. Students in defiant or destructive mode may be willing to attack a teacher and justify their own actions, but the real self behind their temporary persona may already know they are wrong. If the teacher has established that they usually condemn the action but not the actor, the sin but not the sinner, it is easier to reach neutral ground after a temporary flair. Authority does not always lie in stamping on the behaviour at once, but nor does it lie in ignoring it. Reaction may well include a warning, but should also include an explanation, so the actor knows what is being objected to and why.

3) Seen as professional. For all their youth and, in many aspects, ignorance, one thing students know about is teachers. They have sat there and studied them for years, all day every day. They know the usual tricks and empty threats. They know the signs of someone who doesn't mean what they say. They appreciate a real professional, who controls their environment properly. They know that in any rising conflict, the teacher will lose if they start to raise their voice, plead, stand on their dignity or try to intimidate or score small points with sarcasm. They also know it is unfair if, in any single issue conflict, you start to drag previous offences, generalise or display obvious antipathy.

What they expect from a professional is that you will deal with the issue firmly to try to restore calm and get back to the learning. Give the student real choices if appropriate (do this or this but these are the consequences) but also remember that some students, in some conditions, genuinely don't see the world as you do, so can't be expected to make rational choices through a red mist. They may need space to calm down, your help in finding a way back from the edge before penalties are awarded.

Be clear what you want to achieve – not necessarily a public dominance to make you look big but perhaps an easing of tension to allow for a cooling off and an apology later. You may be able to change the location to alter the dynamic (come over here to talk about this). Professionals trying to conciliate look strong. Attempts to look strong at their expense may betray a natural weakness. They can tell the difference. The intention at all times is to retain all students in productive work. Every individual should be learning. If you think first and act afterwards, what is the best reaction to restore normal service to the group?

4) Properly supported. Your professional status should allow you to call on help when you need it, from LSAs, managers, Learning Support, counsellors, school teachers attached to link classes. Students should be able to recognise that you liaise with them for their benefit, and are the front line of a large army, not just some stray victim within range.

Managing the context

Ofsted's report on behaviour (*MCB*, 2005) made some very obvious recommendations. These include:

> Consistency of approach by staff (they stress in FE inconsistency between depts.)

> Clear direction and support for staff by management

> A thorough induction programme

> Regular training

> Using information systems efficiently (to predict and prepare and to analyse patterns)

> Reflection of learning styles, use of short-term targets and feedback to focus on how to improve (to help boys especially)

> Don't use resources that are outside students' life experiences

Tell them, what the lesson is for and what it will contain

Show them respect

In short, a combination of the personal and the organisational. Not all factors will be within your control. Their diet and other life experiences may send them into class hyped up or half-asleep. There are time-honoured ways to manage the energy levels, including the careful use of music and the courageous use of short physical exercises and wall space.

The latter should not be confused with 'brain gym'. This term is trademarked and refers to a set of exercises backed by theories about 'whole-brain learning'. Although listed on the DfES Standards Site, it is was attacked by others for containing glib generalisations and bad science. We do not need to engage in debate with a commercial firm to make a related but much simpler point.

Have you ever sat in a lecture, conference or training session and longed to get up and stretch, or even shout out loud? It should be part of everyone's annual CPD to have to sit in at least three long classes and be talked at until they feel like screaming. It would greatly increase our sympathy for students and cause us to examine our own practice. Recent attention to 'spaced learning' suggests students might do well by focusing on information repeated in short bursts, interspersed with physical exercise. Next time you start a class, gain attention and control their energy levels by asking them to undertake some physical task first. The following examples were donated by a practitioner, who adapted them from sources of her own. If you think you own the copyright, just notify info@bpfe.org.uk and they will be acknowledged or replaced.

Alphabet

Use the attached sheet. Read the capital letters out loud. The letters or sign underneath mean: l - raise your left arm, r – raise your right arm or + raise both arms. Students must react quickly by hearing the capital and translating to the sign below it.

A	B	C	D
l	r	l	l
E	F	G	l
r	+	r	l
J	K	L	M
r	l	+	r
O	P	Q	R
+	l	l	r
S	U	V	W
l	+	r	+
X	Y	Z	
r	l	+	

Lazy 8s

With one arm extended in front of you and your thumb pointing upwards, trace the shape of a figure 8 in the air. The 8 should be on its side and as you trace it out in large, slow movements focus your eyes on your thumb. Without moving your head, trace three 8s in successively larger movements. Now do it with your other hand and then clasp them together and do both.

Names in the air

With your preferred hand write your full name in the air.
Use large movements. Do it forwards and backwards. Now
use your other hand to write your name with both hands
simultaneously. If you are right handed, start in the centre and
work out. If you are left-handed start at the outside and work
in. Try several times before going on to another name.

Rub and pat

Gently rub your hand in a circle on your stomach. Stop,
then pat your head with the other hand gently. Now do both at
the same time and at a similar pace. You should be rubbing
your stomach whilst patting your head. Try to maintain the
difference in each movement. Swap hands.

Finger and thumb

On one hand, hold up your index finger. On the other
hand, hold up your thumb. Then switch as fast as you can, so
the hand that had the finger up now has the thumb up, and the
hand that had the thumb up now has the index finger up.
Repeat several times. Try it standing up.

These exercises allow everyone to stretch and engage their
mind and body in a non-threatening, even amusing warm up.

Once sitting at a desk or working at the lathe, students are
subject to the psychology of the room. You may not have any
authority over that. In FE it is common to share space and you
may have to try to engage students in a room that is
depressingly badly painted with old posters on the wall that
have nothing to do with them or the subject. Years of research
on the effects of colour on the motivation of the workforce
have either never been read or are always ignored because the
budget is too low. If you can, you need to make sure the room
is well lit and ventilated, with appropriate posters that change
often enough to look as if they matter. From time to time,
bring in something unusual just to make it look cared for. A
small bunch of flowers can transform a tatty old room and

send messages about care for the learning environment worth far more than any disciplinary code, and that advice is not gender- specific.

Props related to the lesson might themselves take attention away from peeling plaster and mouldy ceilings, both of which I have taught under, at a time when nobody seemed to notice them or think they really mattered. I found that importing a lemon tree in a pot and an old rocking chair took their minds away from the fact nobody cared enough to decorate or maintain the place. In due course, the chair was broken by overuse, but by then the mould had been removed from the room.

Even arranging the chairs can send useful messages. The U shape is more often found in FE than serried rows. It seems more adult (less like school) and lines of sight generate better student participation.

Music, of course is portable. It can counteract the effects of a cold and empty environment. Muzak in lifts might raise your blood pressure but the idea behind it, that sound affects mood, is effective if wisely applied. Old Beatles tunes played by a cheap orchestra on Prozac might not help, but real music will affect us physiologically. In shops and restaurants, takings will rise if you get the music right. In zoos, rowdy chimps stop attacking each other and pain after surgery is reduced by using the right sounds. Research continues into the choice of classical over popular music, of any music over silence or the use of rhythmic chants to slow heart beats. An experiment in Knowsley in 2003 involved students being given mentors and a specially recorded cd of sounds to relax to, including running water and a gently slowing heartbeat.

Slow, quiet pieces can make periods of quiet reflection more acceptable and thinking more creative. You can speak over it when reading a piece for them to focus on.

More up-tempo pieces are good for kinaesthetic activities, but also as the background for energetic group work.

You can set the pace when they enter and send them off

with a bounce. But you also need to use it carefully, and give their ears a rest after 30 minutes maximum.

You may need to experiment with the right tracks. If you choose music from their era, or to allow them to choose, it may degenerate into a debate on the relative merits of bands and anecdotes about the last concert. Something left-field but universal might be better - baroque, Miles Davis (In a Quiet Way, Spanish Nights) or Mingus (Nobody Here But Us Chickens?). You may choose familiar lyrics to make them feel more comfortable as they arrive but switch to lyrics in another language when they need to use it as background only.

During metacognition discussion, you can encourage them to choose more appropriate rhythms to listen to at home when studying. They may find they remember information better when using the right tape. Too much base or disharmony will distract by taking too much sub-conscious attention. Regular rhythms may help them remember, and chapter 3 has already noted how music helps you remember information when it is sent to a tune. It is also possible to enliven revision for nervous or bored classes by playing music and throwing around a soft ball or a balloon – whoever is holding the ball when the music stops answers the question.

Finally – and it is last for good reasons – we need to consider the principles of effective disciplinary systems.

> In this country we're obsessed with punishment; "Can you whack 'em hard?" But it's got to be about preventing disruption. If you say that people think you're soft, but it's flaming obvious.
> *Sir Alan Steer, Head teacher of 20 years' experience and chair of the government working group on discipline, 2005*

> Most teachers know that the root problem with behaviour lies in the curriculum. Mike Tomlinson

How often do we punish students for our own failings?

Although he is no longer a fashionable reference, R.D. Laing's work at Gartnavel Hospital showed that restraints and drugs had less effect on the behaviour of disturbed patients than improvements in the attitude of nursing staff. He also showed, in *Sanity, Madness and the Family*, that what appears to be an insane reaction may, in fact, be a reasonable response to an insane situation. Students want a world that is

Safe

which means predictable, with clear boundaries and routines, responses that are always the same

Fair

which to their mind means operating rules they understand and approve, praising the good as well as condemning the bad, condemning the act and not the actor

Disciplinary systems exist primarily to control and modify student behaviour, not merely to defend staff. They are part of a coherent package – the college culture – created and managed to engage, motivate and educate students.

However, they may need to defend both staff and other students if they fail to control or change offenders, and should take account of possible extremes of behaviour.

They may also need to defend students against unsuitable behaviour by other students, or by staff, and should take account of the possibility of genuinely different understandings.

They need to be broadly accepted as fair by all concerned, and perceived as jointly owned – no compliance without representation?

They need to be operated in clearly comparable and equitable ways by everyone who uses them.

They need to be employed when required, backed by the whole college/school system and operated consistently. This may also mean not being inconsistent with other systems, e.g. in school.

They need an appeal system that is seen to be fair but also operated quickly and efficiently.

Glib rules are easy to pronounce but vital statements would include:

> Don't have too many rules – more is always less.
> Always apply them – lazy or cowardly exceptions prove them irrelevant.
>
> Get students to buy in early – not just by signing a copy as a mere formality but perhaps by agreeing their own class constitution during induction and exhibiting the agreed rules on the wall to be referred to in any crisis or disagreement.

If students develop their own charter, remember to include

> Start and finish times
> Punctuality (theirs and yours)

It would be interesting to hear anyone argue a case for not being in some way sanctioned for not turning up on time. How long would they be prepared to wait for each other? Why wait at all? What would be a suitable response to anyone being late? Students in week one tend to be more draconian that teachers. They just don't expect anyone to apply the rules they make up, because nobody applies the rules the college makes up. How many 9 a.m. classes start at 9 a.m.?

There is, of course, the problem of 'adjustment time'. You allow students to get used to the rules, to socialise gradually. If you don't start as you mean to go on, you may be seen to be ignoring your own rules and acting weakly. If you apply them all too rigidly you could empty some classes overnight. So rules need to allow for graded responses, which can then allow for adjustment time within reason. How you do that is one of the problems of transition, which is one of the subjects of the next chapter, which also looks at the effects of tutorials on behaviour.

But first, it is worth repeating that your 'problem' with a student or class should not automatically be located on their side of the equation. If students might (or might not) have different learning styles, teachers have different styles and personalities.

> He who is a teacher from the very heart takes all things seriously only with reference to his students - even himself.[30]
>
> Nietzsche, Beyond Good and Evil

When speaking of students, a teacher may use the language of learning styles. When speaking of teachers, psychologists may speak of temperaments or personalities. Keirsey and Bates use four main distinctions:

    guardians
    artisans
    idealists
    rationals.

The Myers-Briggs Type Indicator (MBTI) uses vocabulary developed out of Jungian psychology:

    extroversion - introversion
    sensing - intuition
    thinking - feeling
    judging – perceiving

For children between 6 and 12 there is a special Murphy-Meisgeier Type Indicator (MMTIC)

---

[30] Or herself. In speaking of teachers we have used the inelegant but convenient means of referring to both male and female professionals as 'they' instead of him or her, sacrificing grammatical tradition to social convenience. Nietzsche, of course, really didn't care.

These vocabularies may be combined, for example by Fairhurst and Fairhurst (1995) in a text that typifies both the value and the difficulty of such work. They carefully explain their 'types' then consider the way teachers, techniques, students and styles may be poorly matched, suggesting possible adaptions.

All typologies, whether applied to teachers or students, are subject to obvious dangers. Firstly, they may be quite wrong, unfounded or muddle-headed. How would a lay person know? Even if well founded, they are often complex and take a long time to understand fully. Most teachers have no time for such detailed study. According to psychologists, some tests or questionnaires ought only to be applied and interpreted by qualified psychologists.

Once typologies are popularised, they tend to be over-simplified. The 'types' are used rigidly and no allowance is made for the complexity of real people, who are at best a shifting combination of several types. Nevertheless, when treated with caution, typologies sometimes provoke questions and provide insights which can help to explain situations provide solutions and reduce stress. It is less dangerous to see an individual imperfectly than to see a 'type' with excessive clarity. How can we use the ideas without having to buy in to a single theory, join a fashionable movement or trust a guru?

The following few paragraphs draw partly but not exclusively on the ideas in Fairhurst and Fairhurst and ask teachers to consider their own needs and limitations. It is, as far as possible, a value-free tool for self-exploration. Never mind what some tendency is called by academic researchers. Never mind the labels. Just look at some of the different preferences or tendencies see if you recognise yourself. Do the questions or examples lead to greater self-knowledge or clarity? If so, do they help to explain why you may feel stressed in certain situations, and help you to imagine your way to solutions? After all, there is little point knowing about your students if you don't also know yourself, so you can monitor any mismatch which, perhaps unconscious, is significant and stressful to both parties.

To issue a general caveat that applies to all typologies and much else besides – many people are working hard not to develop their own nature but to become someone else. If a person thinks of themselves as weak they will try to appear strong. Natural sensitivity will be masked by brusqueness, indecision by hurried action. What they appear to be is only what they are trying to be, not what they naturally 'are'. This may be particularly true of a student who has a strong role model, perhaps emulating a peer or an actor or a teacher. Of course, a desire to be 'other', to change and become something else, is precisely what motivates one form of educational activity. But not all kinds. It may be a problem if you take the act for the reality and base your teaching approach on it. Perceiving the dynamics of a personality is not an easy task, especially if it is someone with whom we are in conflict, or ourselves, or both.

To start at the very simplest level, imagine two people opening some flat-pack self-assembly furniture. One of them opens it slowly and reads the instructions. They lay out all the contents and tick them off on the list, as instructed. Then they follow the instructions to the letter. The other rips open the packet, looks at the picture of the final result and starts bunging the bits together, using trial and error as much as any assistance from the instruction sheet. If those two people co-habited, or tried to work together, they might cause each other stress. A successful team may need both of them to make up a full range of complementary talents, but they might need a referee at times to help them find compromise. If one of those people were a teacher and the other a student, the power dynamics would be quite different.

Some people define 'general knowledge' as that which they are generally likely to know. To what extent do we define intelligence or disability by our own preferences? Is an intelligent or educated person one who can do what we are good at? Do we devalue in others what we cannot do and thus do not care about? How can we understand and manipulate someone whose mental processes and motivations are quite different to ours?

Teachers say they want students to be self-motivated. But if a student is really self-motivated they will be immune to the usual teacher tools of feedback and praise. They will be focused on what they want to learn, not on what you want them to do. How many teachers would recognise in themselves and be able to deal with this level of self-absorbtion? Would you consider it healthy or unhealthy? Would your inability to control them cause you stress?

Planning is a strength. So is the ability to cope when plans go wrong. Imagine a teacher who is a careful planner, motivated by a need for order and meeting deadlines. In class, faced with a student who cannot follow their requirements, they might perceive this inability as laxity and feel threatened, insulted or undermined. The teacher values (and needs?) an orderly life. They argue, reasonably, that order is a requirement for learning.

The teacher wants to see a completed product, but their desire to produce it against what appears to be opposition might focus them too closely on the product and less on the process by which it is created. The process might be a lot more important than any temporary product. A focus on the process might lead to solutions to achieve the product, but can the teacher stand back from the stressful experience of seeing their plan unravel?

Conversely, some teachers are very happy to work in creative excitement (=muddle?). Fun, enjoyment, spontaneity. Some students need this and some tutors happily provide it. Other students may find it intimidating. The tutor will frighten or worry them. Is this fun question in the exam? What's the right answer? What do I have to do to earn approval? Some students would prefer more obvious order. Some take a purely instrumental approach to education and too much enjoyment worries them.

Teachers who value thoroughness and attention to detail may encourage that in students, reacting badly to anyone who is unusually untidy. But sometimes attention to detail actually

prevents you from getting to the end of the job. One problem
is to be so tied up with the detail of the early stages you can
never actually get to the end at all. Another is to be so
concerned with planning you never actually start. Some people
never even try to start because they know it will never be
perfect so they would rather not see the imperfect result. By
comparison, it may seem to be more 'healthy' if a student is the
sort who slaps something together quickly, with a few mistakes
and rough edges, but it may not seem so to the over-careful
teacher. How careful is too careful? I am careful, you are fussy,
he or she is obsessive?

Innovators keep some students on their toes and are
appreciated by those students. Other students suffer stress
from the lack of structure and predictability. They prefer
teachers who rely on the tried and tested, who make them feel
comfortable.

If a teacher is motivated by a strong sense of their own
self-worth they may not understand a student who is not and is
thus driven to seek approval too often. The teacher may not
offer approval often enough – they don't need it so they don't
see the need to offer it. Conversely, a teacher who is personally
motivated by a desire for approval may not understand a
student who is not. Being self-motivated, the student won't care
about or respond to praise. They appear to be surly when in
fact they are only behaving quite naturally in the same way as
some teachers. (Those two ideas are not, of course, mutually
exclusive.)

Rules provide order and keep people safe. Bureaucrats waste
time and energy. Most bureaucrats think they are providing
order and keeping people safe. They resent the ingratitude. A
syllabus needs to be interpreted. Do you find you have the
confidence to adapt it? Are you nervous about the
responsibility of ensuring that regulations are applied? If a
student needs more flexibility to respond, would your
personality or temperament make it hard for you to find a way
forward? Conversely, if students are worried about making it
through the educational jungle, would your creative way with

regulations and apparent disregard for small print leave them insecure because they can't trust you to know the syllabus and lead them through the maze?

Some teachers and some students like to see the whole picture before they start to explore details. They enjoy making connections between ideas. They value curiosity for its own sake and may even define 'education' as a tendency to be curious without external cause. They may also be careless of detail in their grand gestures and expansive explanations of the whole picture. Others prefer a step-by-step approach with lists and details. The former will consider the latter to be plodders and may devalue their intellect. The latter may consider the former sloppy and careless and devalue their insights.

Some like theories. They appreciate beautiful abstract ideas. They may descend to facts only to illustrate the theory, like using specks of dust to show a ray of light. Others cannot relate to that at all. If both extremes are teachers they just accept their differences and choose their company accordingly. If one is a teacher and one a student, the dynamics of power are quite different. The student may be devalued and demotivated, the teacher disappointed and frustrated.

Do you feel secure, valued and approved by your peers, managers and students? Does a lack of appreciation cause stress? You may know in your own mind that progress is being made and learning takes place, but is that enough? Do you need external validation, some sign, however, subtle, that you are doing well? Would you prefer that sign to be clear and unambiguous?

Is the job important to you? How important? Is it, in fact, the major or even the only source of validation you have that you are significant and achieving something? When things go wrong, it is healthier if you have another source too? It may be a hobby or family or other relationship, but if work causes a loss of esteem that other source may have to make up for it, and knowing it is there will stop you relying too much on work, and thus over-reacting to situations that are perhaps less significant when in their proper perspective. That also applies to students, of course, who have been shown to learn better when they have outside interests. In fact, most good advice about how we treat students applies to how we treat ourselves, and vice-versa. That includes all the advice about diet and behaviour.

How important to you is the approval of your students? Do you sometimes unconsciously punish or reject them for not giving it to you? One way to maintain a professional life is to adopt a persona. A teacherly mask can be put on in class to enable the person beneath it to remain calm under pressure. The students may also adopt a series of poses, appearing less concerned than they really are. The professional requirement is to locate and understand the real student behind the mask whilst maintaining enough personal distance to ensure that any rejection or abuse is aimed at your persona, which you leave at work, not the real you that goes home. Do you find that idea dishonest or difficult to apply?

Some teachers have a strong personal commitment and a strong sense of personal values. For some students this is inspiring, and the teacher's palpable concern is comforting. But if students reject the lesson or the values the teacher may feel their very self is devalued. What is the difference in practice between being principled and being judgemental, tolerant and weak or vague? Some people are naturally decisive (or precipitate) and others naturally prudent (or indecisive). In a team, do we naturally value our opposites to balance our input, or just find them annoying? In class, do we tend to devalue or even attempt to eradicate tendencies that reflect our opposites?

Taking responsibility is good. Internalising conflict caused by factors beyond your control is destructive. Is there a tension between caring about your students and caring about yourself so you are strong enough to be useful to them? Care is useless without control; control is dangerous without care. The question is not always 'have I done enough?' but sometimes 'have I done the right thing efficiently and effectively?' The phrase 'work smarter not harder' is an irritating cliché but also good advice. Stepping back to analyse the dynamics of conflict, realising it is only your professional self which engages with it, may enable you to view it more dispassionately and thus perceive the solution. It is like trying very hard to remember something, giving up and thus suddenly remembering it. Don't get mad and don't get even but rise above it. More conscious effort can sometimes make only more stress. This, of course, also applies to students. Some of them know that and some don't.

Of course, effective thinking can only take place with sufficient information. That information may only be available through sympathetic perception. Standing back is not the same as switching off – quite the opposite. It is more like switching wavelengths. Hard work is necessary, even gratifying. Overtired and stressed teachers become unresponsive and undermine the relationships necessary to learning. There is no point being up all night making perfect material if you then take it in and snap at the people meant to use it. But nor is there any point rushing in ebullient but with no suitable material. Your temperament and/or personality will partly determine which is the greater danger. That of the students will partly determine how they react.

Action may be needed to motivate the kinaesthetic learner. Some teachers enjoy providing a creative, dynamic, exciting classroom. Some students are quiet and studious and prefer to be left in peace or talked to quietly. Some teachers are good at creating a calm, reflective, studious environment. Some students find this soporific and some find the lack of noise and action unsettling. Some students need a period of relaxation between bouts of activity in order to function well, or at all. Others, finding the pace has been slowed, will suspect that the teacher is resting at their expense and react accordingly.

Sometimes the action is provided by the teacher putting on a show. This might inspire the class, or it might just use them as an audience. If both teacher and student gain from the exchange, it is obviously a successful method, but what enthuses one will overwhelm another. It may be a student putting on the show, perhaps joining in, whilst others just cringe away from the exchange. Miss Jean Brodie inspired in all the wrong ways. Gradgrind never inspired.

There are many means of keeping control. Some teachers, very sensitive to subtle social signals, will themselves respond well in company and readily understand the desires of the other person. Using such signals in class, they may find the students do not respond to them, and fail to recognise that it is a language they simply have not learned. The teacher needs to learn how to make their thoughts and feelings much more clear with direct expression, which will be alien to their nature and may be hard to learn.

Other teachers, more bluff in social exchange, may fail to recognise subtle signals of distress from their students, or peers, or partners. A student who sends signals that are not recognised may then feel confused, frustrated and let down. Withdrawing from the exchange, they are repaying a slight the teacher was unaware of making. Later on, made aware of a lack of co-operation or approval from that student, the teacher may in turn be offended and never find out why.

Some teachers value face-to-face communication. If a student does not, and seems relatively withdrawn, they may think of them as 'not performing' or even suffering from a learning disability, when in fact they are just two different 'types' of people from opposite ends of the spectrum. This problem is exacerbated by the values built in to the syllabus for key skills or functional skills, assuming that all well rounded people should be able to argue reasonably and speak to an audience, forcing the issue on those who come from an extreme that is poor at the former and shuns the latter, persuading them they are not different from but worse than. Can shy students be valued even if they fail the test? Can they be equally valued by all teachers, some of whom have never experienced shyness?

Some teachers are generous and help others. They are likely to value and encourage that tendency in their students. 'Helps others' sounds like a generally healthy statement to be able to make about any student, but some will be too eager to help.

Can we tell the difference between a healthy willingness to help and a dangerous desire to please.

A strong desire to please may lead students (and teachers?) to deny their true nature to achieve that end, acting out a role that they think will win approval. Seeking harmony in dishonesty, they may eventually breed disharmony.

The desire to please may be tied to an inability to accept criticism. Some people can accept it easily because it doesn't matter very much to them. Teachers who can easily live with it may not understand students who go to great lengths to avoid it or react badly when it is offered. What seems to the teacher a helpfully corrective remark may seem to the student a crushing assault on their personality. If that kind of teacher became aware of the fact they would consider the student unnaturally sensitive but, of course, they are least likely to become aware of it. It is not a problem they usually experience themselves so they don't notice it on others. If they notice a dysfunctional reaction they may explain it in other ways, in ways that make more sense to someone of their own tendencies.

A tendency to try to please may be channelled positively or negatively. How it is perceived may depend partly on how far the teacher shares it. Some students may need protection because their desire to help or to please is exploited by peers, practising to be the entrepreneurs of tomorrow.

Competition helps some to thrive. Some students need it as a motivator. Some are risk takers and other risk averse, like some teachers and managers. The movement in the early 21st century is towards greater emphasis on entrepreneurial activities, encouraged by Sector Skills Councils and the need to provide the employment-creators of tomorrow. Some students and teachers will respond well to that atmosphere. Others will draw back. The former may consider the latter to be timid and unrealistic. The latter will sometimes accuse the former of being brash and pandering to motives less worthy or dignified than their own. In fact, both sides will be adopting values that suit their own personal preferences and tendencies, reflecting the diversity of a social group that, as usual, is characterised by mutual incomprehension.

If a teacher-student relationship fails, it would be a reasonable human reaction for the teacher to blame the student, as it stops them having to question their fragile self. If you are operating a professional persona, and have the benefit of a more objective language, it may be easier to achieve self-awareness and thus effective action. Most tendencies and desires can be channelled positively or negatively. Once we have observed, gathered data, reflected and passed beyond judgement to comprehension, we can react accordingly, whether those tendencies are theirs or ours.

In passing, we may note that a great deal we think of as normal or necessary is, in reality, on a temporary element of a local culture. It can be changed, but may have permanent consequences. For example, targets and tests have been part of the primary scene for so long now that 10-11 years olds have started to base their friendship groups on grade scores. They associate success or failure with morality and may drop friends who do badly in tests (TES 9th Feb 2007 p13). The long days and heavy test load we think of as normal in the UK is derided as harmful and unnecessary in other EU countries. If we decided to change it we could make a quite different culture, but would already have hard-wired a generation in ways that may or may not be good for them. Teachers with different temperaments and students with different learning preferences negotiate their relationship in cultures that can change radically in a generation.

Many questions we ask about students may be usefully asked of our own approach to them. The key in both cases is to gather data carefully and look at it honestly.

> What we do in dreams, we also do when we are awake;
> we invent and fabricate the people with whom we
> associate and immediately forget that we have done so.
>
> Nietzsche

Chapter 6

Transition and tutorials, paperwork and reality

In relation to young people, there is a particularly important challenge at key points of transition - often the move at age 16 from school to further learning. .... we will trial models of support which run across the age 16 boundary, so that learning support can be continuous and seamless across different institutions.

DfES (2006) 4.20

In my beginning is my end.......
Time present and time past
Are both perhaps present in time future
And time future contained in time past

Four Quartets, T.S. Eliot

Imagine you are a new student, about to embark on the exciting and intimidating journey that is your new course. You might be young – 14 or 16 or 18 - and full of trepidation about how you will be treated and how you will cope. You could be a mature adult feeling exactly the same way. On your first day, four things have to be achieved:

Fill in forms to register formally, pay deposits and collect codes or cards so you can use the computers, library and photocopier. Become a part of the bureaucracy and thus officially permitted to use the facilities.

Start to understand the nature of the subject you are studying, to see what it entails, what makes it special and why is might be interesting.

To negotiate the social minefield laid by all those faces,
so you can make friends or colleagues.

To learn how to learn in this context – to know what
constitutes success and how to achieve it.

It doesn't need an M.Ed to work out that this list is not in
order of importance. And yet, how many induction processes
take account of the fact that first impression sets the tone for
the rest of the year? How many messages are sent, how
strongly, on that first day about what a student is worth and
how they may expect to be treated, about what is involved in
the rest of the long year to come?

Busy staff, calloused by long years of form-filling and grown
careless of the many new faces that re-appear annually, herd
them in and sit them down to be told a lot of details about fire
escapes and terms dates and overdue book fines and
disciplinary codes which communicate nothing of the
excitement of a co-operative journey of learning. Of course,
official processes are important, and the first student
registration card may be a source of pride or even relief, but
should not remain in the memory as the most important,
certainly not as the only things that seem to matter.

Messages sent and received

In college A the full-time students come in for two days in
week one to register. Forms are filled, codes issued and formal
processes completed. Then they are sent away again until
formal teaching begins the following week

*What matters most is the administration of the college and you must do
whatever is necessary for that to run smoothly, including go home and stay
out of the way if they want to speak to other, more important, people.
College is a big, bureaucratic place and individual students must fit in at
their own expense. It might be boring, time might have to be wasted, and
the college certainly won't go out of its way to accommodate you.*

In college B students start the week by entering a large hall where they are formally welcomed by the Principal then organised past various desks to complete forms on the way out, after which they are divided into classes to meet their tutor. The following day there is a freshers' fair which they can all attend to meet the students' union, student support, college societies etc.

College is large and it has important people in it who want you to listen to them and then do things for them. There is a smaller unit and a friendly face in the centre of it. There is lots going on, which may be interesting, but you will sink or swim. There will be lessons later.

In college C they are directed to a classroom where they first meet as a group of 20 with their course tutor. They are quickly told about toilets and fire bells then ice-breakers are used before an experiment to demonstrate an important principle of the subject being studied. After a tea break, where other classes are also seen, this is discussed and work set for the next week. This is followed by formal registration processes to facilitate that work (enrolment, library cards etc.) spread out over the next few days, which include visits from student support, the students' union, learning support etc.

The small class unit is your home and with these people you will be doing something interesting. To succeed you need to get started with work and keep up the pace. Around you is a larger context you can explore in due course. There are also formal processes that support the learning process and help you succeed. Your tutor will guide you through them.

With so much to manage for so many people, it is hardly surprising that colleges try various ways to simplify the process, but in doing so they often lose sight of the fact that first impressions set the tone for the rest of the year and attitudes need to be managed even more carefully than formal processes. In that sense, W. H. Auden was right:

Thou shalt not worship projects nor
Shalt thou and thine bow down before
Administration.

Under Which Lyre

On the other hand, it is too easy to simply 'rise above' the bureaucracy of a college and ignore or denigrate it, as if class teaching was so important and all those forms simply get in the way of the superior process. Bureaucracy is supposed to serve a purpose that is vital to the learning process. If it doesn't, the systems need to be improved, not side-stepped. What doesn't serve the process will always undermine it – nothing is neutral.

To take the most obvious example, even before induction, how much do you know about the learning needs of the students you are about to meet? How do you know if they are on the right course, with the right support and appropriate personal targets? How will you know if you have 'added value' to their journey instead of just filling in a year of their time? Systems evolve over time and will vary locally, but the general thrust of the national reforms has been to ensure that ensure that:

> Students have a point score in school that can be used to work out their probable percentage chance of success in a given course. This can be used to help decide where to place them, to set personal targets and, later, show that they have achieved more or less progress than other students in the country with similar point scores on similar courses. Have you stretched them or shrunk them?[31]

> They have records of learning difficulties or social needs and any relevant diagnoses that are passed on at interview and become part of the college's file on them. This allows you to recommend the right course (which may or may not be the one you teach) and arrange the

---

[31] *Implementing New Measures of Success*, LSC, June 2005

right kind of support in advance.

In addition to this, local systems will provide screening for learning support and possibly for learning styles. Some of this may at times become tediously bureaucratic, and even impenetrable, but it is important to operate the principle that systems ought to serve the learning experience. If they don't, it may be you have to (a) understand them better (b) reform them. Ignoring or working round them will only retain an element of the organisation that has no right to exist. No process should be followed simply because it is there. It has to be **made** to serve the learning process. The next few pages give examples of how apparently mind-numbing bureaucracy would actually serve the learning process if properly understood and applied, and how this will save time and effort in the long run.

The first example concerns point scores, and it is important to see this in historical context. Most people will be familiar with the old notion of school league tables. Students gain points for passing exams and the total points gained by the school makes up its 'performance' data so it can be ranked in comparison with other schools. Parents are encouraged to use the performance data, along with Ofsted and governors' reports, to monitor their child's school and, if possible, even to choose between schools.

Terminology can be confusing, but **added value** is a term traditionally used for **level 3** qualifications which are **graded** but **distance travelled** is a term used for **other qualifications.** They measure the same thing – how much the student has improved since they started a particular course – and may eventually measure it the same way, but work continues on how to make good statistical sense of the process.

It would be unfair to compare schools directly without allowing for the social mix of their intake. Some students are harder to get through GCSE English than others. Changes were made to allow schools to measure 'added value' so that it was clearer whether the progress made was reasonable given the students' starting point.

Also, at one stage, GCSEs were measured, and vocational qualifications attracted no points. There was no incentive for a school to offer them and, if the students went to college to take them, the school's public record remained the same whether they passed or failed. This did nothing to encourage the growth of vocational options or careful selection for them. Now that vocational options also attract points, and passing them can show added value, it is very much in a school's interest to consider offering them. Changing a system of measurement can change attitudes and behaviour.

Like all new systems, it will be subject to confusion and abuse. A **threshold** is 'a volume of qualifications at a single NQF level'. Measures of performance at the age of 16 use a threshold at level 2. At the age of 18 they will use level 3. The old level 2 threshold was 5 GCSE's grade A-C. The old level 3 threshold was 2 A levels. Now we can also use vocational qualifications to meet the threshold, once it is agreed what value they have by comparison. The TES argued in on 13th January 2006 that if the time spent on a Maths GCSE were spent instead on a vocational qualification worth 4 GCSE's then points per hour would be massively increased. Outsiders will then argue that hard subjects (perhaps "the basics" like Maths and English GCSE) are being dropped for easier subjects, undermining the public valuation of vocational options in the same way that A levels are 'undermined' by too many good results. Another TES article objected that points for cake decorating could be easily obtained then cynically used to inflate a school's league status (TES 4th Feb Opinion p23).

Notwithstanding the imperfection of human systems, it is likely that recent changes to statistical measures will change attitudes and behaviour to improve the learning process in school. Colleges, meanwhile, will be able to use similar point systems. At enrolment, you will know how many points a student has. You will know, nationally, how students with that many points usually manage on the course they apply for. You can consider that when deciding to accept them and, if you accept them, see whether they eventually do better or worse than the national average. This information will be publicly available, which discourages admissions tutors from stuffing an unpopular course with applicants whose chances of success are minimal and calls them to account if they are shown to have done so.

Of course, there have always been reasons why a student with poor point scores at school might flourish in FE. This can be understood by looking at CAT and SAT scores, which are part of the basic terminology in schools and need to be understood by anyone accepting school students.

Schools have a legal obligation to test students and use those tests for predicting and tracking outcomes. Cognitive ability tests (CATS) claim to measure potential. Standard attainment tests (SATS) measure achievement in certain subject areas. Schools can then be asked how well they developed what appeared to be the students' potential. They can use both measures of potential and prior attainment data to allow them to predict outcomes, and to consider suitable methods of differentiation.

CAT or cognitive ability test.

These cover three broad areas:

> verbal reasoning (VR)

> quantitative reasoning (QR)

> non-verbal reasoning (NVR) – which includes spatial awareness

To take the tests, students need to have basic literacy and numeracy, so their success is not independent of subject knowledge – it is not a test of potential in some clean, ideal sense that enables us to see what they are capable of free from previous school experience.

VR scores tend to correlate closely with academic success, as school-based tests in any subject require an ability to read questions and write answers.

NVR tests enable students with poor VR scores to do well because they use visual images for assessment. But the subjects in which such skills are applied may require VR to pass tests and exams.

We are therefore measuring, to a degree, student potential within a system that does not always reflect the learning style most suitable to realising the potential we measure. A typical scattergram of such scores might show implications for learning styles, and thus curriculum management, for the cohort as a whole and for different genders.

As with IQ tests, there are many who argue for the inherent unreliability of CATS, and some school staff may not take them seriously. As with any use of measurements or learning styles info, it is a matter of using data mindfully, not pedantically or carelessly. There is some confusion among teachers, parents and governors about the science behind the tests, and a there is a confusing variety available from commercial firms.

SAT or Standard Attainment Test

The relation between CATS and SATS is complex, and students may do better in SATS than CATS indicate because they are heavily prepared by teachers who need to gain results. They will have been less prepared, less efficiently drilled, for CATS. Tests are taken at certain key stages.

> Key stage two is usually taken at age 11, as they enter secondary school.

> Key stage 3 is taken at age 14, as they choose options for GCSEs taken at 16 (and/or choose vocational links).

An average grade 5 score at KS3 would indicate a potential for at least 5 GCSEs at grade A-C. Grade 6 average indicates potential for 5 grade Bs. Seven indicates As.

But those grades are subdivided into 5a, 5b etc so we might expect fewer grade C's from the weaker end of the grade 5 group. From a grade 4 group we start expecting grade D.

Moreover, marking of SATS is as controversial as any other public system. Formal challenges and requests for review of KS3 English have risen dramatically over the last few years. So what they 'prove' depends on how far you believe in them.

Unless you happen to run a school you may not need to study in detail the methodology behind school measurements But the way students are enrolled and treated in FE will depend to an increasing extent on the logic behind both of them and the new FE measurements, informing the Learner Achievement Tracker (LAT). The Skills Funding Agency can then publish a Learner Achievement Tracker (LAT) which contains "interactive Value Added and Distance Travelled reports". In 2006 it was envisaged that a truly scientific system would be able to use all this data work out the best course for any individual students and then work out whether your teaching had added any value to their stay with you.

> We anticipate that more providers will include predictions from VA and DT for 16-19 learners in their tutoring, monitoring and learner support processes. The VA and DT for 16-19 learners data will also provide information on the potential grades that learners might attain which can be used to ensure that learners are enrolled on appropriate courses ...... information on effective practice in target setting with individual learners will accompany the LAT for the piloting year.

> *New Measures of Success for the Learning and Skills Sector*
> *Frequently Asked Questions (2006) Q49*

How far that has been progressed locally will vary.

On a full time college course, 'success rates' are the number of students who pass as a percentage of those who started the course (not those who remain at the end, which is only an achievement rate). For work-based learning it might be the number of achievers by the original planned date (not the number who pass several months later than intended). There is work to be done for adult students on Accreditation of Prior Experiential Learning (APEL) and on Recognising and Recording Progress and Achievement (RARPA).

Examples

Angelique: CATS show high score on NVT and medium VR. Attendance and discipline has steadily grown worse as she grew older, with poor results in year nine classwork. Her school tutor advised her to take hairdressing but she tells you at a school-based career session she wants to be an engineer. Not interested in GCSEs, she gets quite irritated when they are mentioned.

Sean: Wants to be a web designer and is certainly able to handle IT better than you are. He is withdrawn and isolated at school, with his poor VR results apparently reflected in poor scores at most tests and in most coursework. His mother claims he has always hated tests and he tries to avoid them by being ill when they take place. She also says - in front of him - that he probably won't succeed wherever he goes because he hasn't got the confidence. His Art teacher backs his application.

It could be argued that a good CAT score followed by poor SAT scores would be due to a mismatch of learning styles, unfair assessment regimes and loss of motivation. There is plenty of scope for colleges radically to improve results with a new environment and thus add value, whether in 14+ links or post 16 transitions. Sean may have been permanently damaged by his mother's insensitive behaviour and may have developed a creative relationship with software to escape from other people.

If his Art teacher can find evidence of creative flair, and the FE syllabus does not require on the first year social skills he does not possess and may not develop, he may do well, despite low point scores. But he might equally prove recalcitrant in avoiding challenges. One needs to know more.

There have been occasions when schools and other agencies were unwilling to share information about a student with the FE provider. This was often because they did not trust the interviewer to make a fair judgement, and felt that certain kinds of information would bias the chances of acceptance unreasonably. Protestations that a student was well meaning and keen masked disciplinary record, learning difficulty or criminal conviction that the teacher or probation officer thought it better not to mention as it would not matter on the new course. There was some logic to this – just as a disabled students is not obliged to declare their disability, some past records would certainly lead to unfair decisions by certain kinds of poorly trained interviewing staff.

However, just as the provider has a duty to make fair decisions, they have a right to be informed of potential support needs so that provision may be arranged properly. Trust between partners was increased in many areas as Connexions committees and IF consortia forced the pace of co-operation and forged personal and institutional links. There has always been a legal duty to provide certain kinds of information, but its value has to be carefully weighed.

The **Data Protection Act** (1998) states that data controllers have a duty to tell data subjects the purposes for which information is held and to tell them of third parties to whom it may be passed on. The DFES advised LEAs who advised schools to write to all students, and to parents of those under School Leaving Age, to tell them what is held, how it is used and who it may be given to. The **Freedom of Information Act** (FOIA, 2000) gives students the right to ask to see the records held about them by the provider. The combined effect is to make teachers much more careful about what they write, or store electronically, so that negative comments or caveats which might have been challenged will sometimes become anodyne to avoid unpleasantness.

The **Learning and Skills Act** (2000) brought Connexions into being and had to publish complex paragraphs about who was and was not permitted to obtain data on a given student. Data sharing protocols were organised. Meanwhile, disagreements could arise between admissions tutors and social worker about what ought and ought not to be disclosed before interview, retaining a delicate balance between privacy, the right to a second chance and the duty to protect others and make informed decisions.

In looking at potential applicants or new students, all teachers ought to have:

> A reference or record of achievement that may be accurate but could equally well be ill-informed or anodyne

> Point scores to be used with chances charts

> Information on Literacy and Numeracy which need to be matched with the demands of the proposed syllabus.

> A formal statement of any special educational needs. School Action (stage 2) and School Action Plus (stage 3) are part a code of practice which will mean more to a school's Special Educational Needs Co-ordinator (SENCO) than to most FE tutors, but the formal statement will be the starting point to ask either the providers' Student Support team or the school to explain further what is needed. If students are not 'statemented' but warning signs show up in screening, they may need to be formally processed to release the funding the need for support.

For 14-16 students you may have SATS scores or reading ages.

For ex-link students you have both formal results and internal contacts

You may have or request attendance patterns

You may have interview notes (also subject to the FOIA if formally part of the process)

You may already have screening results for learning support and/or learning styles.

The student may have chosen to disclose a disability, or may do so at interview.

If information is not available it is harder for you to prepare support in advance and gauge the kind of material and learning experience you need to provide. If it is, you need to use it to ensure their first few days start them in the right direction. This brings us to the problem of being a tutor and running tutorials.

Why tutorials?

Tutorials are vital to the learning process because they:

Unify the learning process, so it makes sense

Give students time to reflect on how they learn

Deal with any problems that get in the way of learning

But they only work if the tutor controls the process so that:

The time available serves a serious purpose from which neither will deviate

> There is clarity and agreement on the purpose of the exchange

Tutorials may be group or individual sessions, typically a mixture of the two. As Green (2002) explains:

> Individual tutorials can achieve a range of purposes but for most learners, on most occasions, the one-to-one tutorial offers focused time to benefit the individual's learning. In this sense the purpose relates to:
>
> Improving self-awareness
>
> Increasing self-esteem, confidence and personal growth
>
> Unlocking intrinsic motivation
>
> Promoting a commitment to change where change is needed
>
> Improving performance

The process needs to:

> Encourage personal reflection to clarify where and how progress has been made, where and how progress needs to be made.
>
> Recognise and celebrate achievements to stimulate personal confidence and growth.
>
> Promote high expectations that are challenging but not overwhelming.
> Provide support and encouragement without removing responsibility.

Help resolve conflicting priorities where change is
needed.

Help to set goals and targets.

Green (2002)

If students and tutors are both asked why they attend
tutorials, the replies are usually different, and sometime so
different it is obvious that the occasion is doomed to failure.
Indeed, it is not uncommon to hear comments that tutorials are
a waste of time – teachers do not know what to do with the
time and students can't see a result worth turning up for. The
context for tutorials is wide, but their purpose needs to be
focused. Tutorials only work when the tutor understands the
context in which the student makes decisions. This can include
a large range of factors, of many different kinds:

> financial situation, educational history, personal
> qualities, working habits, family/social situation, skills
> (including study skills); health (mental, physical)
> careers/progression, motivations; plans; personal goals,
> learning style, triggers for action etc.

Faced with such a complex set of factors, and limited time
to complete the interview, it is not unreasonable if some tutors
react by trying to simplify the exchange. But there is a major
difference between choosing a focus and just ignoring the
evidence.

There are not many one-to-ones in the average year, and
they are relatively short. They can affect the rest of the week in
terms of how well students learn, so those moments are
important. To avoid squandering them, they need to have a
clear and agreed purpose. To be practically useful, they need to
have a function that can be managed by the tutor. 'Managed
and controlled by' does not mean 'dominated by', but it does
mean organised to a successful conclusion. Think of the way
you personally prefer to be managed within the system.

The main reason tutorials fail is that they are not planned as part of a whole college policy to use information to locate, guide and support students throughout their study. 'Studying' happens in subject classes and tutorials and tacked on to do something else. If, as discussed in previous chapters, subject tutors were encouraged to use information on previous experience and learning styles and to shape their materials and teaching methods, and students were introduced to debate about how they learn anchored in examples from the syllabus, then

> Tutors would possess information that subject tutors require.

> Students would understand the reasoning behind target setting and self-monitoring.

> Both subject tutors and students would be open to more positive debate about how the learning process could be improved.

In addition to this, of course, personal or practical issues affecting individuals can also be discussed, but this is not the only, much less the main purpose of tutorial time. Part of the difficulty in managing tutorials lies in the expectation that they are for discussing personal problems in some vague and general sense, so that one hears of many cases when students argue that, not having a 'problem', they have no need to attend. A well-planned tutorial programme would have four elements, three of which are common to the institution as a whole:

> Basic information sharing as a group – often necessary during induction, although it can often be speeded up for more advanced students by using printed sheets or intranet sources. It may include careers advice and UCAS guidance, screening for learning support or facts about financial or other support services.

An introduction to thinking about learning, which may involve learning styles and/or other ways to encourage meta-cognition debates, which needs to be anchored to the main programme and inform the way it is taught. This will usually be group sessions.

Regular target setting, review and self-analysis arising from the original debate and linked to progress in the programme as a whole and implementing what was learned during previous discussion. Any personal problem that affects learning will arise in this context and it will probably be a one-to-one session.

Specific matters that affect only certain vocational areas, subjects or levels, such as help with research methods or the Harvard bibliography, advanced safety issues.

In addition to this, some students may also have personal issues that require non-academic support, and some of them may require time during or in addition to tutorial sessions to discuss those issues. This cannot be planned for and some teachers feel less confident in dealing with that personal element. Some, perhaps, are over-confident, and some spend too much time expressing sympathy without making any practical difference. It is important to know when to refer onwards to a more professional service. The tutor is thus engaged in a web of relationships that are interdependent, with

the student

the other people who teach that student

any internal agency that offers support, such as learning support tutors, personal advisers, counsellors, financial advisers etc. (your tutor's handbook ought to list them, with contact numbers, opening times and roles)

they may in turn relate to external agencies, including
schools, PRUs, probation or social services, but may do
so in confidence outside the remit of the tutorial
system

Some providers use subject tutors as class or personal tutors, and many subject specialists will therefore be responsible for a group or several groups within their vocational area. Some will use the 'supertutor' system, where a few well-trained individuals take responsibility for all tutorial sessions across the institution.

At a recent training session it emerged that one college was about to adopt that system just as another as about to abandon it. It was being abandoned because it was impossible for the small group of personal tutors to operate effectively outside the context of day-to-day subject teaching. They didn't know what was happening inside classrooms so couldn't set targets and review progress. The system did not provide information in time, partly because the subject tutors didn't prioritise it, seeing tutorials as someone else's problem and irrelevant to their issues. It was being adopted because too many subject tutors didn't know how to use tutorial time, felt it was an intrusion and were not carrying out what the provider felt to be proper tutorial functions. It is vital that all functions by any member of the provider's workforce are seen to be contributing to more efficient and effective learning, and are understood to have that as an aim, with a track record of achievement that justifies co-operation.

Whatever form tutorials take, they are not optional and will be inspected. Public funding is conditional upon them and automatically includes the expectation that tutorials take place as part of the agreed package of guided learning hours (glh) but will be identifiably different from subject teaching hours. Ofsted noted that the 29 'highly successful colleges' (the top 8% of the total inspected) had a number of factors in common, in particular, an emphasis on effective tutorial systems:

Which are well managed and consistently applied across
the institution.

Tutorials are also where regular progress reviews are
carried out and short- and long-term targets set. All
colleges take this aspect of their provision extremely
seriously and ensure that personal tutors are as expert
in this specialist work as are subject teachers. The
setting of targets is approached sensitively, but also
challenges students to exceed what is predicted:

Many students enter the college with little prior
achievement and low self-confidence. The system
identifies a minimum level to which students should
aspire, based on an analysis of their abilities, and
monitors their progress against this. Students
understand that these are minimum targets and arc
motivated to exceed them.

Ofsted (2004) WCS

They also analysed the 45 colleges who had been deemed to
fail and they were characterised by:

An inability to focus primarily on outcomes for learners
as opposed to processes and procedures ... negative
judgements centre principally on initial guidance, on in-
class learning support and on the quality of tutorials.
Initial guidance is singularly unsuccessful in that a
significant number of students in these colleges would
appear to be on the wrong courses. Interviewing and
induction are flawed. .... In these colleges, it is as if
there is an understanding of what should be done, and
correct procedures are largely followed, but there is
then a lack of resolve about carrying things through.

The recording of tutorials is varied; few set challenging
and measurable targets. Tutorials do not identify

sufficiently the learning needs of students, and individual target-setting and progress monitoring are unsatisfactory. In institutions such as these, where there is no shared understanding of the primacy of students' achievements, it is not surprising that target-setting is neither precise nor evaluated regularly. Nor is it surprising, therefore, that an unacceptably high proportion of students fail.   DfES (2004) WCF

Forms are filled in, routines followed, but nothing happens that makes any difference. If a system does not work it has to be changed. If it is just ignored or paid lip service then it becomes systematic sabotage of both teacher and student, whose time is wasted because they do not take seriously or apply rigorously a system that is supposed to support them.

Individual learning plans (ILP), lesson plans, schemes of work, tutorial report forms and the rest of them are supposed to record briefly a process of thinking which affects learning. If they only take up time and prevent you from thinking about learning, they are badly designed or poorly understood or badly implemented. It is not easy to design a record system that reflects reality. How do you prove something actually happened in the student mind? Often, it is only by recording their success, and your contribution to added value. A sympathetic hearing that does not help them pass the course is recorded as part of a failure, and rightly so. Trying and failing may be understandable sometimes, but it can never be good enough. FE has been too understanding of its own weaknesses, and too quick to accept those of its raw material. The ideal tutorial process uses sympathetic understanding to encourage rigour. It is still too common to observe unsympathetic or overly-indulgent and ill-informed activity that produces paperwork but little else. Subject tutors need to learn more about how students learn, perhaps by asking them, and how to use the information provided for them to inform a rational debate about how to improve learning.

It should be obvious from previous chapters that there is much which could usefully be more openly discussed between tutor and student, not least the very idea of what 'learning' actually means, and how it differs from merely being present and handing in work.

Learners' expectations of College are based on:

> previous learning experiences
> open days
> prospectus/information sheets
> interviews
> experiences/opinions of peers

What were their expectations? Do they have reasons to be confused or disappointed? Do they know and understand your expectations? Did you clearly explain, and check they understood, the expected patterns of:

> work (content, pattern, standard)
> behaviour and responsibilities (yours and theirs)
> set rules and any system for rewards or sanctions

Were these in course information sheets, induction talks, student charter, mutually evolved class agreements stuck to the wall? Were you very clear about what will happen if things don't go to plan?

> Strategies for getting back on track
> Sanctions for poor behaviour

Before engaging them with a scheme of work or lesson, subject tutors need to be clear about the aims of the activity. Do they share those aims? Planning and preparation are important – you need a game plan and need to share it with the students, so they can adopt it.

Of course, the workspace in college is a social situation. The group reacts to each other and their surroundings, to demands made upon them by the system and the tutor. One way to avoid unwanted behaviour is to remove by good planning anything that might cause it. How well did you know the students before you met them, and what kind of planning could you make? What did you know about:

> previous learning experiences
> social skills
> basic skills
> financial pressure
> parental/family/relationship pressure
> other commitments?

Admissions interviews, induction, subject teaching and tutorials and not separable elements. They may be done by different people who never talk to each other, but for the student they are all part of a single experience. The institution acts and they integrate the experience before they react. The student may be the only person who really understands why the institution does not provoke a better response, because only they actually know what the institution as a whole is 'saying' to them.

Tutoring skills

It is often argued that the skills which make for a good tutor are not the same as those which define a good teacher. That may depend on how you define teaching. If teaching is putting on a show and tutoring is quietly listening then it may be true, but that begs several questions.

Certainly, there are skills that any teacher may need to hone in a tutorial context, and others that only some people are likely to deploy successfully. Smart targets are in the former category, motivational interviewing in the latter.

If targets are to be set for students, they need to be

specific - they say exactly what has to be achieved

measurable – students can prove they have achieved them

achievable – they can be achieved in a realistic time frame

realistic - they are within the limits of the student's potential

time-related - they have deadlines (when is the next review, or deadline for the work due and how will progress be monitored?

Whilst this usually sounds pretty obvious, the following as targets set during tutorials in a single college which have clearly missed the point and thus wasted contact time.

Target	Action Plan to achieve it
Understanding the requirements of various course work more	Listening
As previous	Continue with this course *(this entry appeared on four students' IPRs, identically, in sequence)*
Getting up to date	Time management
Complete nine practical assessments	Achieve smart target
Keeping on track	Avoiding distraction
Pass the course	Work harder
Complete portfolio	Finish outstanding assignments

<table>
<tr><td>Complete the course</td><td>Maintain progress</td></tr>
</table>

That fills in the paperwork, but it won't change anything. Setting targets which mean something within the realms of possible student action will clearly take some practice. But if that is how they relate to students as tutors, how do they manage their classes? Are projects and day-to-day directions equally vague?

Some students, of course, seem positively addicted to the kind of behaviour that undermines their chances of success. It is not uncommon for subject tutors to hope that tutorials will address it for them, whilst students in tutorials list the shortcomings of their subject tutors. Both usually have a point to make, placing the personal tutor in a difficult position. In this context, the term 'addiction' may be the clue, and motivational interviewing may be deployed by those who are capable of using it.

Motivational interviewing is particularly useful when students suffer from:

> poor classroom behaviour

> frustration or concern about their future prospects

> low self-esteem

> low confidence in their ability to meet the course requirements

Developed by William R. Miller, Professor of Psychology and Psychiatry at New Mexico and Stephen Rollnick, Professor of Healthcare Communication at Cardiff University, the technique was originally for developing behavioural self-control with addicts. Faced with clients addicted to alcohol, drugs and other self-destructive behaviours they asked "what interventions by well-meaning others might actually work?"

You would think that having a heart attack would persuade a person to stop smoking, but it often doesn't. You might expect that hangovers and blackouts would persuade a person to moderate their drinking, but it doesn't. You might hope that low grades, disciplinary measures and the threat of expulsion would persuade a student to behave differently, but often it doesn't.

Looked at this way, dysfunctional behaviour is an addiction, making typical addict's responses:

> I would like to improve but don't know how
> I will improve later but right now I'm busy
> I don't need to improve
> I don't see the point in trying

Trying to teach whilst the addiction remains as an active hindrance is often pointless. In fact, the student may already feel that attack is the best form of defence:

> It is better to refuse than try and fail
> It is better to be expelled than to stay and look stupid
> If you can't do it, keep quiet and they may not notice, or care enough to chase you

Stages in the change process therefore that the student is able, in sequence, to:

> Recognise the problem
> Care about the problem
> Form an intention to change
> Feel that change is really possible (optimism is a learning tool)
> Commit to a realistic target
> Reinforce that target by checking progress and receiving support

Forming the intention is the first stage, and requires that students actually mean what they say, rather than agree to something to shut you up and get out of the room. The aim of motivational interviewing is not to reason or persuade a student into immediate full-scale change but to enhance their motivation to change. They have to talk themselves in to it, so it is **their** intention.

The dialogue requires 'reflective listening' – the ability to check rather than assuming that you know what is meant. Accurate empathy means knowing what they mean, not what you thought they said. The client/student has to be led to a point where they formulate and accept goals and in such cases mere rational argument is completely pointless. They have to be drawn, not pushed.

It is therefore logical that proper **self-assessment** must precede any other activity.

Some providers like to use self-assessment sheets that link closely to appraisal systems and even grading criteria (on a scale of A* to G, how good are you at x?) but in the early stages it is important to establish that part of a tutorial's function is to build confidence, so it is worth looking for ways to give praise and build self-esteem in more general terms, as well as asking the leading questions that will inform dialogue later in one-to-one sessions. For example:

Can you name a challenge you have overcome?

Can you name a quality you are proud of?

Can you name a skill you have?

followed by

What is your hope for the future?

Is there anything that worries you about the course?

Is there anything you know you need to improve?

It is probably less useful to offer a list of 'qualities' for them to choose from, as with this example -

Honest	Reliable	Good talker	Willing to learn
Polite	Happy	Outgoing	Patient
Noisy	Calm	Short tempered	Enthusiastic
Creative	Ambitious	Confident	Shy
Sarcastic	Practical	Sensitive	Willing to try new things
Helpful	Caring	Kind	Learn from criticism
Dislike criticism	Easy going	Sporty	Good humoured

It looks more like a test with right and wrong answers, so encourages the responder to adopt a suitably impressive facade, and the choice looks like somebody's implicit model for an ideal student, with no chance to question it. On the other hand, some group discussion about what qualities make a good student or prevent learning might be useful as a catalyst.

There may be dissonance between the self-image and the facts of the matter. You can't engage in proper dialogue if you don't start with where the student thinks they are – however mistaken you may think they are. If your own assessment seems alien it will be assumed by them to be wrong. This raises the problem of questioning methods. There are several to consider, but note that tone of voice can be the most important factor in success or failure, whatever the technique.

General principles

You need to allow the student to do most of the thinking, but to use questions to control the evolution of their thoughts. If you confront them you almost inevitably invite them to adopt an opposing perspective, so you need to avoid wasting time on exhausting arguments that will not actually affect behaviour. If you sound as if you have all the answers, the person you are talking to will fall into a passive role and will not work on his/her own to explore and resolve ambivalence. Preaching is even less use than mere reasoning.

Sample exchanges about persistent lateness

1) Do you see a pattern in your lateness?
No.
Would you like to look at the register?
No

Even if they do look (is it confidential?) they will take ages arguing over small details and they can point out they are not the worst in the class anyway…...wasted time.

2) What about your attendance?
What about it?
Is there anything you need to consider?
No.
Are you always on time?
When the buses aren't late and my mum doesn't throw a wobbly when I'm about to leave the house.

Option a –

What was the wobbly about?
Not telling whether this will lead to useful info but they might be waiting to be asked so they can lead you to what they see as

---

a major problem. Will it be more or less important than their lateness?

Option b -

Are the buses often late?
How often have I been late? That's how often. They're crap, but I can't run the bus company?
Given that buses are not reliable, what are the options here? Buy a car?

Might eventually lead to acceptance of an earlier bus and more generous margins, but might also lead to more nit-picking around timetables that you don't have and can't check. If you're going for this, make sure of the facts first and have their address and options in front of you, otherwise it wastes time and you cannot win.

3) How's the attendance problem?
I haven't got a problem.
What's your reputation like for attending on time?

The change of terminology throws them away from facts they can argue about and on to their public image. They can be defensive but not so confident. It would be easy and unproductive to point out that reputations affect references that affect futures. They know that, so it can hang in the air for a while.

Mostly I haven't got a problem, it only that Git Parsons who keeps on about it - always nagging me.
When do you meet that particular person?
Monday morning, Tuesday morning. Wednesday afternoon.
And your disagreements happen in every class?
Mainly Mondays. And Tuesdays.

They will now have to admit a rational reason for 'nagging' Small progress towards accepting that there is a problem and they own it.

Look for the underlying meaning of what is being said and reflect this back to the person. Focus on how the person is feeling, which may be masked by an act they are trying to put on. Avoid labelling and blaming – who is to blame and labels like 'troublemaker' are not to the point here. They get in the way of real reflection. A major contributor to poor effort may be poor self-esteem. This may be a realistic reaction to their daily experience, so you won't find reasons for optimism in their class. In the short term, this interview may be the only source.

Avoid using questions that will elicit a short answer. This prevents elaboration and exploration. (e.g. "Tell me more about these difficulties" as opposed to "Have you had difficulties with this?").

Use two-sided reflections in order to highlight ambivalence. For example, "So, on the one hand, you say smoking makes you feel more relaxed, but on the other hand, you know that it upsets your family and it's not good for your health."

Summarise key statements. Connect motivationally relevant material, allowing the individual to hear their own words and thoughts again.

Create the sense that you are supportive. Reinforce important statements with reflective listening and support. But also be willing to refer onwards if the problem if beyond your skill level.

And that is so because?

Few things are more annoying than being asked for reasons, but if they are genuine rather that rhetorical questions they can lead eventually to discovery:

> I'm usually on time with work but only sometimes I'm late.
> *When you're late it is because....?*
> Well, I didn't have time to finish it?
> *Because?*

Option A – I was busy at work or looking after my
brother or ill or whatever but that will eventually lead
to......
Option B – I didn't have a safety margin because I
didn't start it early enough, because I am not in the
habit of planning for possible problems.

Devil's advocate

The wrong way:

> *How is your portfolio this week?*
> OK.
> *Is there an index and a set of dividers like we discussed as a*
> *target last week?*
> Well, no but….
> *So we'll put it in as it is and just hope they won't mind.*
> Well, no but...
> *And if there's no dividers it doesn't matter about the label being*
> *tatty - we'll just tell them you were busy and they won't mind. Is*
> *that OK with you?*

That sounds like sarcasm, which is not the same thing. Tone of
voice can be the most important factor in success or failure.

The right way:

> And I'm just so fed up with my Dad telling me what to
> do all the time, like I'm some obedient old-fashioned
> girl from some bloody village.
> *Why don't you leave home?*
> Can't afford it, can I?
> *You could go to a hostel.*
> Like a battered wife. Not really. They're horrible places.
> *Then tell him to be quiet.*
> What? He'd go mental!
> *So what are your options then?*

(a bit of tact until you can afford to leave, or accept the
hostel – is it a serious problem or not? If not, move on,
the excuse is not valid.)

Reframing

This is the ability to acknowledge the validity of their
observation but to give it a new meaning:

> And I'm just so fed up with that maths tutor always
> getting on at me.
> *What do you mean by "getting on"?*
> Always moaning at me to finish stuff and moaning it
> isn't good enough.
> *(You could argue that is his job, but that won't wash. What if he
> has some annoying mannerisms that even you find irritating and
> you wouldn't want to be in the student's position? But you have
> professional loyalty.)*
> *It can be annoying when people keep on about deadlines and
> standards, especially if you're doing your best. But it's a lot worse
> if they don't care. If you had to choose between being hassled and
> being ignored, what would you go for?*
> (They'll probably say 'being ignored' but won't entirely
> mean it.)

Social judo

Ordinary judo has a simple basis. You don't push a strong
opponent. You encourage him to push you, then pull him that
way until he falls. Social judo encourages a student to take their
own argument to its logical conclusion so they can perceive its
essential absurdity. Miller and Rollnick give an example of a
counsellor dealing with a heavy drinker

> C: *What other concerns might you have right now?*
> P: (appearing unconcerned) Well, I'm told my liver's
> damaged.

C: (clearly objective tone) Does that concern you?
P: Pardon?
C: Does that concern you?
P: (with a slight frown) Yes.
C: Why?
P: What? What do you think? It's obvious. I'm going to die,
you (expletive) idiot. Look, if I don't do something about
my drinking I'm going to die. Do you think I want that? Of
course I don't. I'm going to have to do something.

Miller and Rollnick (1991) p242

Of course, this kind of approach would make a large
difference to the American context, where previous regimes
had tried to use 'tough love' and shout them into behavioural
change, as if the army were a good model for clinical practice.
Some students, used to a liberal UK regime, will be used to
manipulating well-meaning teachers. But the best response I
have seen to angry students who have been sent in a rage to the
main office after a row with a tutor was to apologise for the
fact they have been upset. "I'm sorry someone upset you,
Jason, now sit down and let's talk about it." They were
expecting a telling off and all geared up for it. By apologising,
the tutor puts them off their stroke. That calms them down (no
need to use aggression as a defence mechanism) and then they
can accept they were wrong.

Normalise ambivalence – accept it as normal and work towards tipping the balance

There is no point arguing that something has to be done and
is important if they feel afraid of doing it. We need to accept
that fear is overwhelming at first and discuss the real possibility
of not doing it, before leading them back to attempting it,
because of the balance of consequences. This means briefly
accepting the possibility of failure because, realistically, that is
where they are most of the time. That is the starting point, but

a hope for success has to be added to it.

An important part of tutorial work may be deal-making. You work out the relative positions of all parties, work out what is possible and persuade them to agree to a deal. It may be imperfect, but it will be the best you can get and will represent real progress, on which you can build. Deal-making is a tough business. Handling students to effect change takes more than tea and sympathy.

Prochaska and DiClemente (1986) developed a useful five-stage model of the process, which has been modified below to include a sixth stage – relapse. When changing behaviours, students might relapse and return to an earlier stage several times before they achieve their goals. Each time this happens they will gain new information about their behaviour and will be able to apply that information in the next attempt.

Pre-contemplation Stage – the student does not believe they have a problem or does not want to change.

During pre-contemplation the disadvantages of change outweigh advantages. You may be concerned about some consequence of your student's poor behaviour, but the student may accept this as okay for them.

Commonly, there is resistance to 'action oriented interventions' and explanations about how to 'behave properly', but relevant information about the student's career goals or the consequences of 'dropping out', and how to avoid this, may be well received.

Use motivational interviewing to help the student explore the advantages and disadvantages of 'being a student'

Contemplation Stage - the student is beginning to evaluate their use and starts to think about change.

The balance of costs and benefits begin to shift, although the student may appear not interested in change. 'I should give up because of all the problems. But what am I going to do instead? I'll miss it and my friends.'

You need to explore this ambivalence using motivational interviewing.

Determination Stage (Readiness to change) - the student decides they do want to change their approach to their studies.

The balance has shifted. The student is preparing to take action and has confidence in their capacity to change. Change is seen as worthwhile. This is often a planning stage. Goal setting, identifying internal and external supports/resources and identifying strategies to support change can help.

Action Stage - -the student changes by adopting a different attitude or conforming to class rules and expected standards. The student is taking steps to change. Support and 1:1 coaching can be provided. Review initial reasons that led to the decision to change.

Maintenance Stage - the student keeps to the class rules or complies with the tutor's instructions.

Changes in behaviour are maintained for several weeks and months and are usually associated with substantial improvements in the student's experience of college life (e.g. tutor relationships, student relationships, improved self-esteem and recognition, better use of college facilities and opportunities). Without such changes, the effort to change may not seem worth it and relapse is more likely.

Encourage students to talk about the positive reasons for maintaining change to reinforce their decisions.

Relapse - the student returns to their previous behaviour.

This is when the student has returned to their previous disruptive or inappropriate behaviour after a period of change. It can be a one off incident or could be a regular occurrence. It is quite common.

Your role is to assist the person to see it as a learning experience, to assess their motivation to change and to develop strategies to overcome the issues involved with going back to their past bad habits.

Other techniques to consider in motivational interviewing include 'scaling questions', to agree the importance of separate issues:

> On a scale of 0-5 how important is it for you to attend lessons?

> On a scale of 0-5 how confident are you about doing well?

You will also need questions to allow the student to build confidence in their ability to change:

> *In the past, what has been helpful when you have tried to finish an assignment?*

Remember that goals will motivate if they are achievable at this stage of development. They need to be negotiated so they are accepted as personal actions by the student who owns them, which may mean making small steps at first towards an eventual minimum condition for passing or remaining on course. They need to be positive (more attendance rather than fewer absences).

Chapter 7

Equal opportunities

> Much concern is expressed about the under-achievement of boys relative to girls. However, other Skills for All research pointed to a disastrous marginalisation or exclusion from the labour market of young women with no GCSE qualifications. The outcome for such young women was considerably worse than for young men. Are 14-16 girls, particularly those having difficulty with basic skills, benefiting to the same extent as 14-16 boys from interventions to raise achievements?
>
> Steedman (2004) p5

> The medical profession is in danger of losing its power and influence because too many women are scaling its ranks, according to the head of Britain's most influential Royal Medical College.
>
> Independent 2nd August 2004

> There is a world of difference between, on the one hand, offering courses of education and training and then giving some students who have learning difficulties some additional human or physical aids to gain access to those courses, and, on the other hand, redesigning the very process of learning, assessment and organisation so as to fit the objectives and learning styles of the students.
>
> FEFC (1996) 4

The arguments have been going on for decades. So, after all the fuss, with the Equality Act working its way into our daily practice[32], what would success actually look like in the context of "equal opportunities"?

---

[32] http://www.legislation.gov.uk/ukpga/2010/15/contents

In what sense, if any, can people be said to be 'equal'? They don't have equal ability or levels of effort. They don't necessarily have an equal right to be in your class – it may not be the right place for them, however much they would like to think so. But they do have the right to be treated fairly. What does that mean?

In the 21st Century there are established legal frameworks to ensure that FE institutions relate to their communities in ways that are not unfair or discriminatory, not even by default or from ignorance. The Disability Discrimination Act Part 4 (Special Educational Needs and Discrimination Act or SENDA, 2001), The LSC's Equality and Diversity Strategy 2002 and the DfES Skills Strategy 2003 all insisted that educational opportunities ought not to be denied to any member of the community by virtue of the laziness, ignorance, incompetence or lack of thought or reasonable adjustment of the local providers. The Equality Act listed protected characteristics[33] and contains an 'Equality Duty' to

> eliminate unlawful discrimination, harassment and victimisation and any other conduct prohibited by the Act

> advance equality of opportunity between people who share a protected characteristic and people who do not share it

> foster good relations between people who share a protected characteristic and people who do not share it

For managers, there are implications for the way the college is run, and these are treated separately in the companion text,

---

[33] Age, disability, gender reassignment, marriage and civil partnership (but only in respect of eliminating unlawful discrimination), pregnancy and maternity, race – this includes ethnic or national origins, colour or nationality, religion or belief – this includes lack of belief, sex, sexual orientation

Managing Teachers in FE. For teachers, there are implications for the way classes are run. Some of these are obvious, whilst others are not. It is easier to say what it means to be treated unfairly than to be treated 'equally', as 'equal' usually becomes a controversial terms whilst 'fair' is a word more easily understood and applied.

The student experience

Decades before these acts came into force, well-meaning teachers in London were trying to ensure that teenage students who happened to be black did not receive any unfair or unequal treatment from their schools or colleges. One of the teachers was showing a group of visitors round their school and explaining how they had adjusted the curriculum to reflect ethnic diversity. Images were carefully monitored to avoid having all white faces and books by African authors had been introduced to avoid an unfair or exclusive focus on 'dead white males' as the only cultural icons worth taking seriously.

Taken to one side for an informal chat, some black female teenagers were asked how they felt about these efforts to 'include' them. "It ain't me", they said. They explained they were not African but born in London and proud of it. They wanted to get a proper education, by which they meant access to the stuff that was traditionally considered proper literature. They felt condescended to, and somewhat excluded, because they were being fed on a diet of 'foreign' authors. African literature was only of any interest to white liberal teachers, not to black teenage Londoners.

There are many questions begged in this small anecdote. The African author Chinua Achebe has since been on the A level syllabus, and the first thing you notice when reading the set text is an epigraph from Yeats. Achebe directs our attention to African experience and makes a claim for an African 'literature' in the European sense of the word, whilst simultaneously making it clear he has mastered the European canon. The message the teacher wanted to send was that black writers were of equal merit. The message received was that black students were excluded from studying white writers, and they resented being treated as different. He tried to be fair; they felt unequal. He tried to 'include' them but in his haste to be fair he had not bothered to listen to them. That is not to say that other students from ethnic minorities might not appreciate having their world mirrored in the teaching material and their culture validated by being included. But we do not treat people equitably by making unwarranted assumptions about them.

Youth culture is now pervaded by an international and largely non-white patois, with urban whites sounding vaguely West Indian to try to fit in. Classes are full of Ali-G wannabes, hoodied and blinged. What has 'authority' within our culture is a complex question and what counts as 'including' can be too superficially defined. From a practising teacher's point of view, less time will be wasted if we start by asking what kind of action or omission might be excluding and unreasonable, and it would be useful to start by moving the focus away from the obvious clichés attached to notions of race and gender. Some of them, for example the assumption that black males achieve less well in educational contexts, could too easily become self-fulfilling prophecies. An expectation of achievement may be the most significant factor in assuring it. Also, of course, we need to keep up with our data - by 2008 it was being argued that poor white males were most likely to leave at 16 and black males are closing the GCSE gap.

It is not so long ago - and certainly within living memory of some senior citizens - that left handed students in schools learned to become right handed by having their left arm tied behind their back. More recently, we have learned to accept that left handed students may be left in peace, although most tools and keyboards are still designed for right handed users. Mostly, we never think about that. They just learn to manage. There is, of course, a supplier who can solve the problem with specialist adaptions[34], so a small amount of effort and some cash will make the world as accessible for left-handers as for right-handers. The only question is how much effort and cash we wish to put into the problem, instead of asking them to adapt to us.

Providing equal opportunities to learn is not about treating people the same. It is about treating them in ways that suit their learning needs, so they are equally able to learn. Equal Opportunity means treating people differently so they have equal access to learning chances, but doing so with sensitivity and in consultation.

It maybe you had never thought about left handed students. What about tall students or short students? I once taught a secretarial student who was so small she needed a special chair and cushion to access the keyboard, and disappeared behind the reception desk until adjustments were made. Physical adjustments were easy. More difficult was to stop staff from being so worried about saying the wrong thing ("is it insulting to use the word dwarf?") that their tone or expression implied unease and made her feel she was causing discomfort by being there.

How do teachers with limited experience react to students with limited mobility or hearing or sight or reading ability, students with strong regional accents or unusual personal beliefs or green eyes or red hair? When does a difference become an impediment in its own right, and not just because you choose to mention it too often? How many kinds of difference can one practitioner reasonably deal with in such a way that the learning experience is fairly available to all?

What is fair?

Eric was a student on a level 2 English course that involved an oral presentation to the class. He was also an evangelical

---

34 See bpfe.org.uk/links

Christian, so he spent his time telling the others about the love of God and how Jesus could save you from sin. He was failed because (a) his sermon was not well structured and (b) he had clearly not considered the needs of his audience, one of whom led a local Jewish youth club and was not at all happy to be subjected to it.

Eric appealed against the decision on the grounds it was unfair and he was being denied free speech. It was upheld on the grounds that oral presentations were not to be used to insist unreasonably on beliefs that, in Popperian terms, could not be falsified. A case was also cited where a student insisted on the veracity of alien abductions in ways that did not allow the audience to engage in reasoned debate.

In both cases, it was not the belief but the manner of its presentation that was failed. Both students remained convinced they had been discriminated against by unbelievers who would not allow them a fair hearing.

This was in the days before the Darwin vs Genesis debate had started to affect UK schools, and before an Academy the UK suggested to its students that Hitler was defeated by an act of God.[35]

'Equal opportunities' does not mean that all teachers should be able to teach everybody equally well, with equal outcomes, regardless of their background, social or behavioural problems or any disability. We all have different talents and limitations, and to try to undertake a task for which you are not trained or temperamentally suited would be to let down the person you

---

[35] Emmanuel College in Gateshead, sponsored by the Vardy Foundation, which was led by an evangelist (TES July 23 2004 p3). Note also TES March 18th 2005. p6, on the bid for schools by Exclusive Brethren through Focus Learning Trust. FE Focus 13th Jan 2003 Bill Rammel suggested a chaplain in every college would help students explore their spirituality. If that question came to public prominence now, would the same result be supported?

try to help. It **does** mean that nobody should be unreasonably denied access to the learning experiences you offer to others. In other words,

> nobody should be denied access to your class or course because you have not made the necessary effort to try to accommodate them by informing yourself of their difficulties and potential solutions and,

> once in your class, nobody should learn less than the others because you do not make the necessary effort to accommodate their difficulties.

To fail to make a reasonable effort is not only unprofessional but often illegal. To pretend you can solve all problems for all applicants is irresponsible. How can you steer a sensible course between these extremes?

The obvious starting place is to look back at previous chapters. If the student files describe or even imply information about a condition that might affect learning chances then it would be unprofessional not to look into that question before the class starts. You may need to take advice, become informed, obtain specialist equipment or support. You may not, but if you didn't ask you are not making a reasonable attempt to ensure equality of opportunity. It may be something as simple as remembering that some students will be hungry and less able to concentrate during Ramadan, or auditing your material so it portrays a world the students would recognise, with names, pronouns problems and practical contexts that are drawn from their world and not that of the teacher of a previous group.

If you and the student are in personal contact before the academic year – perhaps during interviews or information days – then you may give them opportunities to declare a potential barrier so you can act in time. Some pro-formas that guide interviewing procedures will ask students to declare any disability, but equally some students will fail to declare it because (a) they fear it will lead to non-acceptance or (b) they feel it is personal and best kept private to avoid discrimination. It is therefore even more important that conversation about learning during the early stages of the course will encourage them to talk positively about how they will manage their own learning process, and what kinds of actions on both your parts would make it easier. What was kept private during interview may emerge when talking about meta-cognition, because the context and tone allows for disclosure.

Chapter 3 explored the problems of differentiation, and clarified some of the ways you can inform yourself of important differences between students. Whether it is reading age, gender, learning style, previous experience of education or cultural background, you are aware that materials and techniques need to be developed on the basis that people are different, and your teaching must allow for those differences if you are not to find yourself helping only a small minority of the group for whom you are responsible. It also made clear that the process of allowing for such differences will often enliven and simplify the process even for the minority that might just have coped anyway. Good teaching will automatically allow for many differences. Good class management will discover those which require particular effort, and seek out advice. There are further external sources below, although your student support service would normally be the first port of call, and probably know about those sources already.

Self-awareness, or mindfulness, is the *sine qua non* of good teaching, and all that is required to fulfil your professional obligations is to ensure that you understand what is possible, what is within the range of a reasonable person who wishes to help the community to learn. That will also cover your legal duty, if you and the courts can agree on what we mean by 'reasonable'.

What is reasonable?

Marlene enrolled in a construction skills class as a link student from school aged 15. She was the only girl. Her father was a builder. At 16 she wanted to gain an apprenticeship elsewhere so she could eventually come back and take over the family firm. The local admissions tutor argued in private that no construction firm would take on a 16 year old girl so he would be wasting his time in asking them. He knew he could not refuse her on those grounds, so combed her file seeking other reasons. She did not know this.

.. the majority of employers (70%) agreed that recruiting more young people of the non-traditional sex into their sectors would help solve skills shortages.....71% thought (it) would be good for business (but) there were fewer career opportunities for female ex-apprentices in the male-dominated sectors - Fuller et al 2005

Some customers in diverse households are happier to have tradeswomen in their home.... women tended to have communication and interpersonal skills that enable business to be more competitive (but) women found it much harder ... to secure work experience placements....faced overt and covert discrimination ... laughed at ... bullied ... given the worst jobs to do...
Dale et al (2005)

The admissions tutor may be right in his analysis, but is acting illegally. Local employers might be unusually unwilling, but how far is it reasonable to assume a negative response and by doing so reinforce the tendency? When is realism a name for laziness? On the other hand, students trying to force the pace in gender atypical training are more likely to leave under pressure (see Evans et al 2003). When Marlene enrolled, was any attention paid to the problem of progression? If not, was that ground-breaking or irresponsible?

Julie enrolled as one of several 16 year old girls in motor vehicle. The general conversation among the male students could sometimes be crude and lascivious. This was no different to their general conversation in school and in social environments – it defined their social group. The course tutor argued that most garages were likely to be the same, so if Julie wanted to make a living in them she would have to toughen up and deal with the vocational culture. The same argument defended the soft-porn calendar hanging in the tool cupboard. The tutor was undergoing a divorce at the time. For Christmas, to cheer him up, the male students presented him with a blow-up woman. He taped up her mouth and hands and hung her from the office wall. It stayed there for two weeks until a senior student counsellor made him take it down. Julie never complained about it.

There are mentoring systems to help young women who find it hard to cope with the aggressively old-fashioned 'maleness' of certain occupational cultures. There is a case to be made for warning Julie what she may have to face when seeking work, but none at all for behaving in a college in ways that might give offence or cause distress (calendar) and the almost incredibly insensitive example of the hanging doll is included here just to show how far some tutors can transgress without realising the distance they have travelled from what is reasonable in an educational (or any) environment.

Ludmilla suffered from a number of physical illnesses during her first term on the Psychology Access course. She was having difficulty with her written English so the tutor arranged learning support. She had difficulty understanding the basic principles of a research project, so a mentor was arranged from the local university. She was absent for illness so often she fell behind. More mentoring time was requested, but refused for lack of budget. She could not complete the work and left.

Mentors can help within reason, but should not be asked to deal with situations that demand counselling or try to make up for poor teaching or bad management. On the face of it, Ludmilla was enrolled for a course for which she was not suited – an unfair act if perhaps well-intended. Her chances were never equal, and it may be that no attempt to help would have made them so. The unreasonable act was to accept her, and to ask a mentor to solve the ensuing problem. To set students a task they cannot achieve is not fair or productive (see Maslow in Chapter 5). If they are in a class where they cannot reasonably be expected to succeed, then arranging more support may only compound the problem.

Charles enrolled as a post-graduate on a journalism course within FE. His physical disability, which became worse during the second term, made it difficult for him to gain regular access to the college's computer systems on the seventh floor of a tower block. This made it hard to complete the course. His tutor arranged for Student Support to supply a special computer at his home, so he could word process his submissions and email then. It was designed so it only accepted the programmes needed for the course, delivered and installed by the tutor. When the course was officially over, Charles asked for an extension because he had been ill.

Providing the technology was reasonable, and funds exist to cover it. How far any illness can excuse later delivery is an individual question, but if the course is to prepare for a career as a journalist, it is questionable whether too much sympathy would be unrealistic. Stephen Hawking writes books. If the technology exists, why can't this student get the work in?

A member of College X visited school Y to explain the range of options for 14-16 year old students. He was told by a female careers adviser there were 'not enough options for girls', by which she meant that she wanted lots more hairdressing places and not so many in engineering.

> Fewer than a third of Pathfinders reported
> interventions relating to gender issues
>
> Haynes et al (2005)

> Employers believed that schools ... do not encourage
> young people to apply to non-traditional sectors.
>
> Fuller et al (2005)

To pander to the call for more hairdressing places would be unreasonable, unless there were a demonstrable shortage in the area. That is unlikely. But to offer only engineering to try to force the pace of change in society is also unreasonable. How do you balance consumer demand against labour market information against your own views of what makes for a civilised society?

> EBP managers and work-experience co-ordinators
> tended to see their priority in provision of choice for
> pupils, rather than widening opportunities or addressing
> workforce issues. Francis et al (2005)

It is easier to try to give people what they want, but it is irresponsible not to try to widen their range of potential requests, to open their eyes to new possibilities. The college's job here is to help the school to engage with employers to educate both staff and students about potential markets.

A gay male mature student was placed in a class with adolescent males. He complained about homophobic bullying. Students called each other 'gay' when they meant 'weak' of 'useless' and an empty wrapper from a fudge bar had been left on his desk (with apparent reference to a slang term for male homosexuals). The Head of Dept. called in the young males complained of and was worried because they were among his best students, whom he and the course tutor thought unlikely to be guilty of deliberate bullying, but at the same time he wanted to be fair to the complainant and to be seen to take his complaint seriously.

The formal evidence was not enough for decisive action either way. Using the word 'gay' in a generally derogatory sense is so common among adolescents that, although offensive in its effect, it was used in innocence of any bullying intent in that instance. As part of the formal hearing, it was necessary to discuss in detail how meanings were generated by listeners not by speakers, and to explain to the young males the difference between what they thought, what they said and what other may assume they thought. They were then able to apologise for any unintended offence and to accept a request not to repeat it even by accident. Whatever their real intentions, their behaviour in college could then be monitored on the basis of a new set of rules that all sides agreed to be 'fair'.

The problem here may or may not have been one of generation and not of sexual orientation and homophobia. It is not always easy to separate out individual factors when asking why some people do less well or feel less welcome.

> It is difficult to separate factors such as ethnicity from social class from religion from the effects of subtle or overt racism   Modood and May 2001

Nor is it easy to act 'fairly' at all times. If boys do less well than girls in certain educational environments it may be partly because they let the girls offer the answers and never feel the need to put up their hand. That means they never feel the need to formulate possible answers, so they focus less on what is said and how it might be translated into their own words. It would be fairer to make them join in by directing questions to them. A campaign of sustained victimisation would render the learning experience more equal.

Part of Equal Opportunities work is to strive to create a culture free of racism and other forms of prejudice – which asks more of the college than is achieved by the society it supposedly reflects. Given the range of differences to allow for and respond to, it asks more of staff members than is asked of any other citizen on a regular basis. Racial diversity can increase homophobia, as 'batty boys' are mocked by rap songs. Social diversity increases racism if the new intake are poor whites who think all the council houses went to asylum seekers. One of the many ways teachers continue to learn in their chosen profession is to discover more each year and more about how diverse our society really is, how many different ways a person can be disadvantaged within it, how little we seem to do to understand and to help each other and how, if you read the papers, it is often all our fault. You don't have to accept the blame to know you can contribute to the solution, nor solve everything to feel you are making progress.

Teaching is changing society one person at a time.

That's a long job. But very satisfying.

Good luck.

Bibliography

Ainley 2005	*For Free Universities* Inaugural Lecture by Professor Patrick Ainley Greenwich University 19th January 2005 Isbn 1 86166 210 6 published by marketing office Uni of Greenwich
Ali 2004 and 2005	*Adult Learning Inspectorate* *Annual Report of the Chief Inspector 2003-4 or 2004-5*
ALI 2004 (b)	*Creating a virtuous circle - Successful provision in Business Administration, Management and Professional* National survey report 2004
Ashcroft and James ed (1999)	*The Creative Professional – Learning to Teach 14-19 year olds* Ed. Kate Ashcroft and David James, Falmer Press, ISBN 0750 707402
Ausubel (1963)	Ausubel, D. (1963). *The Psychology of Meaningful Verbal Learning.* New York: Grune & Stratton.
Ausubel (1978)	Ausubel, D. (1978). *In defense of advance organizers: A reply to the critics.* Review of Educational Research, 48, 251-257.
Barnes 1975	*From Communication to Curriculum* Douglas Barnes Penguin 1975
Becker et al 1968	*Making the Grade; the academic side of college life.* H Becker, B Geer, E Hughes 1968 USA John Wiley
Birminghn am 2003	*A study of children and young people who present challenging behaviour,* School of Education, The University of Birmingham, directed by Dr John Visser Senior Lecturer in Special Education, November 2003.
BMA 2006	*Child and Adolescent Mental Health – a guide for healthcare professionals.*
Bruner (1967)	*Toward a theory of Instruction.* Cambridge, Mass. Harvard Uni Press 1967
Coffield et al (2004)	*Learning styles and pedagogy in post-16 learning : A systematic and critical review* edited by Frank Coffield, David Moseley, Elaine Hall, Kathryn Ecclestone. LSRC 2004 isbn 1 85338 9188
Coffield et al (2004b).	*Should we be using learning styles? What research has to say to practice.* edited by Frank Coffield, David Moseley, Elaine Hall, Kathryn Ecclestone. LSRC 2004 isbn 1 85338 914 5
Coffield 2008	Just suppose teaching and learning became the first priority ... Frank Coffield, LSN, 2008, isbn 978 1 84572 708 6

Cox and Smith 2004	*From little acorns – towards a strategy for spreading good practice within colleges.* Philip Cox and Vikki Smith 2004 LSDA isbn 1 85338 937 4
Dale et al 2005	*Women in non-traditional training and employment,*Angela Dale, Nors Jackson, Nicky Hill, EOC Working Paper Series No. 26
Day (1999)	*Developing Teachers: the challenges of lifelong learning* Day C. 1999 Falmer
Desmedt et al (2003)	*There are two refs:* *Learning style awareness:why should it work? In search of a theoretical explanation for a self-evidence conception,* Desmedt E and Valke M and *Comparing the Learning Styles of medicine and pedagogical sciences students* Desmedt E, Valke M, Carrette L and Derese M Both are in *Bridging Theory and Practice,* Proceedings of the Eight Annual European Learning Styles Information Network Conference, University of Hull
DfES 2003	*Using the National Healthy School Standard to Raise Boys' Achievement,* 2003, ISBN 1-84279-128-1
DfES 2005	*14-19 Education and Skills,* February 2005 Cm 6476 HMSO
Dfes 2005 (b)	*Key Stage 3 National Strategy Behaviour and Attendance Strand Toolkit unit 1, Leadership and management,* DfES 1260-2005
Dfes 2005 (c)	*Developing emotional health and well-being: a whole-school approach to improving behaviour and attendance* Behaviour and attendance training materials Core Day Status: Ref: DfES 0182-2005 G - 4
Ecclestone 2002	*Learning Autonomy in Post-16 Education – the politics and practice of formative assessment.* Kathryn Ecclestone Routledge and Falmer, ISBN 0 415 24741 1
DfES 2006	*Further Education: Raising Skills, Improving Life Chances* March 2006, Cm 6768, HMSO 167682 3/06 JW4524 http://www.dfes.gov.uk/publications/furthereducation/
DFES 2007	*2020 Vision Report of the Teaching and Learning in 2020 Review Group* DFES Jan 2007
Elton 1989	*Discipline in Schools:Report of the Committee of Enquiry.* HMSO DES 1989
Ekirch (2006)	*At Days Close, a history of nightime,* A. Roger Ekirch , London, Phoenix, isbn 13 978 0 7538 1940 1/ 10 0 7538 1940 6
Fairhurst and	*Effective teaching, effective learning: Making the personality connection in your classroom.* Palo Alto, CA: Davis-Black.

Fairhurst (1995)	
Evans et al 2003	*Gender matters; gender autonomy and VET policy and practice* Karen Evans, Gerald Heidegger, Bettina Hoffman and Anke Kampmeier LLearning and Skills Resarch. Autumn 2003
FEFC 1996	*Inclusive report of the Learning Difficulties and/or Disabilities Committee*, Further Education Funding Council (1996) John Tomlinson. London: HMSO.
Francis et al 2005	*Gender equality in work experience placements for young people.* Dr Becky Francis, Ms, Jayne Osgood, Dr. Jacinta Dalgety, Dr Louise Archer London Metriopolitan University EOC Working Paper Series no. 27 -
Fuller et al 2005	*Employers, young people and gender segregation (England)* Alison Fuller, Vanessa Beck, Lorna Unwin, University of Leicester Working Paper Series n 28 Spring 2005 see
Goodwin and Thompson 2001	*Dyslexia Toolkit*, produced for The Open University by Vicki Goodwin & Bonita Thomson, 2001
Green 2002	*Improving one-to-one tutorials*, Muriel Green, LSDA .ref 021111
Harkin 1995	*The impact of GNVQs on the communication styles of teachers –* paper for UCET conference October Oxford School of Education, Oxford Brookes University cited by Lucas.
Harkin 2006	*Behaving like Adults; meeting the needs of younger learners in further education*, Joe Harkin LSDA/LSC isbn 1 – 84572 – 388 - 0
Harrison 1984	*The Common People* J.F.C.Harrison Flamingo 1984 ISBN 0-00-654020-1
Haynes et al 2005	*Equality and Pathfinders* Gill Haynes, Caroline Wragg, Keith Mason Uni of Exeter Working Paper Series 36
Hughes et al 2004	*A cut above – customising a curriculum for excellence in skills development* Maria Hughes, Barry Smeaton, Graeme Hall, LSDA 2004 isbn 1 85338 955 2
Ivanic˘ and Tseng (2005 and 2009)	*Understanding the relationships between learning and teaching: an analysis of the contribution of applied linguistics.* Roz Ivanic˘ and Ming-i Lydia Tseng. National Research and Development Centre for Adult Literacy and Numeracy Feb 2005. Book of the project was published by Routledge in 2009 as *Improving Learning in College: Rethinking Literacies Across the Curriculum*
Illich 1971	*De-schooling Society* Ivan Illich 1971 page refs to Pelican 1979

Kidd 1975	*How Adults Learn* J R Kidd New York Association Press, 1975
LSC NMS 2006	*Piloting New Measures of Success: the Quality Improvement Pack* LSC Jan 2006
LSRC 2004 (a)	Learning styles and pedagogy in post-16 learning : A systematic and critical review F. Coffield, D Moseley, E Hall, K Ecclestone et al.
LSRC 2004 b	*Should we be using learning styles?* F. Coffield, D Moseley, E Hall, K. Ecclestone et al. Hard copy or download from LSRC
Lucas 2004 (a)	*Teaching in Further Education – new perspectives for a changing context.* Norman Lucas, Bedford Way Papers, Institute of Education, University of London. ISBN 0 85473 700 6.
Lucas 2004 (b)	*The Fento Fandango: national standards, compulsory teaching and the growing regulation of FE college teachers* was in The Journal of Further and Higher Education Volume 28, Number 1 February 2004
LSRC 2004(a)	*Emerging Policy for vocational learning in England – will it lead to a better system?* Cathleen Statz and Susanah Wright LSRC 2004 isbn 1 84572 000 8
LSRC 2004 (b)	*Learning Styles for Post 16 Learners - What Do We Know? A summary of the report to the Learning and Skills Research Centre from the School of Education, Communication and Language Sciences, University of Newcastle.* Published by LSRC Feb 2004
Margot et al 2006	*Freedom's Orphans, Raising Youth in a Changing World,* Julia Margo and Mike Dixon with Nick Pearce and Howard Reed. IPPR isbn 186030303x download exec summary from http://www.ippr.org.uk/publicationsandreports/publication.asp?id=496
Marzano (1998)	*A theory-based meta-analysis of research on Instruction.* R. J. Marzano, Aurora, CO; Mid-continent Regional Educational Laboratory.
Miller and Parlett 1974	*Up to the Mark – a study of the examination game* London Society for Research into Higher Education.
Miller and Rollnick (1991) and (2002)	*Motivational Interviewing,* William R. Miller, Stephen Rollnick, second edition, Guidford Press2002. Original edition 1991.
Modood	*Multiculturalism and education in Britain: an internally contested*

and May (2001)	*debate,* Tariq Modood and Stephen May Inermational Journal of Educational Research 35 (2001) 305-317
Moseley et al (2004)	*Thinking skill frameworks for post-16 learner; an evaluation.* David Moseley, Viv Baumfield, Steve Higgins, Mei Lin, Jen Miller, Doug Newton, Sue Robson. Joe Elliot, Maggie Gregson. LSRN 2004 isbn 1 85338 916 1
OECD 2003	*Paragraph cited from Policy Briefing Paper 30, Beyond Rhetoric: Adult Learning Policies and Practices, LSDA*
NLT 2012 (1)	*Literacy: State of the Nation* *A picture of literacy in the UK today* *Deeqa Jama and George Dugdale* National Literacy Trust Last updated 10 January 2012
NLT 2012 (2)	*Young People's Writing in 2011* *Findings from the National Literacy* *Trust's annual literacy survey* Christina Clark April 2012, National Literacy Trust
Ofsted MCB	*Managing Challenging Behaviour,* March 2005 HMI 2363
Ofsted WCS	*Why Colleges Succeed* November 2004 HMI 2409
Ofsted WCF	*Why Colleges Fail* November 2004 HMI 2408
Postman and Weingartne r 1969	*Teaching AS A Subversive Activity* Neil Postman and Charles Weingartner USA 1969 page refs to Penguin 1971
Prochaska, and DiClement e 1986	Prochaska, J. O. and C. C. DiClemente (1986). *Toward a comprehensive model of change.* Addictive Behaviors: Processes of Change. W. R. Miller and N. Heather. New York, Plenum Press
QIA 2006	*Pursuing excellence: an outline improvement strategy for consultation.*
Spencer 1893	*Education* Herbert \Spencer Williams and Molrgate 1893
Steedman et al 2004	*Disengagement 14-16: Context and Evidence* Hilary Steedman (CEP) and Sheila Stoney (NFER) October 2004 Part of research summaries from Skills for All project.
TLRP 2006	Learning how to learn – in classrooms, schools and networks Teaching and Learning Research Briefing 17, July 2006
Tribus (undated)	*Quality Management in Education* Myron Tribus, Exergy Inc Hayward CA. Download, part of the Continuous Quality

	Improvement (CQI) Server at the Department of Industrial Engineering, Clemson University (USA)
Tomlinson (1995)	Tomlinson, Carol, *How to differentiate instruction in mixed-ability classrooms*. Alexandria, VA: Association for Supervision and Curriculum Development.
VanderEyken and Barry 1975	Learning and Earning – aspects of day release in FE ed W. Van der Eyken and S M Kaneti Barry NFER 1975
Venables 1967	*The Young Worker at College*, Faber and Faber 1967 (reprinted 1973)
Yurchak 2005	Alexei Yurchak *Everything was forever, until it was no more: the last soviet generation*. Princetown December 2005 isbn 0 691
Zemke 1984	*30 Things We Know For Sure About Learning*, Ron and Susan Zemke, Innovation Abstracts, Vol VI, No 8, March 9, 1984

FE Training and Consultancy

includes mentoring and interim management

www.bpfe.org.uk

Managing Teachers in FE

ISBN 978-0-9926088-4-2